AF600243

THE CATHOLIC UNIVERSITY OF AMERICA
CANON LAW STUDIES
Number 80

FORCE AND FEAR

As Precluding Matrimonial Consent

AN HISTORICAL SYNOPSIS AND COMMENTARY

A DISSERTATION

Submitted to the Faculty of Canon Law of the Catholic University of America in Partial Fulfillment of the Requirements for the Degree of

DOCTOR OF CANON LAW

BY

REV. JOSEPH V. SANGMEISTER, A.B., J.C.L.,
Priest of the Archdiocese of Philadelphia

THE CATHOLIC UNIVERSITY OF AMERICA
WASHINGTON, D. C.
1932

Nihil Obstat:

VALENTINUS T. SCHAAF, O.F.M., J.C.D.,
Censor Deputatus.

Washingtonii, D. C., die xx Aprilis, 1932.

Imprimatur:

✠ DIONYSIUS CARDINALIS DOUGHERTY,
Archiepiscopus Philadelphiensis.

Philadelphiae, die xxi Aprilis, 1932.

Printed by
THE PAULIST PRESS
New York, N. Y.

TO MY MOTHER

FOREWORD

THE pages that follow represent an attempt to determine the effects of force and fear on matrimonial consent according to ecclesiastical law. The frequency with which the validity of the marriage contract is attacked on these grounds is sufficient justification for the endeavor. It is always unpleasant to be compelled to any action simply to satisfy the selfish ambitions and scheming designs of another. To be forced into marriage through these or similar motives constitutes a gross violation of justice.

At all times a most zealous guardian of the rights of the individual, the Church has in every age striven to protect the freedom of the marital state. The historical study, despite its necessary brevity, clearly reveals the legislation found in the Code of Canon Law as a grand culmination to her untiring efforts in this regard. The canonical part of the treatise is devoted to a detailed exposition of the principles governing this point of ecclesiastical matrimonial discipline. Doubtful and disputed matters receive careful consideration. Examples are used arbitrarily and are intended only to illustrate the principles. The numerous references to the decisions of the Roman Rota serve to indicate the mind and practice of the foremost judicial tribunal in the Church.

The writer gratefully acknowledges the direction and assistance of the members of the Faculty of Canon Law at the Catholic University in the preparation of the monograph. He is also greatly indebted to all who have contributed to its final completion by their kindly interest and generous encouragement.

TABLE OF CONTENTS

PART I

PRELIMINARY DISCUSSION

CHAPTER I

MATRIMONIAL CONSENT

SINCE the problem of this canonical study deals with one aspect of vitiated matrimonial consent, that in which the act of the will is influenced by violence, moral compulsion and fear, a brief review of matrimonial consent in general becomes imperative, in order to obviate misunderstanding. The voluntary act termed consent is the constitutive element of a contract. It is the instrument by means of which rights are transferred and obligations incurred. Upon its reality depends the validity of the contract.

As referred to contracts in general, consent is defined as a deliberate act of the will expressed between two or more individuals, which results in an agreement or consideration regarding a well-defined object and including within its ambitus everything comprising the essence thereof and substantially inseparable therefrom.[1] The genuineness of this act is the vitalizing factor which legalizes the transaction. As the validity of a contract depends upon the reality of consent, so the reality of consent is conditioned upon certain positive characteristics. The lack of these marks denotes the presence of negative qualities which are denominated defects of, or obstacles to, that reality and which vitiate the contract in a degree more or less definitely determined by natural or positive law.

From a positive point of view, consent, to be a real expression of the will sufficient to conclude a valid contract, must be internal, free and deliberate, externally manifested, and mutual. Consent must be internal or true, not merely external or feigned, because the transfer of rights with the obligations arising therefrom can only proceed from the wills of the contracting parties. It must be true and deliberate, or posited with that advertence and liberty required for a perfect human act, since the parties impose on themselves obligations binding in strict justice. Communication of the common

[1] D'Annibale, *Summula Theologiae Moralis,* II, n. 411; Gasparri, *De Matrimonio,* n. 872.

agreement is necessary: consequently the internal consent must be externalized in some recognizable manner. The form for manifestation is usually determined by positive law for various kinds of contracts, so that words, signs, actions, or even silence may produce the required effects. Finally, the minds of the contracting parties must meet upon the same thing in the same sense. In other words, consent must be mutual, or given by each of the parties concerned in such a way that it corresponds with the intention of the other.[2]

The binding force of any contract may be weakened by circumstances that directly or indirectly vitiate the genuineness of consent. These circumstances are error, misrepresentation and fraud, coercion, duress, fear and undue influence, and condition. A brief explanation of each will suffice. Error is present when the contracting parties do not have the same thing in mind, or when one or both, while meaning the same thing, have formed mistaken conclusions as to the subject matter of the agreement. When one of the parties has been led to form such conclusions by statements innocently made, or facts innocently withheld, by the other, misrepresentation is had. Fraud consists in inducing such conclusions by intentional misrepresentations or active concealment by the other party, or intentional concealment where there was a duty to disclose, for the purpose of deceiving. Coercion or duress is verified when the consent of one of the parties has been extorted by actual or threatened violence. Fear and undue influence are brought to bear on consent when circumstances render one of the parties morally incapable of resisting the will of the other, so that his consent is no real expression of intention. Condition is a circumstance to which consent is attached and on which the value of the contract depends.[3]

Since matrimony is a strict bilateral contract,[4] the most irrevocable and inviolable possible of formation, consent is an essential and necessary requirement for its validity. Present ecclesiastical

[2] Genicot, *Institutiones Theologiae Moralis,* I, nn. 585-586; Pruemmer, *Manuale Theologiae Moralis,* II, n. 255; Noldin, *Summa Theologiae Moralis,* II, nn. 530-533.

[3] Clark, *Law of Contracts,* § 129. Cf. Genicot, *Institutiones Theologiae Moralis,* I, nn. 588-592; Pruemmer, *Manuale Theologiae Moralis,* II, nn. 256-258; Noldin, *Summa Theologiae Moralis,* II, nn. 544-547.

[4] Cappello, *De Matrimonio,* n. 23; Wernz-Vidal, *Jus Matrimoniale,* n. 34; Petrovits, *Church Law on Matrimony,* n. 4.

discipline states that the consent of parties juridically competent, when properly manifested, constitutes marriage.[5] Moreover, matrimony as a sacrament has its proper matter and form consisting in the mutual transfer and acceptance by the contracting parties of rights to their respective bodies. This exchange can only be effected by consent expressed in some sensible and intelligible way.[6] The necessity of consent on the part of both parties is further emphasized by the law itself which declares that it cannot be supplied by any human power. Hence, matrimony, whether considered as a natural or sacramental contract, is unintelligible unless consent be regarded as of its essence; in fact, so absolutely and exclusively necessary, that nothing else is required for its essence.[7]

The nature of matrimonial consent consists in an act of the will, whereby the parties transfer and accept the exclusive and perpetual right to each other's body for the purpose of performing acts apt for the procreation of children.[8] Both parties must deliver and accept what pertains to the essential object or substance of marriage. Two formal and distinct acts are not required, because one and the same act of transference virtually contains the acceptance, and *vice versa*. An explicit act of the will is not necessary as long as the act implicitly excludes nothing in a positive manner from the essence of the contract. The essential object is the right to each other's bodies, which must be perpetual and exclusive in accordance with the essential properties of marriage, *viz.*, unity and indissolubility.[9]

The qualities requisite for the validity of matrimonial consent are similar to those demanded by law for other contracts. Matrimonial consent must be true, free and deliberate, mutual, manifested by external signs, and exchanged between two juridically competent persons. The consent must be a true internal act, actuated by the will. A feigned, fictitious, or interpretative act, without matrimonial intent,

[5] *Codex Juris Canonici,* c. 1081, § 1.

[6] Cappello, *De Matrimonio,* n. 571.

[7] St. Alphonsus, *Theologia Moralis,* lib. VI, n. 879; Gasparri, *De Matrimonio,* nn. 8, 871; Wernz-Vidal, *Jus Matrimoniale,* n. 451; Vlaming, *Praelectiones Juris Matrimonii,* n. 512.

[8] *Codex Juris Canonici,* c. 1082, § 2.

[9] Gasparri, *De Matrimonio,* nn. 872, 874, 877; Wernz-Vidal, *Jus Matrimoniale,* n. 453; Cappello, *De Matrimonio,* n. 574; Vlaming, *Praelectiones Juris Matrimonii,* n. 513.

cannot effect a valid marriage. The internal act must be deliberate since marriage is fraught with obligations of a most serious nature, which no one is considered willing to assume unless he consents with perfect freedom. The bilateral nature of the marriage contract requires that consent be mutual, that there be a union of minds and wills on the rights and obligations involved. This true, deliberate, mutual consent must be manifested in proper form, because a reciprocal transfer of rights cannot be understood unless the intention of so doing is expressed in an unmistakable, external fashion. For this consent to be effective, the persons giving it must in no way be disqualified from entering into valid marriage by the divine, ecclesiastical, or civil law.[10]

The formation of a valid marital pact depends, therefore, upon the genuineness of consent endowed with all these essential qualities. Whatever militates against the reality of consent sufficiently to destroy any one of these requisites will render the union null and void. According to ecclesiastical law, obstacles or defects preventing matrimonial consent from possessing the characteristics outlined above can exist on the part of the intellect or on the part of the will. The former are want of proper discretion, or ignorance, and error; [11] the latter, simulation, violence, moral compulsion and fear, and condition.[12] In accordance with the particular subject-matter of this canonical monograph, attention will now be directed to some fundamental considerations of the factors which make for defective matrimonial consent under the head of violence and fear.

[10] D'Annibale, *Summula Theologiae Moralis,* III, n. 443; De Becker, *De Sponsalibus et Matrimonio,* pp. 26-27; Genicot, *Institutiones Theologiae Moralis,* II, n. 457; Cappello, *De Matrimonio,* nn. 575-576; Farrugia, *De Matrimonio,* nn. 17-23; Petrovits, *Church Law on Marriage,* n. 397.

[11] *Codex Juris Canonici,* cc. 1082-1085.

[12] *Codex Juris Canonici,* cc. 1086-1087, 1092.

CHAPTER II

FUNDAMENTAL NOTIONS OF VIOLENCE AND FEAR

In all of its legislation on the matter of acts and transactions vitiated by the defects of violence and fear, the Code understands these terms according to the commonly received explanations of their nature and divisions and acknowledges the general principles determining the moral and juridical value of human acts performed under their influence. It will be advantageous to recall these notions for the sake of clarity and, because of the subjective element in fear, to devote some space to certain useful psychological observations.

Article I.—Definitions and Divisions

Violence or force, in its most general sense, signifies strength or energy actively displayed or exerted. It is usually defined as being an impetus of a degree greater than can be resisted.[1] It consists in an impulse from without compelling the object against which it is directed to do or to suffer something against its natural inclination. In moral and legal matters, violence is the use of force by an external agent to compel another to do what is opposed to his will.[2] Force greater than can be resisted is applied by an external agent, thereby compelling the passive subject, without concurrence on his part, to perform or to refrain from some action. In a word, the fact of violence is verified when a person is forced by another to act in such a way that he cannot do the contrary.[3]

A distinction is made by some between violence or force *(vis)* and coercion *(coactio)*. The former is regarded as the genus and referred equally to both animate and inanimate objects, while the latter is specifically applied to animate beings.[4] For example, the impetus given to move a stalled automobile into a garage would be

[1] Dig. 4, 2, 1, 2.
[2] Callan-McHugh, *Moral Theology*, I, 20.
[3] St. Thomas, *Summa Theologica*, 1, q. 82, a. 1.
[4] St. Thomas, *Summa Theologica*, 1, 2, q. 6, a. 5 et ad 2.

termed "force"; that applied to a stubborn beast or obstinate person to compel action would be designated "violence" or "coercion." In both English and American law a person who suffers violence is said to be "under duress." [5] Inasmuch as violence is being considered in its relation to the voluntariness and validity of human acts, the various shades of meaning which differentiate violence, force, coercion, duress, etc., may be disregarded and the terms may be used without distinction.

Violence is distinguished into absolute or physical and relative or moral, also termed conditional or causative. Absolute violence is that understood in the strict sense, that which cannot be resisted in any way whatsoever. Certain conditions must exist in order to have it verified. In the first place, the force must originate from an extrinsic principle, i.e., an agent external to the passive subject. "The violent is that, the origin of which is from without." [6] No one can do violence to himself since he cannot be a principle external to himself. If the impulse were to proceed from an internal principle, the action would be more or less voluntary, or at least spontaneous.[7]

Secondly, the will must in no way give its approval or consent to the action, otherwise it cannot be attributed to violence. Unless this interior resistance is made, the will to suffer the force is present in the passive subject and, although he does not actually consent by willing the action, nevertheless he gives a virtual consent by being willing to suffer the violence.[8] Hence the action must be posited without any volitional concurrence on the part of the one who suffers the force.

Finally, the passive subject must not hold himself negatively or indifferently, but actually, virtually, or at least constructively *(interpretative)* opposed to the force. In this sense, violence is equally done to a person who is murdered while asleep or awake. Wherever, accordingly, force is exercised against a person who both interiorly dissents and exteriorly resists, the fact of absolute violence is verified.

[5] Slater, *Moral Theology,* I, 17-18; May, *Marriage Laws and Decisions,* p. 27.

[6] St. Thomas, *Summa Theologica,* 1, 2, q. 6, a. 6, ad 1.

[7] Walsh, *De Actibus Humanis,* n. 346.

[8] St. Thomas, *Summa Theologica,* 1, 2, q. 6, a. 5, ad 2.

Relative or moral violence is accepted in a two-fold sense. According to some, it is had when the passive subject can resist or at least diminish the onset of the force but fails to do so. Others term violence relative when the person cannot indeed resist it, but at the same time does not altogether dissent interiorly or suffer it unwillingly.[9] It is this latter species of violence, moral compulsion, which excites fear in the subject who suffers it.

Whereas violence is something external to a person, fear is a subjective state intimately affecting the individual. Canonists and moralists generally adopt the definition of Roman law[10] and explain fear as a perturbation of mind caused by the apprehension of an imminent or future danger. The words *perturbation of mind* distinguish it from a purely sensible fear, the *passio timoris* of the Scholastics, since the definition describes fear which is perceived by the mind and influences the will. The designation of the disturbance as mental, without any explicit allusion to the motions of the sensitive appetite which ordinarily accompany the emotions, is not intended to signify that the fear in question is an agitation of the mind only to the exclusion of any sensitive alteration.[11]

It cannot be denied that the degree of organic disturbance which accompanies fear is variable, depending to a large extent upon the character of the subject and the nature of the danger or evil. Since certain pertinent remarks on this matter will be made further on, suffice it to say in this place that in so far as fear constitutes an obstacle to voluntary action, it appears always to include some sensible, nervous alteration and this is the more profound as the exercise of liberty is more strongly impeded. If, as may happen, the mind coldly considers a danger and weighs the reasons for avoiding or sustaining it, this should be attributed to the habit of prudence rather than to the absence of fear. For this reason the mental

[9] Cf. St. Thomas in IV *Sententiarum,* d. 22, q. 1, a. 1; Schmalzgrueber, *Jus Ecclesiasticum Universum,* lib. IV, tit. I, n. 384; St. Alphonsus, *Theologia Moralis,* lib. VI, n. 1045; Ballerini-Palmieri, *Opus Theologiae Moralis,* I, tr. I, n. 115; Wernz, *Jus Matrimoniale,* n. 261; Noldin, *Summa Theologiae Moralis,* I, n. 57.

[10] Dig. 4, 2, 1.

[11] Cf. Bouquillon, *Theologia Moralis Fundamentalis,* p. 636, who seems to favor this restricted meaning.

perturbation is more truly understood as affecting both the sensitive and intellectual nature of the passive subject.[12]

The evil or danger exciting the fear may be of the physical or moral order, such as death, bodily injury, financial loss, damaged reputation, etc. It need not immediately threaten the person fearing, since threats made against relatives or associates can produce the same effects. While it is not necessary that the object of fear be actually present, it should be instant or of the immediate future: a remote evil ordinarily causes no mental agitation. Death is an evil from which man naturally shrinks, but as long as it does not appear immediately imminent he thinks little about it and cannot be said to "fear" it. Finally, the evil or danger must be such that it can be overcome only with great difficulty, otherwise it is not the source of fear.[13]

Fear is distinguished according to its origin or cause, mode or manner, and degree or intensity. From the viewpoint of its origin, fear assumes the nature of the cause producing it. If the cause of the apprehended evil or danger partakes of a supernatural character, the resulting fear is styled supernatural. Such is that inspired by a belief in God's omnipotence, or by an evil privative of supernatural good, as eternal punishment or loss of eternal life, or by qualms of conscience.[14]

Natural fear finds its cause in some natural evil or danger and may be *ab intrinseco* or *ab extrinseco*. Fear from within results from a necessary cause or natural event, whether internal or external to the individual, the existence of which does not depend on a free human agent. Examples are death, virulent disease, earthquake, fire, shipwreck, etc. Fear from without is that caused by a free human agent, i.e., an individual who threatens evil to obtain some end.[15]

[12] Cf. Bouuaert, "De Metus Influxu," *Jus Pontificium*, III (1926), 105-106.

[13] Ballerini-Palmieri, *Opus Theologicum Morale*, I, tr. I, n. 123; Pruemmer, *Manuale Theologiae Moralis*, I, n. 67; Noldin, *Summa Theologiae Moralis*, I, n. 54.

[14] Gasparri, *De Matrimonio*, n. 946.

[15] Sanchez, *De Matrimonii Sacramento*, lib. IV, disp. XII, n. 2; St. Alphonsus, *Theologia Moralis*, lib. VI, n. 1046; Laymann, *Theologia Moralis*, lib. I, tr. II, c. 6, n. 2; D'Annibale, *Summula Theologiae Moralis*, I, n. 138; Gasparri, *De Matrimonio*, n. 947; Pruemmer, *Manuale Theologiae Moralis*, I,

According to the mode or manner of its infliction, fear from an extrinsic free cause is just or unjust. It is just when it is inflicted for a reason really meriting it by a competent person and in a lawful manner. An authorized judge who threatens a delinquent tax payer with the penalty provided by law for such offense induces a just fear. If fear is inflicted for no adequate reason or for a cause not connected with the evil threatened, or if the one inspiring the fear has no right or authority to threaten an evil, the fear is unjust. Should the above taxpayer be free from guilt, or should the judge be incompetent or threaten a penalty exceeding that determined by the law, the fear inflicted would be unjust.[16]

According to its quality, intensity or degree, fear is grave or slight. Grave fear arises from a serious evil that is certainly or very probably imminent. Slight fear is induced by a trifling evil or from little danger of the evil ensuing. Grave fear may be absolutely or relatively grave. It is absolutely grave if the evil or danger is objectively serious and will intimidate any one of ordinary prudence and courage, even though in some extraordinary case it might not disturb an exceptionally courageous person. Relatively grave fear is caused by an evil which might not affect the average person, but which in relation to certain individuals, considering circumstances of sex, age, health, disposition, character, and education, becomes serious. For this reason absolutely and relatively grave fear are

n. 68. According to another distinction, fear is termed extrinsic when it is due to an external cause, whether necessary, natural or free, while intrinsic fear is that resulting from a cause internal to the individual. Cf. Ballerini-Palmieri, *Opus Theologicum Morale,* I, tr. I, n. 123; Wernz, *Jus Matrimoniale,* n. 261; Cappello, *De Matrimonio,* n. 604; Noldin, *Summa Theologiae Moralis,* I, n. 55; Maroto, *Institutiones,* I, n. 397. Although this division may be more logical, the one given above appears more in accord with the tenor of the Code in understanding fear *ab extrinseco* to be that inflicted by a free agent. Either distinction may be accepted for, as Genicot (*Institutiones Theologiae Moralis,* I, n. 28) observes, fear *ab intrinseco* and fear *ab extrinseco* due to a necessary or natural cause are practically of the same import in moral matters. For a discussion of this point cf. Vermeersch, "De Metu ab Intrinseco vel ab Extrinseco," *Periodica,* XVII (1928), 141*-143*.

[16] Ballerini-Palmieri, *Opus Theologicum Morale,* I, tr. I, n. 129; Genicot, *Institutiones Theologiae Moralis,* I, n. 28; Pruemmer, *Manuale Theologiae Moralis,* I, n. 68; Augustine, *Commentary,* V, 246. A thorough analysis of just and unjust infliction *quoad substantiam* and *quoad modum* will be given in Chap. VI, Art. II, § 3.

considered equivalent wherever there is question of the voluntariness and validity of a human act.[17]

In this connection mention must be made of reverential fear. This usually has its origin in the desire not to offend one's parents or superiors, so as to avoid incurring their wrath, displeasure, or indignation. In itself, reverential fear is slight; but, as will be seen, it may become grave under certain circumstances.

A further distinction must be made between antecedent fear and concomitant fear, according as the act is performed *ex metu* or *cum metu.* Fear is concomitant when it is not the cause of the act, but is merely occasioned by it and would rather prevent the action if that were possible. It is not the cause which moves to action since, even if it were not present, the latter would nevertheless be performed. The agent acts, not because of, but apart from or in spite of his fears. Thus the martyrs suffered with a natural fear their horrible tortures and deaths, but fear of their sufferings was not the cause of their martyrdom. Fear is antecedent when it is the cause of the action, inasmuch as it is anterior to the action and moves the will to act. Were the fear not present, the action would not be done. The fear of suffering and death moves the apostate to deny his faith. It is clear that the principles about to be stated refer only to antecedent fear.[18]

Article II.—Moral and Juridical Principles

With the above distinctions clearly in mind, it is now possible to state several general principles regulating the moral and juridical value of acts performed under the influence of violence and fear. They may be conveniently formulated as follows:

I. *Absolute violence entirely destroys the voluntariness of an act and consequently excludes consent. Conditional violence does not destroy but merely lessens the voluntariness of an act and therefore admits consent.*

[17] Ballerini-Palmieri, *Opus Theologicum Morale,* I, tr. I, n. 126; Noldin, *Summa Theologiae Moralis,* I, n. 55.

[18] Walsh, *De Actibus Humanis,* n. 324; Pruemmer, *Manuale Theologiae Moralis,* I, n. 68; Noldin, *Summa Theologiae Moralis,* I, n. 54.

Absolute violence cannot be done to an act elicited by the will, because it proceeds from an intrinsic principle whose essential property is freedom, whereas violence comes from without. To have an act at one and the same time free, as elicited by the will, and forced, as caused by an external agency, is a contradiction in terms. Violence can compel actions distinct from and external to the will *(actus imperati)*. But the proper act of the will *(actus elicitus)*, since it is intrinsically free, is by its very nature proof against every directly constraining action. Hence, an act due to violence is involuntary and consent is impossible.[19]

Conditional violence does not necessarily destroy the voluntariness of an act but merely diminishes it because either the resistance which could and should be employed is omitted, in which case the act is indirectly willed; or the will is not entirely opposed to it, with the result that there is some degree of consent.[20] This violence, which is exercised by means of fear proximately creating a disturbed mental state, affects the elicited acts of the will. While it does not usually destroy voluntariness and freedom entirely, as absolute violence, still it hampers or diminishes freedom to an extent which prevents complete and perfect consent. Since conditional violence, or moral compulsion, induces the state of fear, the two are related as cause and effect. The former considers the obstacle to consent from the viewpoint of the active agent who causes the fear; the latter from the viewpoint of the passive subject who suffers the fear.[21] In practice, accordingly, since acts due to moral compulsion are equivalent to those performed through fear, the same principles find application.[22]

[19] St. Thomas, *Summa Theologica,* 1, 2, q. 6, a. 5; Ballerini-Palmieri, *Opus Theologicum Morale,* I, tr. I, nn. 116-118; Pruemmer, *Manuale Theologiae Moralis,* I, nn. 64-65. Cf. *Codex Juris Canonici,* c. 2205, § 1.

[20] Ballerini-Palmieri, *Opus Theologicum Morale,* I, tr. I, nn. 119-122; Noldin, *Summa Theologiae Moralis,* I, n. 58.

[21] St. Thomas, *Summa Theologica,* Suppl., q. 47, a. 1; Schmalzgrueber, *Jus Ecclesiasticum Universum,* lib. IV, tit. I, n. 384; Feije, *De Impedimentis et Dispensationibus Matrimonialibus,* n. 125; Noldin, *Summa Theologiae Moralis,* III, n. 633.

[22] Maroto, *Institutiones.* I, n. 396; Pruemmer, *Manuale Theologiae Moralis,* I, n. 66, coroll. 2.

II. *Unless fear is so great as to deprive the agent of the use of reason, it does not destroy but merely diminishes the voluntariness of an act, and consequently consent is not excluded.*

Fear may be so intense as to deprive the agent of the use of reason. When this occurs a human act is impossible. The "deliberate will" [23] necessary for such an act is completely lacking. The intellect neither adverts nor forms a judgment; the will makes no voluntary choice nor gives consent. Such an action is merely an *actus hominis,* without moral or juridical value.[24]

Excepting this case of complete mental collapse, fear does not entirely destroy the voluntariness of choice. This is apparent from the fact that fear is not like violence which cannot be overcome. Experience proves that an individual of ordinary firmness and prudence can resist its influence. No matter how great that influence may be, as long as the use of reason is retained, sufficient knowledge and freedom exist to posit a human act. The intellect adverts to the matter and forms a judgment, whereupon the will freely makes its choice. Certainly if physical force cannot compel the will, *a fortiori* the gravest fear cannot have this effect.[25] As Roman law expresses it, *quamvis si liberum esset, noluissem, tamen coactus volui.*[26] The same truth is witnessed to in the axioms: *qui mavult, vult* and *coacta voluntas est semper voluntas.*

Fear, nevertheless, diminishes the voluntariness of choice. The exercise of liberty involves judgment on the part of the intellect and choice on the part of the will. Though they are spiritual faculties, both intellect and will depend objectively for the exercise of their functions upon the sensitive faculties. Since these latter are organic and therefore subordinate to the integrity and normal functioning of the organism, volitional liberty depends for its exercise upon the same material conditions. When a strong emotion, such as fear, pervades consciousness, the sensitive faculties in their disturbed condition upset the mind. This uneasy mental state directly affects the intellect and indirectly influences the will. The mind is rendered

[23] St. Thomas, *Summa Theologica,* 1, 2, q. 1, a. 1.

[24] Noldin, *Summa Theologiae Moralis,* I, n. 53.

[25] Pruemmer, *Manuale Theologiae Moralis,* I, n. 69.

[26] Dig. 4, 2, 21, 5.

less robust in its effort to counteract the impressions of evil. The will in its turn, inclined in the direction of escape, chooses one course of action in preference to another, merely as a means to avoid the imminent danger or evil.

Thus fear indirectly, and in no less degree because the manner is indirect, determines the will to elect an act precisely and exactly on account of the impending evil. If the latter did not threaten, or did other circumstances prevail, the will would withhold its act of choice. The Scholastics expressed this truth in the terse proposition: *Actus ex metu productus est voluntarius simpliciter et involuntarius secundum quid.*[27] The action is voluntary because the will freely chooses it under existing conditions. Voluntariness is diminished, however, as far as the intellect is hindered in its normal operation. The act is voluntary only in a restricted sense, or better, involuntary in a certain respect, because the will is adverse to what it chooses. The course of action is adopted, not because it appeals as being good, but rather because it is considered favorable or preferable as the lesser of two evils.[28] The will, moreover, by making a choice is understood to give consent. For this reason, beyond the exception noted above, consent is not excluded when the will acquiesces under the influence of fear. But its freedom is vitiated to the degree in which the voluntariness of choice is affected.

An illustration will serve to clarify the point in question. Domineering parents threaten their daughter with disinheritance if she refuses to marry in accordance with their wishes. The girl is filled with grave fear as she faces the repugnant alternatives: the unwelcome marriage or the threatened evil. To avoid incurring the latter, she yields to her parents' wishes. Her consent is voluntary *simpliciter* inasmuch as she freely chooses what she considers here and now as most desirable. But it is involuntary *secundum quid,* since her will is opposed to the marriage. If all circumstances are considered, the daughter's consent to marry is voluntary, while it is involuntary if only the marriage itself is regarded. To paraphrase

[27] St. Thomas, *Summa Theologica,* 1, 2, q. 6, a. 6.

[28] Ballerini-Palmieri, *Opus Theologicum Morale,* I, tr. I, nn. 130-132; Pruemmer, *Manuale Theologiae Moralis,* I, n. 69; Noldin, *Summa Theologiae Moralis,* I, n. 56; Genicot, *Institutiones Theologiae Moralis,* I, n. 29.

the text of Roman law cited above, although the girl would be unwilling to marry if she were free, nevertheless, since she is compelled by circumstances, she gives consent.

III. *An act posited under the influence of physical violence has no juridical value. An act due to grave and unjustly inflicted fear is valid, unless the law rules otherwise; but it can be rescinded.*

Human acts posited to produce a special effect or to establish a definite juridic status are either valid or invalid. The act is valid when it enjoys all the essential conditions required by law to produce the particular effect or status. If it lacks but one of these requisites, it is invalid. This distinction especially finds application where there is question of sacraments, contracts, vows, oaths, etc. According to the nature of the act, the essentials for validity may be regulated by natural or positive law. Thus, consent is required for the validity of marriage by the natural law; positive law makes necessary its celebration according to a prescribed form. Valid acts are either rescindable or non-rescindable, according as they can be deprived of their force by competent authority, or are so firm and binding, that no authority, at least no human authority, can deprive them of their force.[29]

The above principle states ecclesiastical legislation in general concerning the validity of acts, which are a source of obligation or effect a juridic status, when due to physical violence or grave and unjustly inflicted fear.[30] Since the nature of physical force of necessity excludes free consent, an act posited by reason of such influence can have no juridical value whatever. While the action is performed physically, juridically it is considered as though it were not done. The interior will withholds consent to the external action, and without consent a juridic transaction is impossible.[31]

A juridic act influenced by grave, unjustly inflicted fear is usually valid. This is a consequence of the principle that fear does not

[29] Ballerini-Palmieri, *Opus Theologicum Morale,* I, tr. I, nn. 13-16; Noldin, *Summa Theologiae Moralis,* I, n. 41.

[30] *Codex Juris Canonici,* c. 103.

[31] Ojetti, *Commentarium,* II, p. 147; Maroto, *Institutiones,* I, n. 396. Cf. *Codex Juris Canonici,* c. 2205, § 1.

destroy consent, but merely diminishes it. If this principle holds for the forum of conscience, there is all the more reason for its application in the external forum. Otherwise obligations could easily be evaded and contracts deprived of their force, on the pretext that the acts were vitiated by fear. As a rule, however, such acts can be nullified. One who posits under the influence of grave fear an act which is a source of obligation suffers a grave injury because of the violation of his rights. In the interests of justice, the law provides that the act can be deprived of its force through a judgment rendered by competent authority, which will release the injured person from all obligation and restore him to his former status.[32]

To defend the individual against injustice, positive law in addition to these provisions declares certain juridic acts *ipso jure* null and void, should the necessary conditions be fulfilled.[33] Invalidity is decreed, not because consent is lacking or involuntary, but rather on account of the indissoluble nature of the act, the sacredness of the obligations involved, or the possible harmful consequences to the common good. The law wishes the act to enjoy the fullest degree of liberty possible and consequently invalidates it when it is unduly influenced by moral compulsion and fear. The conditions required for these defects of consent to invalidate a juridic act depend upon its nature as well as positive legislative enactments. The general tenor of the present Code is that fear must be grave and unjustly inflicted by a free extrinsic cause in order to have an invalidating effect.[34]

[32] *Codex Juris Canonici,* cc. 1684-1689.

[33] *Codex Juris Canonici,* cc. 185; 542, § 1; 572, § 1, n. 4; 169, § 1, n. 1; 1087; 1307, § 3; 2238.

[34] Wernz-Vidal, *De Personis,* nn. 37-38; Maroto, *Institutiones,* I, n. 398; Ojetti, *Commentarium,* II, 150-153; 156-160. Cf. Bouuaert, "De Metus Influxu," *Jus Pontificium,* III (1926), 107-111. Under certain circumstances positive laws, whether human or divine, will not oblige under grave fear because the legislator is understood as having the intention of not binding subjects when grave inconveniences will result from observance of the law. Exceptions are: (a) if the violation of the law should endanger the common good; (b) if the transgression implies contempt for religion or ecclesiastical authority. Cf. *Codex Juris Canonici,* cc. 2205, § 2, § 3; 2229, § 3, n. 3; Pruemmer, *Manuale Theologiae Moralis,* I, n. 70.

ARTICLE III.—PSYCHOLOGICAL CONSIDERATIONS

Nothing need be said from the psychological viewpoint concerning absolute violence. Physico-motor actions can be forced to conform to another's will and the internal sensitive faculties may be affected by conflicting emotions. But judgment and choice can preserve their independence in the presence of such violence, since it is an influence external to the subject and certainly without any psychical bearing that determines the action.

Fear, however, offers a different problem because of its subjective nature. Its presence means an unhealthy mental condition which interferes with the normal operations of the intellect and will. Deliberation and consent are proportionately affected. Since the psychical nature of fear excludes direct knowledge of its existence and intensity, these can be deduced only mediately from external manifestations. Acquaintance with the physico-psychological reactions to the emotion of fear will be of no little assistance in passing just and equitable judgment upon the juridical value of a transaction alleged to have been concluded under its influence.

Psychologically considered, fear is a prospective emotion looking to the future and acting as a stimulus of activity. It springs from an apprehension of evil about to befall and prompts flight in the direction of safety. The emotion is purely painful and for this reason has been defined as the pain of anticipated pain.[35] This anticipation cannot be called actual prevision, but rather a highly-generalized fore-feeling, itself unpleasant, that a more painful state impends. The *élan vital* of the victim is more or less checked in its momentum or narrowed in its range by the intimation that it may be still further arrested. Continual concentration on the "what next" and the "about to be" becomes a most intense psychic experience. The future dominates the present in the fear-state and gives it a new significance in addition to its own. This protensive or futuristic attitude may be termed the specific property of the psychic condition called fear.[36]

[35] Maher, *Psychology*, p. 430; McCosh, *The Emotions*, p. 113.

[36] Cf. Hall, "A Synthetic-Genetic Study of Fear," *Journal of Psychology*, XXV (1914), 149.

Just as physical pain, so too the ideal pain of fear is identified, understood and explained by certain physical and mental facts and conditions. On the physical side, in common with all emotions, fear is accompanied by various organic or physical phenomena which are the product of the feelings and indicate the interior state. It is true that the manifestation of certain of the ordinary signs of fear is highly improbable in the case of a person being forced by moral compulsion to give his consent to some repugnant transaction, chiefly because the fear suffered in a distressing situation of that kind is predominantly mental rather than emotional. Since a variety of circumstances, however, make possible their manifestation, the organic symptomatology is given somewhat in detail.

The usual and obvious signs of fear imply organic derangement and muscular relaxation accompanied with vigorous efforts in particular directions. The result on the whole is a noticeable lowering of vitality, depreciation of active energies, and a loss of power, as inertness, torpor, and a certain sense of being fettered or rendered incapable of action pervade the whole system. The countenance is contracted and pale, or possibly flushed. The eyes are pallid, the brows furrowed, the lips quiver and the tongue falters in conversation. Cold perspiration may even exude and bathe the face in the moment of crisis. Certain motor-vocal reactions incline the agonized victim to cry or scream, or at least to denote the inward anguish by words of distress, pain, or prohibitive commands, uttered in a husky voice, loud and high, or hushed and low. Some of the cardio-respiratory and vaso-motor reactions, such as the increased strength and rate of the pulse, can practically never be observed. But the very marked chest movements of deep and rapid breathing, the swelling of blood-vessels of the neck, face and arms, the pale or flushed color of the skin, are readily apparent. Posture and movement vary, as the body may be rigid and motionless, or charged with nervous agitation indicated by trembling, shivering, drawing back, shrinking away, looking to others as though for assistance, ending sometimes in attempted or actual headlong flight. The hands may be clenched or shaking, the arms thrust forward or thrown up toward the face as if to ward off or close out the object or idea identified as dangerous and causing fear. A general attitude of desire not to be alone is manifested, as well as refusal to go to certain places or do certain things.[37]

The more important mental characteristics and effects of fear reveal the emotion as it is consciously experienced and as it influences conduct and sways the destiny of the victim. The disagreeable state of consciousness produced by the representation of an evil or danger plays great havoc with the normal functioning of the internal faculties. Fear produces an agony and anxiety about the heart and paralyzes the soul in such a manner as to render it insensible to almost everything but its own misery. Concentration upon the object of fear and excessive hold of related possibilities of evil result in a "fixed" idea amounting almost to obsession. Gloomy excitement and depression mark the general mental tonality, to which must be applied the strongest descriptive figures: apprehension, dread, terror, horror, worry, melancholy, despondency, despair. The excited imagination exaggerates impressions and gives distorted representations of reality. It introduces irregular, eccentric, and disproportionate pictures which may serve to augment mentally the objective reality of the evil already serious in itself. The lack of a definite image to control or steady the movements of the imagination makes possible the reception of anything that the chance course of the thought-stream may light upon. The victim is tossed to and fro in uncertainty and distraction. Thus there naturally ensues a painful and voluminous state of excitement under the ordinary laws of thought and feeling. Every trifle is suggestive, there is a large amount of incoherent speculation, the exact *where, when* and *what* is rather obscure. This depressive mental condition grows and deepens in proportion to the length and acuteness of the fear-state.[38]

Under such circumstances it is inevitable that the mind is shaken from its calm center of orderly operation in the way of judgment and choice. Volition is a complex act involving the conception of some object or end as good or desirable, advertence to the possibility of alternative courses of action, a judicial act of preference, and a consequent active inclination on the part of the will to that side. This

[37] Perrin-Klein, *Psychology*, pp. 162-163.

[38] Bain, *Emotions and Will*, pp. 151-154, 157-158; McCosh, *The Emotions*, pp. 140-144.

final tendency is determined by what is called a motive. Whatever moves or influences the will is a motive. The apprehension of any object as desirable, whether ultimately elected or rejected, constitutes a motive. Strictly speaking, the motive is not the thing possessed of objective reality or existence, but this thing as apprehended by the mind and represented as desirable or preferable. The force of a motive fluctuates in consequence, depending upon the vividness with which it is retained. Its attractiveness will depend partly on the thing itself, partly on the general character of the person, but especially and more immediately upon the extent to which it is permitted to absorb the attention. The ultimate acceptance of a course of action, or its rejection, as determined by the play of motives, constitutes the act of choice. For this exercise of choice there must be the self-conscious reflective cognizance of at least two possible alternatives. Thereupon follows a free practical judgment of the intellect as to which is to be preferred, and the will embraces one side, acquiesces to it, adopts or chooses it.[89]

Apply these general findings of psychology to the case of a person laboring under a grave fear induced by being unjustly brought face to face with the obnoxious alternatives of an undesired marriage or of suffering a serious evil, damage or loss. It is but natural that the engrossing persistence of these elements will blind his view to consequences generally and overturn rational calculation to a large extent. The fear-state distracts his mind as the various intellectual adjuncts, collaterals and causes strongly engage the attention of his irritated consciousness. It apparently consumes the powers of thought and the intellect fails to operate in a normal manner. The equilibrium of an otherwise healthy mind is upset and the faculties of sound judgment and reasoning disordered. The will, blind faculty that it is, suffers in turn. The volitional property of fear to be a stimulus to the will is a characteristic feature already noted. To avoid instinctively what is apprehended as evil, to shun danger, is an innate tendency of human nature. Faced with the above-mentioned alternatives, the will is led to follow a course of action which ordinarily of itself it would not adopt. Marriage, though repugnant, appears as the only definite avenue of escape and the will chooses it

[89] Maher, *Psychology*, pp. 340, 380-384.

as the one means to avoid the threatened evil. Precisely by this juxtaposition of two evil alternatives is a completely free choice and consent prevented. Under normal conditions the will would never be determined in either direction. Under the influence of fear, however, it consents to what appears the lesser of two evils. The freedom or voluntariness of that choice is necessarily diminished in proportion to the motivating force exerted by the imminent evil or danger.

PART II

HISTORICAL DEVELOPMENT

CHAPTER III

THE ATTITUDE OF ROMAN LAW

FREEDOM of consent is today so universally recognized as necessary for the validity of marriage, that the absence of this requirement in ancient times may occasion surprise. The intended brevity of the present historical study makes impossible a thorough and detailed investigation of liberty of choice or freedom of matrimonial consent among ancient or primitive peoples.[1] Nevertheless, to clarify the gradual evolution and ultimate position of Canon Law in the matter of compulsory marriage, the legislation of Rome is of particular interest and importance. The recognition of violence and fear as an invalidating factor of the matrimonial contract cannot be termed a strict principle of Roman Law. It is beyond doubt, however, that this very fact served to determine the Church's legislation. To understand more completely Roman legislation relative to marriage contracted because of coercion and fear, it is necessary to explain that central notion of Roman family life, the *patria potestas*, and to discover to what extent it was weakened in the course of time. Next matrimonial consent will be examined together with the juridic value of a compulsory marriage. Finally, a particular piece of Roman legislation will receive consideration.

ARTICLE I.—NATURE OF THE *Patria Potestas*

The term *patria potestas* in Roman law refers to the mutual relations of father and child, or more strictly, to that right which the father exercises over the property and person of the child.[2] From natural law alone the father has power over the physical, mental and moral education of his child, and this is in the nature of a duty rather than a right or privilege.[3] Primarily, the fulfillment of this obligation rests with the father, although secondarily it affects also

[1] Cf. Westermarck, *History of Human Marriage*, ch. X.
[2] Morey, *Outlines of Roman Law*, p. 240; Vidal, *Institutiones*, n. 337.
[3] Vidal, *Institutiones*, n. 337.

the mother as the associate of the father.[4] But in Roman law the authority of the father had a special character from the fact that it was a strict legal right vested in him alone and in no way pertaining to the mother.

In ancient times the sovereignty of the *paterfamilias* was practically absolute and unlimited and was exercised over both the persons and property of those *in potestate*.[5] It was admirably summed up in the comprehensive term: *jus vitae necisque,* the power of life and death over those in the family, though this jurisdiction, even to the point of imprisonment and capital punishment, was true only of the early Roman period. He could sell his children by mancipation to another.[6] If one *in patria potestate* committed some crime or offense, the father had to answer and had the alternative of making redress or noxal surrender *(noxac deditio)*.[7] In addition, he had the right of exposing his children.[8]

As regards the right of the *paterfamilias* over the property of the *filiusfamilias,* the latter, on principle, was incapable of having anything as his own. Whatever he acquired, he acquired for the head of the family. At a very early date, however, the father was in the habit of giving his children certain goods of which they had the management and with which they could carry on some kind of business.[9] These goods were termed *peculium profectitium,* i.e., *a patre profectum,* and were symmetrical to the *peculium* of the slave.[10]

[4] St. Thomas, *Contra Gentiles,* III, c. 122; Meyer, *Jus Naturale,* II, 110; Wernz-Vidal, *Jus Matrimoniale,* n. 602; Cappello, *De Matrimonio,* n. 741.

[5] Those subject to the *patria potestas* were: (a) all children born of a lawful marriage, provided the father himself was *sui juris* and not a *filiusfamilias,* in which case the children fall under the same *potestas* as their father (Inst. 1, 9, 3): not only did the children of the marriage fall under *potestas* but likewise all remoter issue through males; (b) children born out of lawful wedlock, but legitimated by subsequent marriage (Inst. 1, 10, 13; Cod. 5, 27, 11; Nov. 89, c. 11), or by imperial rescript (Nov. 74, c. 1; Nov. 89, cc. 9-10), or by *oblatio* to the *curia* (Cod. 5, 27, 3; Inst. 1, 10, 13); (c) all persons adopted or arrogated into the family (Dig. 1, 7; Inst. 1, 11; Cod. 8, 48).

[6] Gaius, I, 117.

[7] Gaius, IV, 75. Noxal surrender was effected through a mancipation by which the son was taken from the authority of his father and given in reparation to the victim of the delict. Cf. Gaius, IV, 79.

[8] Plautus, *Amphitrio,* I, 3, 3.

[9] Gaius, II, 87; IV, 69, 73.

[10] Cod. 4, 26, 10; Dig. 15, 1, 5, §§ 3, 4.

This *peculium* did not cease to be the property of the head of the family since he reclaimed it, despite any contrary disposition, on the death of the *filius*.[11] Finally, since the *filiusfamilias in potestate* had no patrimony, he could make no will.[12]

This brief exposition of the *patria potestas* clearly demonstrates how significant an institution it was in Roman family life. Sohm's words give an exact appreciation of it:

> Whatever a filiusfamilias acquires he acquires for the paterfamilias. Whatever rights he acquires, be they rights of ownership or obligatory rights, nay, even the marital power over his own wife and the paternal power over his own children, vest not in him, but in his father. For according to early Roman law there exists in every Roman household but one ownership, one marital and paternal power: that of the paterfamilias.[13]

Hence Mommsen has reason for observing: "All in the household were destitute of legal rights—the wife and the child, no less than the bullock or the slave."[14] In view of such an extensive jurisdiction, it is not surprising that the *paterfamilias* exercised considerable authority in so important a domestic affair as marriage.

Article II.—Modification of the *Patria Potestas*

The extraordinary and unlimited extent of the *patria potestas* was gradually restricted. Its extreme harshness and primitive severity were relaxed and toned down. This modification was accomplished partly through the evolution of classical law along with the efforts of the censors and praetors under the Republic, partly by the reformed legislation of emperors who were influenced by economical and political conditions and by Christian principles of justice and equality, which were especially favorable to women and children.[15] But the limitation of the *patria potestas* with the corresponding liberation of the *filiusfamilias* was more truly verified in the law relating

[11] Cod. 12, 37, 5.

[12] Ulpian, *Liber Singularis,* XX, 10.

[13] *The Institutes,* p. 177.

[14] *History of Rome,* I, 64.

[15] Troplong, *De L'Influence du Christianisme sur le Droit Civil des Romains,* p. 115.

to "things" than in that treating of "persons." In other words, the capacity of the *filiusfamilias* was enlarged rather in connection with possession and ownership of property, the contracting of obligations, and rights of inheritance and succession, than with respect to paternal authority over matters purely personal and domestic.

In the early Empire, through a series of changes, the *filiusfamilias* came to acquire a distinct proprietary position. He obtained a three-fold *peculium*: the *peculium castrense*, the *peculium quasi-castrense*, and the *peculium adventitium*, introduced successively by the emperors Augustus, Diocletian, and Constantine.[16] Justinian went still further when he expressly gave him the absolute right to acquire any property whatever as his own.[17] Thus the *filius* became a real *dominus* of the property he acquired. Included in this proprietary capacity was the power to dispose of the *peculium castrense* and *quasi-castrense* by juridic acts with his father or others,[18] or by a will.[19]

It would be wrong to suppose that the *patria potestas* was weakened or diminished to an equal degree in matters that were purely personal. Although the *jus in rebus* of the father had been restricted, yet the right of the father *in personam filii* and *filiae* was rather more clearly defined than actually limited. Practically all the modifications of the *patria potestas*, which were the product of changes in social conditions and a more just conception of the natural rights of individuals, were intended to mitigate the extreme rigor and not to do away with it entirely. The reforms sought to check the abuses of that power and to release children from the unjust oppression to which they were liable. The old principle of the *jus vitae necisque* had fallen into desuetude long before the time of Justinian.[20]

[16] Inst. 2, 12, pr.; Dig. 36, 1, 27; Cod. 6, 60, 1. *Peculium castrense* embraced whatever the son acquired in military service (Dig. 49, 17, 4, pr., 11, 13; Cod. 12, 37, 1); *peculium quasi-castrense* comprised all the son earned in civil service or received as a gift from the emperor, and subsequently everything gained in a professional capacity (Cod. 3, 28, 37, pr.; Cod. 2, 7, 4; Dig. 36, 1, 50); *peculium adventitium* covered all property coming to the son as heir of his mother and later also that acquired through marriage (Cod. 6, 60, 1, 2; Cod. 6, 61, 4, pr.).

[17] Cod. 6, 61, 6; Inst. 2, 9, § 1.

[18] Dig. 18, 1, 2, pr.; Cod. 6, 61, 6, 1, b.

[19] Inst. 2, 12, pr.

[20] Morey, *Outlines of Roman Law*, p. 240.

> In the Empire patria potestas no longer conferred on the father the full and unlimited powers of the old jus civile, but only those powers of chastisement and correction which the jus gentium recognized as naturally appertaining to the paternal authority.[21]

Should this power be found inadequate, the father might invoke the assistance of a magistrate to whom alone the infliction of serious punishments was now reserved.[22]

Despite the various changes, there were still certain aspects of the *patria potestas* which preserved a vestige of its ancient supremacy. Besides having the right to correct and chastise his children, the father's authority remained a controlling influence in the household. The paternal home was the necessary legal domicile of the child before the age of puberty.[23] If one subject to him were detained by a third person, the father could reclaim him by a vindicatory action,[24] or by the interdict *de liberis exhibendis et ducendis.*[25] He could designate a tutor for those in his power who had not as yet reached puberty and could also make a will for them if they died before that age.[26] Finally, all *in patria potestate* required the consent or permission of the *paterfamilias* in order to contract marriage.[27]

Article III.—*Patria Potestas* and Matrimonial Consent

In view of the nature of *patria potestas,* its relation to matrimonial consent is inevitable. According to Roman law, *nuptiae, sive matrimonium est viri et mulieris conjunctio, individuam vitae consuetudinem continens,*[28] or again, *nuptiae sunt conjunctio maris et feminae, consortium omnis vitae, divini et humani juris communicatio.*[29] Properly speaking, marriage was not considered by the Romans as a contract in the complete juridic sense of the term, but was

[21] Sohm, *The Institutes,* p. 483.
[22] Cod. 9, 15, 1, un.; Cod. 8, 47, 3.
[23] Dig. 43, 30, 1, pr.; 3, pr.
[24] Dig. 6, 1, 1, § 2.
[25] Dig. 43, 30, 1, pr.; 3, pr.
[26] Inst. 1, 13, 3.
[27] Inst. 1, 10, pr.
[28] Inst. 1, 9, 1.
[29] Dig. 23, 2, 1.

a domestic union, legally regulated and protected, of a man and woman for the purpose of lifelong mutual companionship.[30] The accord of wills effects the marriage but does not constitute a contract because it has for its immediate end not the creation of obligations, but merely the realization of the *consortium vitae.* Not the wills of the parties, but the law fixes the consequences of that association. Briefly, marriage is a status realized by the agreement of the parties and regulated by the law.[31]

An indispensable requisite to a valid marriage was consent. The legal term *consensus* as applied to marriage implied both the consent of the contracting parties and the consent of the respective heads of their families.[32] The Roman concept of marriage demanded a free and mutual consent on the part of the parties themselves. Marriage was an exalted and sacred institution. Its existence depended upon the mutual love and affection of the parties: *ex affectu omnes introducuntur nuptiae.*[33] As long as *maritalis affectio* endured, the marital state existed. Once it was at an end, the marriage also ceased and a legal separation or divorce was in order. This notion of marriage accounts for the scarcity of texts in the sources dealing directly with matrimonial consent. Nevertheless, some evidence concerning it is found in certain passages. Thus, it is stated: *nuptias non concubitus, sed consensus facit.*[34] This passage distinguishes between the *affectio maritalis* and the *affectio concubinaria.* The intention to live as husband and wife, in the state of *nuptiae,* demands *maritalis affectio.* This factor differentiates *justae nuptiae* from that cohabitation which amounts to a mere concubinary union. In another place the law decrees: *sufficit nudus consensus ad constituenda sponsalia,*[35] and again: *libera matrimonia esse antiquitus placuit.*[36] Furthermore, it is expressly held that matrimonial consent cannot be supplied by another, e.g., in the case of one who is insane.[37] The logical conclu-

[30] Sohm, *The Institutes,* p. 452.

[31] Cf. Desforges, *Étude Historique sur la Formation du Mariage,* pp. 54-59.

[32] Vidal, *Institutiones,* n. 322; Roby, *Roman Private Law,* pp. 131-132; Bernard-Sherman, *Roman Law,* n. 258.

[33] Cod. 5, 4, 26.

[34] Dig. 50, 17, 30.

[35] Dig. 23, 1, 4. Cf. Dig. 23, 2, 16; Dig. 23, 2, 22; Dig. 23, 2, 2.

[36] Cod. 8, 39, 2.

[37] Dig. 23, 2, 16, 2; Dig. 1, 6, 8, pr.

sion to these passages is that the mutual consent of the parties themselves was necessary for the existence of a valid marriage. Personal love and mutual affection rather than other alien interests must be the efficient cause of the union.

As far as the *filius* is concerned in the matter of self-determination relative to marriage, there is little difficulty in accepting the tenets of the law at their face value. Neither in the sixth century A.D. nor in the classical period could a father betroth his son against his will. Paul's words: *filiofamilias dissentiente sponsalia nomine ejus fieri non possunt* [38] indicate, it is true, that absence of dissent rather than express consent was sufficient for espousal. But there is no reason for denying to the son an unlimited liberty of dissent. Consequently, the law protected in a negative way, at least, his freedom of choice by decreeing that a promise of future marriage could not be made if the son resisted. If dissent or resistance rendered it impossible to conclude *sponsalia,* the same principle *a fortiori* must have held where marriage was in question.

The case of the *filia,* however, is much less clear and doubt might be entertained as to whether she had a very great power of free choice. Such expressions of the law as *filiam in matrimonium collocare, tradere, dare,* contrasted with the *uxorem ducere* used of sons, appear to demand a negative answer. But the difference is mainly one of terminology. It is sufficiently explained by keeping in mind what marriage meant to the girl and her family. She left the household of her father for that of her husband—the *deductio in domum mariti* of the sources. This was especially the case in the *manus* marriage when she passed from the *potestas* of her father to that of her husband or his *paterfamilias.* But even in the form *sine manu* she departed from her family.[39]

Various texts of Roman law seem to suggest that children had little choice in the matter of their marriage. Such a conclusion is not entirely justified, since the passages in question can be reasonably explained by giving them constructions more in harmony with the facts. When Ulpian, for instance, writes: *et utrique consentiant, si*

[38] Dig. 23, 1, 13.
[39] Corbett, *Roman Law of Marriage,* pp. 2-4; 54-56.

sui juris sunt, aut etiam parentes eorum, si in potestate sunt,[40] he seems to imply that according to the ancient practice it was for the father, as being *sui juris,* to determine the choice of a partner for all who were in his power. This is not necessarily the meaning, inasmuch as the text can be explained as requiring the consent of the *paterfamilias* over and above that of the immediate parties. The probability of this interpretation increases when it is recalled that a dowry or financial consideration accompanied every marital agreement. Furthermore, when the praetor's edict[41] declares free of liability the *filius* or *filia* who contracts a double betrothal or marriage in obedience to the will of the father and punishes only the latter, the decision can be understood in the nature of a concession to the moral duty of obedience rather than an admission that the *sponsi* or *nupturientes* had nothing to say in the matter of their marriage.[42]

In addition to the consent of the immediate parties, the consent of the *paterfamilias* was required, or of those in whose *potestas* the parties were constituted.[43] This condition resulted from the *manus* marriage as a further inference of the principle: *nemini invito heres suus adgnascitur.*[44] Even later it still survived in the free marriage where no agnatic connection was established between the bride and the husband's family. Hence, the real reason for it must be found in the fact that frequently marriage involved a dowry and the nature of the *patria potestas* demanded that the *paterfamilias* have something to say in the financial negotiations. Moreover, as a protection to minors and as a safeguard against clandestine unions, the rule was of great value and consequently was maintained without relaxation. If the one who was supposed to give consent refused it or was incapable of giving it, e.g., on account of absence or insanity, permission could be obtained from a magistrate.[45] In this way the old marriage transaction, concluded by parents with the consent of their children, gradually came to be concluded by the children with the consent or

[40] Reg. 5, 2.
[41] Dig. 3, 2, 1.
[42] Cf. Corbett, *Roman Law of Marriage,* p. 54.
[43] Dig. 23, 2, 2; 18; Inst. 1, 10, pr.; Cod. 5, 4, 7; 12.
[44] Dig. 23, 2, 9, pr.; Dig. 23, 2, 16, 1.
[45] Dig. 23, 2, 19.

authorization of their parents.[46] The father's privilege of dictating marriage for his sons declined into a conditional veto with the evolution of society, and it seems that even daughters at length enjoyed a certain amount of freedom in the choice of a husband.[47]

The primitive autocratic nature of the *patria potestas* is a sound basis for assuming that in ancient Rome both the *filius* and the *filia* were frequently married off at the discretion of the *paterfamilias*. Even after the *patria potestas* was diminished in its extent, the father still had it in his power to play a despotic part, inasmuch as his consent was required for a valid marriage. The boy had some protection from the law itself, since he could not be compelled to marry. With the girl it was a different question. She naturally played a more passive part in the proceedings and would ordinarily be less resistent to authority. Consequently, the possibility of successful constraint in her case must have been considerably greater. The head of the family would probably be content to depend upon his own influence to make the daughter act the part of consenting bride.[48] In spite of these conditions, however, mutual consent was an essential requisite for a valid marriage. As *consensus* came more and more to be recognized as the constitutive element of marriage, its real significance was more clearly understood.

Article IV.—Juridic Value of Compulsory Marriage

What, then, according to Roman law, was the legal value of compulsory marriage? If the force or coercion were physical or absolute, the marriage was necessarily null and void, if for no other reason than that the element of *maritalis affectio* was completely lacking. The law explicitly states: *Neque ab initio matrimonium contrahere neque dissociatum reconciliare quisquam cogi potest. Unde intellegis liberam facultatem contrahendi atque distrahendi matrimonii transferri ad necessitatem non oportere.*[49] The use of moral compulsion was likewise condemned: *Ne filium quidem familias invitum ad ducendam uxorem cogi legum disciplina permittit. Igitur, sicut de-*

[46] Bernard-Sherman, *Roman Law,* nn. 258-259; Girard, *Manuel,* p. 153

[47] Maine, *Ancient Law,* p. 138.

[48] Corbett, *Roman Law of Marriage,* pp. 58-67.

[49] Cod. 5, 4, 14.

sideras, observatis juris praeceptis sociare conjugio tuo quam volueris non impediris, ita tamen, ut in contrahendis nuptiis patris tui consensus accedat.[50]

Admitting, however, that a marriage was contracted under circumstances of fear and moral coercion, the law expressly declares that it is valid and binding: *Si patre cogente, (filius) ducit uxorem, quam non duceret, si sui arbitrii esset, contrahit tamen matrimonium, quod inter invitos non contrahitur; maluisse hoc videtur.*[51] This law admits that marriage is not contracted between persons who are opposed to it: *inter invitos non contrahitur.* Nevertheless, in the case of marriage concluded because of paternal pressure, the marriage was held to be valid: *maluisse hoc videtur.* This phrase appears to signify that the coerced party is considered to have ratified the marriage afterwards by giving consent, that is, the *maritalis affectio* and the intention of living together as husband and wife.

As an examination of the sources reveals,[52] Roman law had an extensive system of legislation and jurisprudence to cover the points of violence and fear influencing transactions. But, outside of the single case of enforced emancipation,[53] moral compulsion, understood as *vis compulsiva,* had no annulling or abrogating influence whatsoever. The transaction, no matter what its nature, was valid but rescindable on appeal. Hence the dictum of the praetor: *quod metus causa gestum erit, ratum non habebo.*[54] Even though no definite case can be found in the sources, it is not at all improbable that these principles applied to marriage also, at least in so far as the dowry rights were concerned.

As for the marital union itself, since *maritalis affectio* never really existed, the association had only the appearance of marriage. Where consent had never been given subsequently, the legal remedy was divorce. The marriage could be dissolved on proposal. To examine thoroughly the question of Roman divorce is not necessary. It is sufficient to indicate that in this case the dissolution would be voluntary and manifested by the act of one party. *Repudium,* as it

[50] Cod. 5, 4, 12.
[51] Dig. 23, 2, 22.
[52] Cf. Dig. 4, 2; Dig. 44, 9; Cod. 2, 19.
[53] Dig. 40, 9, 9.
[54] Dig. 4, 2, 1.

was called, proceeded from either the sole will of one or the other of the parties concerned, or from the will of the head of the family. Outside of the simple agreement of the parties, and the presence of witnesses to the *libellus repudii,* the dissolution was effected without any particular form.[56]

It seems reasonable to conclude, therefore, that a diriment impediment of force and fear not only did not exist but was unnecessary in Roman law. On the one hand, marriage could not stand without *maritalis affectio,* a requisite which was incompatible with coercion, compulsion, or constraint. On the other hand, with the possibility of divorce so easy, it was not necessary to declare the forced marriage *ipso jure* null and void. It sufficed to regard it as voidable, similarly as any other transaction entered into because of duress or undue influence.[57]

Article V.—Legislation of Emperor Honorius

It is well at this point to refer briefly to a piece of Roman civil legislation which helped in no little way to discourage the practice of forcing marriage upon those opposed to it. In the year 409 the Roman Emperor Honorius enacted a law whereby marriages which had been contracted on the face of an imperial rescript were declared *ipso jure* null and void, if the official order had been obtained by the allegation of a falsehood.[58] This legislation was later repeated in the codification of Justinian.[59] A previous constitution of Honorius had made it lawful to obtain a decree from the emperor for the purpose of removing a legal or personal impediment so that a marriage, which had been earlier agreed upon, could be validly contracted.[60] Abuses of this privilege soon made their appearance. Unscrupulous persons sought the imperial rescripts under false pretenses in order to force an unwilling person to contract marriage. The legislation of Honorius was the measure taken to put an end to so odious a practice.

[56] Dig. 24, 2; Cod. 5, 17. Cf. Vidal, *Institutiones,* nn. 328-331; Sohm, *The Institutes,* pp. 474-477; Leage, *Roman Private Law,* pp. 96-97; Sherman, *Roman Law in the Modern World,* II, 484-492.

[57] Freisen, *Canonisches Eherecht,* p. 259.

[58] Cod. Theod. 3, 10, 1.

[59] Cod. 5, 8, 1.

[60] Gothofredus, *Codex Theodosianus,* I, 330.

The substance of the law was to declare that a rescript could not be validly obtained for a marriage that was against the will of either the parents or the parties immediately concerned. Gothofredus interprets the law as follows:

> It sometimes happens that certain persons lie to the emperor and seek for themselves *ex praecepto* a marriage which they do not merit (i.e., to which they have no right because the parents or the parties will not consent) and in order to obtain the imperial mandate, they allege false statements[61] about the consent of parents or children. Whoever thinks to obtain marriage under such circumstances is condemned. . . .[62]

In other words, the law decreed that a rescript could not be validly asked for the purpose of forcing a marriage that was contrary to the wills of the parties concerned. Their consent could not be extorted by imperial authority, because *sua sponte matrimonia decurrere oportet.*[63] That the validity of the marriage depended upon the truth of the cause alleged to obtain the rescript is apparent from the penal sanctions attached to the law. Besides loss of property, deportation, and impossibility of pardon in the future, any children born of such a forced union were declared illegitimate. This drastic measure shows that no valid effects could follow from a marriage extorted under false pretenses. No more definite legislation could be desired to safeguard matrimonial freedom from this form of abuse or to outlaw the use of coercive authority to secure consent to marriage. Furthermore, the law makes it clear that no external power or person, not even the emperor, might supply consent for one who was unwilling to marry.[64]

[61] The law makes use of the terms *obreptio* and *subreptio* without discrimination. Brunneman, *Commentarius in Codicem Justinianeum*, p. 552. Cf. *Codex Juris Canonici*, c. 42.

[62] *Codex Theodosianus*, I, 329.

[63] Gothofredus, *Codex Theodosianus*, I, 330.

[64] Brunneman, *Commentarius in Codicem Justinianeum*, p. 552.

CHAPTER IV

EVOLUTION OF ECCLESIASTICAL LEGISLATION

At what precise date the law of the Church first declared that gravely unjust restraint of liberty in marriages makes the contract null and void is impossible to ascertain. Many centuries passed before Canon Law arrived at a clear and coherent conception of this doctrine. For the longest time, whenever its expression is met with, it is found in a most rudimentary form, in contrast to laws of more urgent demand which were clarified into definite legal formulae at comparatively early dates.[1]

For kindred reasons, the historical development of ecclesiastical legislation to the effect that violence and fear invalidate matrimonial consent is not characterized by a wealth of detail. The present crystallized form of the law of invalidity must be read from indirect law to the particular, and from the particular to general definite legislation. Meagre and scattered as is the evidence for this historical evolution, it offers sufficient testimony to the unceasing endeavor of the Church to surround marriage with the freedom so sacred a relationship demands. It carries indubitable conviction that the Church was instrumental in asserting the natural rights of individuals against the absolutism of secular and parental authority, as practised especially in regard to the marriages of daughters by their parents under heathen civilization. How this was accomplished down through the centuries to the present time is conveniently demonstrated from a consideration of the evidences offered previous and subsequent to the time of Gratian.

Article I.—Developments Previous to Gratian

§ 1. *Doctrinal Position of the Church*

It has been seen that, while Roman law condemned the use of coercive measures relative to marriage, it viewed as valid the union which was the result of duress or constraint. The same law, how-

[1] Freisen, *Canonisches Eherecht*, p. 259.

ever, which provided for contracts in general by rescinding them if they had been forced upon anyone, permitted the dissolution of such a marriage on proposal because it was considered rescindable. This notion was altogether in conformity with Roman law since it did not recognize marriage as an indissoluble union.[2]

Accordingly, it was only to be expected that the Church would establish the impediment of fear for the protection of liberty. From the very outset her policy was necessarily dictated by the conception of marriage as an indissoluble bond. The divine revelation committed to her care taught that it was dissoluble by death alone.[3] In this Christian view there was no possibility of rescinding the marriage contract once it had been validly made. If matrimony was to be truly indissoluble, it had to be valid or invalid from the moment of celebration. A law therefore had to be enacted that would make marriages due to violence and fear invalid from the beginning.

By elevating matrimony to the dignity of a sacrament, the Son of God conferred upon the Church complete jurisdiction to regulate everything that pertained to the valid and licit celebration of marriage.[4] According to the more common opinion, He did not determine the essential constituents *in infima specie,* but left it to the Church to specify those elements of matter and form which were best suited to express the intrinsic nature of the sacrament.[5] In making marriage a part of the sacramental system, Christ did not wish to change the conditions of the contract, but to elevate it, just as it was, so that as often as it was a valid contract between baptized persons, it would also have the nature of a sacrament.[6] Despite the fact that in Gratian's era the notion became obscured, the Church

[2] Cf. Wernz-Vidal, *Jus Matrimoniale,* n. 498; Cappello, *De Matrimonio,* n. 614.

[3] Gen. 2: 24; Matth. 19: 6; Mark, 10: 11-12; Luke, 16: 18; Rom. 7: 2-3; I Cor., 7: 10-11; 39.

[4] Conc. Trid., Sess. XXIV, *de sacramento matrimonii,* cc. 2, 4, 12; Schmalzgrueber, *Jus Ecclesiasticum Universum,* lib. IV, tit. I, n. 360; Cappello, *De Matrimonio,* n. 57.

[5] Salmanticenses, *Cursus Theologiae Moralis, De Sacramentis in Genere,* c. IV, n. 48; Lugo, *De Sacramentis in Genere,* disp. IV, n. 86; Billot, *De Ecclesiae Sacramentis,* I, 35, 171; II, 297; Van Noort, *De Sacramentis,* n. 101.

[6] Lugo, *De Justitia et Jure,* disp. XXII, n. 392.

may be said to have adopted substantially the municipal law concerning matrimonial consent.[7] The dictum of the Roman jurisconsult, *nuptias non concubitus sed consensus facit,*[8] found its counterpart in the later words of St. Ambrose: "Not the deflowering of virginity, but the conjugal agreement makes a marriage." [9]

Nevertheless, the indissoluble nature of Christian marriage prevented ecclesiastical law from adopting the Roman concept of mere consent unqualified in any way, [10] as well as the principles of voidability and dissolution on proposal. Marriage due to extorted consent could not be held valid and rescindable by annulment or divorce. At the same time, the interests of the common good and the right of the individual to matrimonial freedom prohibited that compulsory marriages be regarded as valid and binding. Accordingly, to provide for the liberty of marriage in perfect harmony with her doctrine of a permanent and enduring marital bond, the Church made use of the jurisdiction she possessed and regulated this point of matrimonial discipline in her own distinctive and peculiar way. This was to declare that matrimonial consent must be free and uninfluenced. Where force and fear intervened, the marriage was not valid and voidable, but null and void from the beginning.[11]

§ 2. *The New Testament and the Fathers*

The New Testament may be minutely scrutinized but no express word will be found to uphold the freedom of marriage or to condemn the use of violence and coercion for the purpose of compelling marriage. On the contrary, various passages [12] seem to assert or assume the power of the father over his children and of the ruler over his subjects in the matter of marriage, although St. Paul [13] apparently

[7] Smith-Cheetham, *Christian Antiquities,* I, 435.

[8] Dig. 50, 17, 30. Cf. c. 1, C. XXVII, q. 2.

[9] *De Inst. Virg.* c. 6.

[10] Schulte (*Eherecht,* p. 119) holds that the *consensus* of Roman law implies free consent. Freisen (*Canonisches Eherecht,* p. 258) and Zhishman (*Eherecht,* p. 607) view it as signifying an unqualified consent.

[11] Wernz-Vidal, *Jus Matrimoniale,* n. 498; Freisen, *Canonisches Eherecht,* p. 259.

[12] Matth. 24: 38; Luke, 17: 27; I Cor., 7: 38.

[13] I Cor., 7: 39.

considered widows free to marry at their own discretion. The inference is that, in accordance with the ideas prevalent at the time, children and subjects were not always free to marry of their own choice, but were under the control of others who could marry them off as they thought best. Only after centuries had passed was there seen in St. Paul's teaching on marriage [14] an analogical argument that persuaded the necessity of matrimonial freedom. Marriage, as a sacrament, signified the voluntary union between Christ and His Church. Consequently, matrimony should be voluntary and free, in order that the sign may correspond to the thing signified.[15]

It is not strange that the Fathers, educated as they were under the laws of Rome and guided by the teachings of St. Paul, should have little or nothing to say, directly or indirectly, concerning matrimonial freedom or extorted consent. Still some evidence is at hand to show that they wished so solemn a union to be concluded freely and without constraint. Writing in 202, Clement of Alexandria states that not every one should marry. If one does so decide, the choice of a partner should be given some consideration. A mutual love must exist between husband and wife, and not that which is due to force or necessity.[16] St. Basil (329-379) likewise decided that there was no place for constraint or coercion in marriage.[17] Those who carried off virgins by force and would not restore them were to be treated as fornicators and were not to be admitted to communion with the Church until they had done penance; those to whom the virgins had been espoused were free to accept or refuse them in marriage.[18] Accomplices in these abductions incurred the same censure, but the crime is only then committed when violence is employed.[19]

Commenting on the words of St. Paul that a widow may marry whom she wills, St. Ambrose says she should marry one whom she thinks most suited to herself, because a marriage contracted unwill-

[14] Ephes, 5: 23-33.

[15] Panormitanus, *Commentaria,* lib. IV, tit. I, c. 13, n. 7.

[16] *Stromata,* lib. II, c. 23—*MPG,* 8, 1087. Cf. Probst, *Sakramente und Sakramentalien,* p. 450.

[17] *II Epist. Can. ad Amphil.,* n. 199—*MPG,* 32, 715.

[18] *II Epist. Can. ad Amphil.,* c. 22—*MPG,* 32, 722.

[19] *II Epist. Can. ad Amphil.,* c. 30—*MPG,* 32, 726.

ingly is wont to have unhappy results.[20] But it seems to have been the opinion of the same writer that it was not in keeping with maidenly modesty for a girl to choose her husband and more praiseworthy to await the decision of her parents in the matter.[21]

A letter of St. Augustine reflects somewhat the viewpoint of his time. The Bishop Benenatus had written to him concerning an orphan maiden whom a civil magistrate had requested Augustine to rear as a ward of the Church. She seems to have declared that if she were of full age she would refuse every proposal of marriage because she wanted to be a nun. Speaking of the possibility of her marrying when of age, the Bishop of Hippo declares that, although the girl has been placed under his guardianship, she cannot be given by him to whomsoever he chooses. When she becomes of age, she has a legitimate right to choose for herself.[22] In another letter to the pagan Rusticus, who had sought the hand of the same girl for his son, Augustine bluntly denies his request and refers him for the reasons of refusal to his correspondence with Benenatus.[23]

In no more lucid fashion than above illustrated do any of the Fathers write of the liberty of marriage or the freedom of matrimonial consent. This fact will occasion no surprise when it is remembered that they necessarily shared and were influenced by the ideas and customs of their day. In no Christian writing, however, has it ever been maintained that a forced marriage, contracted against the will of either party, is valid and binding.[24]

§ 3. *Conciliar Legislation*

The historian who seeks for distinctly formulated canons establishing the liberty of consent or the nullity of the forced marriage contract in the early Church is destined to be disappointed. Although definite conciliar legislation is not to be found in the first centuries,[25] it cannot be concluded that freedom of choice was unknown or that the condemnation of compulsory marriage was for-

[20] Cf. *Dictum Gratiani ad* C. XXXI, q. 2.
[21] *De Abraham,* I, c. 9, n. 91—*MPL,* 14, 453.
[22] *Epist.* 233—*MPL,* 33, 1069.
[23] *Epist.* 234—*MPL,* 33, 1070.
[24] Fulton, *Laws of Marriage,* p. 182.
[25] Cappello, *De Matrimonio,* n. 614.

eign to ecclesiastical discipline. To infer the non-existence or non-necessity of a thing from its non-accentuation is clearly illogical.[26]

The earliest semblance of legislation in this connection is to be found in the penal laws which were enacted against those guilty of the crime of abduction.[27] Even on this point, however, very little is to be found, since the high moral tenets of the new religion made such a violation of the liberty of marriage a very rare occurrence among the Christians.[28] Moreover, ecclesiastical prescriptions were not so necessary in view of various civil laws which declared abduction a capital crime.[29]

When conditions were such as to make them imperative, however, canonical prohibitions made their appearance. One of the most direct condemnations of violence is to be found in the *Apostolic Canons.* The sixty-sixth canon of this collection anathematizes anyone who by means of force takes a virgin not betrothed to another and keeps her for himself.[30] Neither the antiquity nor the authenticity of this canon can be satisfactorily established. It is certainly not of apostolic origin.[31] Because in point of severity it holds the middle course between the ancient ordinance of the Council of Ancyra (314) and the more recent rule of the Council of Chalcedon (451), some conclude that it must be referred to the period between these councils and even go so far as to regard it as an imitation of the latter's legislation.[32] Whatever the truth may be, the canon has its value as indicating the opinion of Roman Pontiffs, Councils, and Fathers,

[26] Freisen, *Canonisches Eherecht,* p. 260.

[27] Knecht, *Katholisches Eherecht,* p. 568; Freisen, *Canonisches Eherecht,* p. 262.

[28] Wernz-Vidal, *Jus Matrimoniale,* n. 309.

[29] Cod. Theod. 9, 24, 1; Dig. 48, 6, 5, 2; Cod. 9, 13, 1.

[30] Mansi, I, 57; Hefele, *Conciliengeschichte,* I, 391.

[31] The date of the composition of the Apostolic Canons cannot be determined with certainty. The first fifty canons of the collection were accepted as authentic by the early Popes and Fathers. The remaining were looked upon as apocryphal by Gelasius (492-496) and were not included in the collection of Dionysius Exiguus (c. 500). Cf. Mansi, I, 57; Funk, *Die Apostolischen Konstitutionen,* pp. 187-191; Maroto, *Institutiones,* I, nn. 43, 50; Vermeersch-Creusen, *Epitome,* I, n. 12.

[32] Cf. Hefele, *Conciliengeschichte,* I, 821, note 1.

from which sources it may well have been taken,[33] and as reflecting the attitude of the early Church on the use of violence or coercion in order to secure a wife.

More authoritative is a similar prescription of the Council of Ancyra held in Galatia in the year 314. Among the canons of the Council is one which condemns force and violence. It orders that betrothed girls who have been carried off by others shall be given back to those to whom they have been espoused.[34] The latter were at liberty to receive their affianced brides or to dismiss them.[35] The freedom given the injured party to accept or quit the engagement was doubtlessly prompted by the desire to protect him against injustice. At the same time it indicates that the marriage contract was safeguarded from anything resembling compulsion.

The first universal prohibition against violence is found in the Fourth Oecumenical Council held at Chalcedon in 451. Its twenty-seventh canon anathematizes all who forcibly carry off women under pretense of marriage.[36] It furthermore decreed that all who assisted the abductors by actual coöperation or conspiracy, as well as all who approved their action, incurred the same censure. Coöperators were those who actually gave assistance to the abductor and abettors, those who lent moral support by words of counsel or encouragement.[37] In this general prescription against violence, with all that it implied, can be seen the first steps of a legislation that would eventually forbid every species of coercion and duress for the purpose of securing marriage.

Further indirect evidence can be drawn from another source. A Council held at Hippo in 393 ruled that deacons should not be ordained and virgins should not be consecrated until they were twenty-five years of age.[38] Later, in the year 418, a general African Synod at Carthage permitted the bishop to dispense with this law

[33] Mansi, I, 57.

[34] C. 11—Mansi, II, 518; Hefele, *Conciliengeschichte,* I, 230.

[35] Van Espen, *Jus Ecclesiasticum Universum,* III, 129; Knecht, *Katholisches Eherecht,* p. 439.

[36] Mansi, VII, 370; Hefele, *Conciliengeschichte,* II, 527; c. 1, C. XXXVI, q. 2.

[37] Van Espen, *Jus Ecclesiasticum Universum,* III, 260.

[38] C. 1 (*second series*)—Hefele, *Conciliengeschichte,* II, 56.

for a just and reasonable cause.[39] Among the reasons enumerated were those in which the girl was in danger of losing her virginity because of being demanded in marriage by an influential person, or because of threatened abduction by violence. In other words, an exception was made to an important general regulation in favor of personal liberty. To prevent one who wished to consecrate himself to God from being forced into marriage, the Council saw fit to allow a dispensation. While this legislation directly protected the freedom of religious profession, it argues, at least indirectly, that marriage was not to be forced upon anyone contrary to his will.

With the vast missionary activity of the fifth and sixth centuries which witnessed the Gospel spread rapidly beyond the confines of the Roman empire,[40] the church was confronted with the problem of inculcating the principle of matrimonial liberty upon primitive barbarians whose mode of living, customs, and practices differed widely from those of the highly advanced social culture of the Empire. Similar to the *patria potestas,* but not identical with it,[41] was the *mundium* or paternal authority among these peoples. Although the actual extent of the father's rights in ancient times, when the races had no written laws, is unknown, still the religious basis which the family institution enjoyed endowed paternal authority with a strong religious character.[42] Consequently marriage, of its very nature domestic and religious, was under the full jurisdiction of the father. This dominion over marriage was not confined to parents or superiors of the individual family. Princes and rulers claimed for themselves the royal prerogative of marrying their subjects. Regardless of the wishes of others, they arranged marriages in accord-

39 Mansi, III, 822; Hefele, *Conciliengeschichte,* II, 119.

40 The Gospel had been introduced into Gaul, Spain, Germany and Britain much earlier, but these sporadic incursions of missionaries were as nothing compared with evangelizing efforts and successes of later years. Cf. Funk, *Manual of Church History,* I, 35-39; 122-133.

41 Laboulaye, *Recherches sur la Condition Civile et Politique des Femmes,* p. 80; Mackenzie, *Studies in Roman Law,* p. 104; Inst. 1, 10.

42 Cf. Fustel de Coulanges (*The Ancient City,* p. 116): "In primitive antiquity the father is not only the strong man, the protector who has power to command obedience; he is the priest, he is heir to the hearth, the continuator of the ancestors, the parent stock of the descendants, the depository of the mysterious rites of worship, and of the sacred formulas of prayer. The whole religion resides in him."

ance with their own interests and machinations.[43] Evidence of these abuses is readily seen in a study of the civil laws. By denying this power to inferior potentates, the kings of the Franks and Visigoths did not eradicate the practice but rather restricted it to themselves.[44]

The Church faced the issue with as firm a stand as circumstances permitted and sought to correct the abuses with legislation aimed both at ruler and subject. If a canon of doubtful authority to be found in Gratian [45] and enacting that widows before professing continence may marry whom they will, that virgins may do the same, and that none should be forced to marry a husband, be excepted,[46] the earliest ecclesiastical enactment found outside of the Empire seems to belong to an Irish Synod. In one of a series of synods, held between 450 and 456, it was declared that a girl should do the will of her father, "for the head of the woman is the man." Nevertheless, the will of the girl is to be inquired of the father.[47] While this law acknowledges paternal authority, it expressly insists that the will of the child be not entirely disregarded.

Perhaps the first condemnation of the practice of kings to marry their subjects was promulgated by the IV Council of Orleans held between 541 and 545.[48] The disciplinary measure which condemned the use of royal authority to force persons to marry was sanctioned with a sentence of excommunication for offenders.[49] The reason offered for this drastic measure was: *ne conjugium velut captivitas judicetur.* Captivity in its real sense meant slavery in those days, and a marriage due to coercion and constraint was deemed equivalent to captivity and slavery.

The III Council of Paris, convened around the year 557, made a similar prohibition. Men were accustomed to seek from the king

[43] Freisen, *Canonisches Eherecht,* p. 260; Esmein, *Mariage en Droit Canonique,* II, 255-256.

[44] Moy, *Eherecht,* p. 328; Wernz-Vidal, *Jus Matrimoniale,* n. 498.

[45] C. 38, C. XXVII, q. 1.

[46] Mansi (VIII, 629) attributes it to the IV or V Council of Arles (524, 554). Richter (*Corpus Juris Canonici, Proleg.* p. XXI) recognizes it as the tenth canon of the III Council of Toledo (589).

[47] Mansi, VI, 526.

[48] Mansi, IX, 122; Baronius, *Annales,* IX, 614, n. 9; Hefele-Leclercq, *Histoire des Conciles,* II, 2, 1164.

[49] Mansi, IX, 117.

authorization to acquire things belonging to others when such permission had been refused by the Bishop or priest. They went so far as to secure imperial orders for the purpose of forcing marriage upon those opposed to it.[50] To defend the liberty of marriage and to prevent kings from assuming powers to which they had no right, the Council decreed that anyone who presumed to take by force a widow or the daughter of another for his wife, or attempted to secure her on an order from the king, incurred excommunication.[51] As in the above ordinance of Orleans, nothing is said concerning the consent of the parties. This may be explained as due to the ascendancy of parental authority. Parents, as Christians, would only then consent to a marriage when it was in accordance with the laws of the Church and the wishes of the children. At all events, the Bishops of the Council followed the earlier legislation in an effort to guarantee matrimonial liberty.

The legislation of the II Council of Tours (567) requires some consideration. The twentieth canon [52] among its disciplinary measures was intended to correct certain abuses connected with the relinquishment of the religious habit by women. After punishing with excommunication virgins, widows and others who ventured to put off the religious habit for the purpose of returning to the world and contracting marriage, the canon condemns an excuse frequently offered by such persons in extenuation of their action. This was the practice of girls sometimes to enter the convent, not with the intention of dedicating themselves to God, but simply to escape being forced into a repugnant marriage. When the danger no longer threatened, they abandoned the religious life, re-entered the world, and married in accord with their own inclinations or aspirations. This pretense of taking the veil in order not to be forced into a disadvantageous or undesired marriage is roundly condemned and forbidden. The Council of Carthage, it has been seen, supposed the case of a virgin who took the veil because she feared being forced into marriage when she really wished to consecrate herself to God.[53] The present

[50] Mansi, IX, 748-749.

[51] C. 6—Mansi, IX, 756; Hefele, *Conciliengeschichte,* III, 13; Hinschius, *Kirchenrecht,* IV, 800, n. 6; cf. c. 6, C. XXXVI, q. 2.

[52] Mansi, IX, 798; Hefele, *Conciliengeschichte,* III, 26.

[53] C. 126, (18)—Mansi, III, 822.

canon excludes the danger of forced marriage as an excuse for temporarily taking the veil with the intention of later relinquishing it.

Following the reprobation of this custom is an observation amounting practically to a direct testimony of the solicitude of the Church for the liberty of the marriage contract. The canon counsels that those fearing violence should, without receiving the veil, take refuge in the church until parents or relatives find means to liberate them from their fears through the aid of the Bishop or the king. By following this course of action, they will remain free to marry; but once clothed in the religious habit, they must persevere in their resolution.[54]

Several decades later witnessed similar legislation in Spain. It is of special interest for several reasons. In the first place, it is evidence that the Church of Spain defended matrimonial freedom with the same constancy and solicitude among the Visigoths as did the Bishops of the Frankish kingdoms. Secondly, the personal liberty of the immediate parties is more specifically upheld than in any previous legislation. In 589 the Council of Toledo, which marked the revivification of the faith in Spain with the conversion of Recarred,[55] was summoned by the king so that the Bishops might instruct the people once again in the true principles of Christianity.

The doctrine concerning marriage was embodied in the tenth canon.[56] A widow was not to be compelled to marry. If previous to having vowed continence she chose to marry, she was to do so of her own choice and a husband was not to be forced upon her. The same legislation was made with regard to the unmarried. It was forbidden to compel them to marry against their parents' or their own will, nor were they to be prevented from entering religion if they so desired.[57]

[54] Mansi, IX, 800; "Quaecumque ergo timet violentiam et non vult habere maritum, refugiat ad ecclesiam donec propinqui possint eam principis imperio, aut sacerdotis vel ecclesiae liberare et defensare, ac condigno sociare marito. Nam quae se veste mutaverit, absque dolo in eo proposito quod disposuit, perseverare procuret."

[55] Hefele-Leclercq, *Histoire des Conciles,* III, 122.

[56] Mansi, IX, 995; Hefele, *Conciliengeschichte,* III, 51.

[57] Cf. c. 16, C. XXXII, q. 2; c. 38, C. XXVII, q. 1.

The terms employed to express this legislation now become somewhat more definite. For the first time is found an explicit declaration that marriage must be the result of free choice: *si nubere elegerint, illis nubant, quos propria voluntate elegerint habere maritos.* Nor can anyone be compelled to re-marry: *nulla vi ad nuptias iterandas venire cogantur.* Particularly noteworthy is the definite mention now made of the will of the party immediately concerned: *ne citra voluntatem suam cogantur maritos accipere.* Here at last are notions which in succeeding centuries would be subjected to a thorough analysis until they yielded the crystallized form of canonical legislation found in the Decretals.

The beginning of the seventh century witnessed the Council of Rheims (625) renew the legislation of the Councils of Orleans, Paris and Tours.[58] Marriage was not to be forced on anyone, and not even on the pretext of imperial authorization or the mandate of anyone was a virgin or widow to be compelled to marry.[59] In the same century the Council of Trullo (692) reiterated the regulation of the Council of Chalcedon.[60]

The following century produced scarcely more accurate legislation. A Synod held at Rome in 721 under Gregory II, after forbidding marriage within certain degrees of consanguinity and affinity, once more repeated earlier prohibitions concerning violence relative to marriage.[61] About twenty years later an important Roman council convened by Pope Zachary corroborated these statutes.[62]

Enactments of some significance were included in the canons of the Council of Compiegne convened in 756. A decision was given regarding the forced marriage of a free-born step-daughter. If any man gave such a one in marriage against her own will and the will of her mother or relations, she was not bound by the marriage. She could refuse the man and, should she desert him, her relations had the right of giving her another husband. If the girl herself, of her own initiative, took another husband, they were not to be separated.[63]

[58] Mansi, X, 591; Harduin, III, 569; c. 6, C. XXXVI, q. 2.
[59] C. 23—Mansi, X, 597.
[60] C. 92—Hefele, *Conciliengeschichte*, III, 341.
[61] Cc. 10, 11—Mansi, XII, 264; Hefele, *Conciliengeschichte*, III, 362.
[62] C. 7—Mansi, XII, 383; Hefele, *Conciliengeschichte*, III, 516.
[63] C. 4—Harduin, III, 2005.

The first point to be noted is the express mention of the girl's own will similarly as in the decree of Toledo. Secondly, the validity of the marriage must have depended on freedom of personal choice, otherwise a second marriage would never have been permitted, much less could the girl have continued to live with a second man of her own choice. Likewise given consideration is the case of a serf who seems to have been constrained to marry a certain woman, in order that his lord might the more securely hold him to an estate of which he had just come into possession. After living with the woman for some time, the serf abandoned her and married another. The Council rendered a decision in favor of him retaining the second woman as his wife.[64] Whether compulsion was actually used by the lord is not clear. But this seems to be implied and, in view of the peculiar relationship existing between lord and serf in feudal times, no other reason for the decision seems more probable than that the latter had never freely consented to the first union.

A synod held at Pavia (Ticino) censured violence and excommunicated those guilty of the offense. The decree reads:

> Concerning those who use violence, we decree that this must be held in accordance with the statutes of the ancient fathers: if they force those who have been betrothed with the sacerdotal blessing, although they violate them, nevertheless they are to be separated from those who forced them and returned to their spouses. As regards those who are widows, or have not as yet been espoused, and are coerced against their own wills and the wills of the parents, they too must be restored to their relatives and they may marry others if they will; for they can never be the legitimate wives of those who have contrived against them with force.[65]

The mere perusal of this legislation discloses the important implications it contains. The Church's determination to uphold the liberty of marriage and to outlaw the use of force is particularly evident in her treatment of the case of those who were not as yet engaged. The express mention of the will of the parties is altogether in keep-

[64] C. 6—Harduin, III, 2005.

[65] C. 10—Mansi, XIV, 934; Harduin, V, 28; Hefele, *Conciliengeschichte*, IV, 177.

ing with the gradual evolution of that element to greater prominence in ecclesiastical law.

Other councils and synods of the pre-Gratian period which legislated more or less directly on the matter under discussion might be cited.[66] The decrees, however, to which reference has been made, are adequate enough to reveal the tenor of conciliar legislation during these centuries. Moreover, the canons indicated were all couched in the general terms of earlier canonical statutes. Councils which made no explicit mention of the matter did so implicitly by declaring that all the ancient canons heretofore enacted were to be observed. Such an expression as found in the legislation of Ticino, *antiquorum patrum statuta sequentes,* is typical and is to be understood of all previous legislation on that particular point of matrimonial discipline.

§ 4. *Pontifical Decisions*

So far only conciliar decrees have been offered as evidence that the Church in the centuries preceding Gratian championed the liberty of the matrimonial pact and condemned the use of force and compulsion to secure its conclusion. To suppose, however, that the supreme pontiffs were silent in this matter would be erroneous. In keeping with his position as the shepherd of the flock of Christ, the chief ruler of the Church is naturally expected to indicate to his subjects the correct rule of action in any particular situation and to make use of his sovereign authority in the prosecution of that end. Although the Popes were not found wanting in regard to guidance in the matter of the forced marriage contract, it must be confessed that evidence to substantiate the claim is not abundant. Whereas the Roman Pontiffs were frequently the prime movers in

[66] I Synod of Orleans (511), c. 2—Mansi, VIII, 352; Synod of Trullo (692), c. 92—Mansi, XI, 982; Council of Aix-la-Chapelle (817), cc. 22-24 (*3rd docum.*)—Hefele, *Conciliengeschichte,* IV, 27; Synod of Verneuil (844), c. 6—Hefele, *Conciliengeschichte,* IV, 111; Synod of Meaux-Paris (845-846), cc. 64-69—Mansi, XIV, 834-835; Synod of Worms (868), c. 77—Mansi, XV, 882; Synod of Ravenna (877), c. 6—Mansi, XVII, 338; German Reform Council of Metz (883), c. 11—Mansi, XVIII, 80; French Reform Synod of Trosly of Rheims in the diocese of Soissons (909), c. 8—Mansi, XVIII, 286-288; Council of Vienne and Tours (1060), c. 9—Mansi, XIX, 928; Council of Aran (*Strigonium*) (1114), c. 153—Mansi, XXI, 109.

the assemblage of Councils and Synods that numbered among their disciplinary measures condemnations of violence and coercion,[67] the majority of the anathemas were issued from local or provincial assemblies. Nevertheless, when they were consulted or asked to render a decision in a particular case, their pronunciations were in complete accord with the principle that marriage is a state of life to be freely chosen. Assuredly the Popes, who never sanctioned or approved an ordination or religious profession obtained by force,[68] must have proceeded against compulsory marriage in a similar fashion.

Leo I (440-461), writing to Rusticus, Bishop of Narbonne, testifies to the freedom with which those entering either the religious or married state should act. He condemned those who *non parentum imperio,* but *spontaneo judicio,* took up the religious life, only to abandon it afterwards in order to marry.[69] The wording of the reprobation makes it clear that persons must be free from influence or coercion in their choice of a state of life. Once that had been selected, however, they were to persevere in it. If the election were due to some external pressure, they were evidently at liberty to forsake it.

In a letter of instruction to Caesarius, the Bishop of Arles, Pope Symmachus (498-514) strongly reprehends those who used violence to secure a wife. All offenders of this kind were, in his opinion, most detestable because of the enormity of the crime. Those especially were to be punished who attempted forcibly to marry virgins consecrated to God, whether they were willing to marry or not: *quos pro tam nefandissimi criminis atrocitate a communione suspendi praecipimus.*[70]

Mention may here be made of a letter canonized in the Decree of Gratian[71] as well as in the Decretals of Gregory IX[72] and spur-

[67] Thus e.g., Gregory II called the synod of Rome in 721, and Zachary that of 743.

[68] Hinschius, *Kirchenrecht,* I, 110.

[69] *MPL* 84, 768.

[70] *Epist. ad Caes.,* c. IV—Jaffé, *Regesta,* 764; Mansi, VIII, 212; Hinschius, *Decretales Pseudo-Isidorianae,* p. 567; Thiel, *Epistolae Genuinae,* I, 725.

[71] C. 2, C. XXXI, q. 2.

[72] C. 1, X, *de despons. impub.,* IV, 2.

iously ascribed to Pope Hormisdas (514-523).[73] This document states that one who was unwilling to marry could not be forced into the contract by his father, if he were an adult. A son not yet of age could be promised in marriage. Later he should observe and fulfill his father's pledge, but nothing is said of an obligation to marry.[74] Gregory I (590-604), when consulted by the Bishop Maximian concerning a marriage which had been *violenter adversis persuasionibus puellae ipsius junctum,* termed the situation a great evil which must be corrected at once, because in matrimony the will should be free.[75]

The manner in which Nicholas I (863-866) disposed of the attempted divorce of Lothair II from his lawful wife Theutberga in order to marry his mistress Waldrada furnishes some indication of the Church's attitude toward a marriage influenced by fear. It is unnecessary to enter into the complicated details of the long controversy which ended only with the death of the king.[76] What is of paramount interest is that, in the early days of his marital difficulties, Lothair wrote to Nicholas and asked that legates be sent to examine into the rights of his case. To strengthen his cause he assured the Pope that his father had originally given him Waldrada as his wife but that afterwards, because of threats made against his kingdom and himself, he had been unwillingly compelled to marry Theutberga.[77]

[73] Cf. Thiel, *Epistolae Genuinae,* I, 1006. Difference of opinion is found as to probable authorship and date of composition. Van Espen (*Opera Omnia,* III, 635-636) believes the letter is apocryphal. Berardi (*Gratiani Canones Genuini,* I, 384) is inclined to agree with this opinion but thinks it may be the work of Honorius II (1124-1130). Richter-Friedberg (*Corpus Juris Canonici,* I, 1113, II, 672) classify it as a *caput incertum.*

[74] *Bullarium Romanum,* App. I, 458-459; Mansi, VIII, 530.

[75] Epist., lib. III, ep. 12—*MPL,* 77, 682; Mansi, IX, 1164.

[76] Cf. Mansi, XV, 548, 615; Hefele, *Conciliengeschichte,* IV, 224-227; 251-254; Funk, *Manual of Church History,* I, 271-272; Mann, *Lives of the Popes,* III, 79; Schaff, *History of the Christian Church,* IV, 275-276; *Dictionnaire de Théologie Catholique,* IX, 2119.

[77] Mann, *Lives of the Popes,* III, 72; Ernouf, *Histoire de Waldrade et de Lothaire,* II, 3. It cannot be definitely settled whether Lothair freely consented to his marriage with Theutberga. A gloss to c. 4, C. XXXI, q. 2 speaks of the king as *mendaciter* relating the circumstances of fear to the Pope. In his instruction to the legates, Nicholas does not seem to put much faith in the

Nicholas dispatched two legates with orders to convoke a synod at Metz, examine the case of the king, and send the acts to him for his approval.[78] He likewise gave them a letter of instruction as to how they should treat the matter.[79] They are ordered to investigate diligently whether the king had been legitimately united to Waldrada as he claimed. If this is substantiated, they are to find out why she had been repudiated in favor of a marriage with Theutberga. Regarding Lothair's assertion that he had married the latter out of fear, the Pope remarks with apparent irony that so great a king ought not be the victim of fear.[80] If it is proven that the marriage of Waldrada is not legitimate, because not contracted according to canonical norms, they are to exhort Lothair to become reconciled to Theutberga.

This document reveals the views of Nicholas regarding the forced marriage contract. The fact that Lothair appealed to fear and duress as a reason for declaring his marriage to Theutberga null and void argues that marriage contracted under those circumstances was not always considered valid. The Pope admits as much when he berates the king for proposing such a cause and implicitly makes another distinction. By scorning the idea of a great ruler being forced into marriage through threats, he acknowledges that a person not so powerful or influential might suffer from such coersion. Here is evidence of fear being distinguished as grave or slight, absolute or relative. When Nicholas finally says: *suggerite illi, ut non moleste ferat legitimam sibi reconciliari uxorem,* he states his opinion that the marriage is valid in the presence of a fear insufficient to effect nullity.

More definite than these decisions are two that have come down from Urban II (1088-1099) and have been received by Gratian as canons in his Decree.[81] The first concerned the case of a certain Raynald, son of Rodelus, who had prevailed upon the weak-willed

monarch's story. Cf. Baronius, *Annales,* XIV, 542, nn. 28-29 (*ed.* Theiner); Hefele-Leclercq, *Histoire des Conciles,* IV, 238, note 1.

[78] Mansi, XV, 367; Mann, *Lives of the Popes,* III, 72.

[79] C. 4, C. XXXI, q. 2; Mansi, XV, 367-368; Hefele, *Conciliengeschichte,* IV, 263.

[80] Cf. Freisen, *Canonisches Eherecht,* p. 261.

[81] C. 1, C. XXXI, q. 2; c. 3, C. XXXI, q. 2.

Jordan to betroth his daughter to him despite her tears and protests. When later Raynald demanded her in marriage, Jordan refused, alleging coercion and claiming that the girl was entirely opposed to the union and declined to accept him as her husband.[82]

Urban's answer upon being consulted was definite and decisive. If his representative establishes as true all that the agents of Jordan have reported, namely, that under duress he espoused his daughter, that her mother and relatives were opposed to the betrothal, and that the girl herself resisted it with all the power at her command, then the canons and laws which do not approve such a procedure must be observed. Lest his decision appear too stringent to those who are ignorant of these principles, the Pope accommodatingly modifies his ruling by making several distinctions. If Jordan, with the consent of his daughter and all concerned, should now wish the marriage, then it may be contracted. If they do not desire it, the papal legate will hear both sides of the case. Should the facts of coercion and undue influence be verified and the girl refuse to live with the man, then, in accordance with the injunctions of ecclesiastical laws, he does not forbid her from marrying another if she so wishes.[83]

The second decision is of similar exactness and precision. Sancho, King of Aragon, because of some urgent necessity had promised under oath to give his niece in marriage to one of his soldiers. This was done without her knowledge or consent and she set herself positively against the proposed marriage.[84] When the king inquires whether he can make the girl consent to the marriage, Urban answers, *aequitate dictante,* that if she continues to refuse and persists in her opposition to the soldier, the king cannot compel her to marry. Those whose bodies become one must be one also in soul and spirit, and those who are unwillingly joined together are in danger of sinning against the precept of the Lord and the Apostle by fornication.[85]

The value of these decisions is considerable. They offer strong

[82] *Glossa* to c. 1, C. XXXI, q. 2.

[83] C. 1, C. XXXI, q. 2; Jaffé, *Regesta,* 5382 (4311); Freisen, *Canonisches Eherecht,* p. 261; Wernz-Vidal, *Jus Matrimoniale,* n. 498.

[84] *Glossa* to c. 3, C. XXXI, q. 2.

[85] C. 3, C. XXXI, q. 2; Jaffé, *Regesta,* 5399 (4113); Mansi, XX, 713; Freisen, *Canonisches Eherecht,* p. 262.

evidence that at the time of Urban various laws and canons condemned not merely physical violence but also *metus compulsivus*. Appealing to what he terms the *canonum et legum auctoritas,* the Pope holds as a well-established law that violence and fear have no place in the matrimonial contract. He follows the dictates of these laws and canons and the demands of canonical equity in deciding that an injured party has the right to marry another. The fact that those compelled to marry are in danger of fornication points to the invalidity of the union. Despite the apparent recognition of such a factor as *metus compulsivus* in the age of Urban II, its exact content and significance was scarcely endowed with the precision of later ages.[86]

§ 5. *Penitential Books*

The study of the evolution of any particular piece of ecclesiastical legislation requires that some consideration be given to the Penitential Books of the early Church. These are particularly valuable as a source for the historical examination of canonical statutes. In ancient days the canonical form of penance was of highest importance and many canons were prescribed for its performance. Inasmuch as these are a practical application of ecclesiastical norms, they serve as a means to determine the *vigens Ecclesiae disciplina* of the times in which they were in use.[87]

Concerning the use of violence for the purpose of securing marriage, the Penitential Books reveal a discipline in harmony with conciliar legislation. The *Poenitentiale Valicellanum I,* which seems to date from the first half of the eighth century,[88] lists the anathemas of Gregory I, the seventh of which condemns all who in any way are involved in an action which forces a widow to become the wife of another.[89] Among the penitential canons is one which recalls the legislation of Chalcedon, later repeated at Trullo in 692 and the two Roman Synods of 721 and 743, and lays down a penance for

[86] Smisniewicz, *Die Lehre von den Ehehindernissen,* p. 76.

[87] Schmitz, *Bussbuecher und Bussdisciplin,* p. 1; Maroto, *Institutiones,* I, n. 56; Vermeersch-Creusen, *Epitome,* I, n. 16; Probst, *Sakramente und Sakramentalien,* pp. 296-335.

[88] Schmitz, *Bussbuecher und Bussdisciplin,* p. 237.

[89] Schmitz, *Bussbuecher und Bussdisciplin,* p. 247.

those guilty of infringing that discipline.[90] The *Poenitentiale Valicellanum II,* consisting of *canones poenitentiales vetustiores,* likewise sets a penance for those who commit such an offense.[91]

The *Poenitentiale Arundel* contains an interesting canon:

> Si quis uxorem rapuerit, absque ejus voluntate et parentum suorum, eam, nisi illa sponte sua voluerit, uxorem habere non poterit, sed per separationem ipsa, si velit, alteri nubat. Raptor vero VII annos peniteat. Quod si ipsa, antequam alteri jungatur, illius conjunctioni assensum praebuerit, habeat eam uxorem, sed tamen praedicto modo poeniteat.[92]

From this it is evident that the validity of the marriage, as it is termed today, depended upon a consent that was *sponte sua,* otherwise what is the import of the consequence: *eam uxorem habere non poterit?* On the other hand, the marriage, once invalid, was convalidated by consent afterward given.

The Penitential Book attributed to Theodore of Canterbury and dating from around the year 684 is really illuminating on the matrimonial discipline of that era. A boy was under the authority of his father until his fifteenth year. Thereafter he could enter a monastery if he desired. A girl of sixteen or seventeen years was permitted to do the same, but previous to that age she was subject to her parents. After this age a father was not permitted to give his daughter in marriage contrary to her will. Unless an espoused daughter positively resisted to marriage with her bethrothed, parents were not permitted to give her to another. Moreover, if a girl did not wish to marry the man to whom she was betrothed, she could not be compelled to do so. The matter might be adjusted, as far as the ends of justice were concerned, by returning to her fiancé the dowry money with the addition of a third part.[93]

In the so-called *Excerpta* of Egbert, Archbishop of York in the eighth century, it is stated that women are not to be united in

[90] *Poen. Valicell. I, c.* 17—Schmitz, *Bussbuecher und Bussdisciplin,* p. 270.

[91] C. 26—Schmitz, *Bussbuecher und Bussdisciplin,* p. 361.

[92] C. 65—Schmitz, *Bussbuecher und Bussdisciplin,* p. 455.

[93] *Poen. Theod.,* lib. II, c. 20—Schmitz, *Bussbuecher und Bussdisciplin,* pp. 547-548.

marriage if they are absolutely opposed to it.[94] The collection of penitential canons attributed to Halitgar, Bishop of Cambrai, imposes penances to be performed by those guilty of marrying by force or forcing others to marry.[95] Books imposing similar penances are the Penitential of Paris[96] and that credited to Cummaeus who died around the year 661.[97] By reason of the severe punishments they levy against those who make use of force and violence to coerce a person to marry, all are eloquent witnesses to an ecclesiastical discipline which constantly sought to defend matrimonial freedom.

Article II.—From the Decree of Gratian to the Code

The period about to be considered saw the Church's doctrine concerning marriage contracted under the influence of violence and fear emerge from the vague and indistinct expression of the previous centuries to the sharply defined formulae that have passed practically unchanged into existing canonical legislation. The whole of matrimonial discipline developed so remarkably during the late middle ages that it is somewhat difficult to account for this phenomenon. One reason is that by this time there was a generalization of the Christian faith in civil society. A natural consequence was the admission of the exclusive competence of the Church over the sacrament of matrimony.[98] Moreover, due to the influx of Roman and Germanic elements, marriage legislation was in a greatly muddled and confused condition and some kind of unification was sorely needed. Conciliar legislation and canonical compilations had handed down many norms of action woefully lacking in systematization and codification. A complete inventory of ecclesiastical legislation was demanded and, difficult though it was to supply, it was gradually achieved in these centuries.[99]

94 *Excerp. Egbert.*, lib. II, c. 20—Schmitz, *Bussbuecher und Bussdisciplin*, pp. 565-573.

95 *Poen. Halit.*, lib. IV, ch. 16—Schmitz, *Bussbuecher und Bussdisciplin*, pp. 477, 725.

96 C. 123—Schmitz, *Bussbuecher und Bussdisciplin*, p. 694.

97 *Poen. Cumm.*, cap. VIII, c. 1—Schmitz, *Bussbuecher und Bussdisciplin*, p. 659.

98 Chenon, *La Rôle Social de l'Eglise*, pp. 74-75; Pollock-Maitland, *History of English Law*, I, 106; II, 364.

99 *Dictionnaire de Théologie Catholique*, IX, 2125-2130.

Relative to the particular point of matrimonial consent there was no end of controversy. The rescript of Nicholas I to the Bulgarians decreed that mutual consent, provided it had the requisite qualities, sufficed to conclude marriage.[100] Opposed to this teaching was the theory, ascribed to Hincmar of Rheims,[101] that marriage is begun by consent but perfected by the conjugal act.[102]

Even before this dispute was settled by Alexander III,[103] canonists and theologians focused their attention more critically on the subject of matrimonial consent. If the consent of the parties gave rise to marriage, its nature had to be more specifically determined. Not every or any consent would suffice, but only that which was endowed with the proper requisites. The intellectual skill and acumen of the age little by little fixed the kind of consent essentially required for marriage. The factors of condition, error, ignorance, violence, moral compulsion and fear received earnest consideration in order to discover to what extent they vitiated that consent. The scientific renaissance of Roman Law in the eleventh century[104] revived many of the ancient notions and furnished a fitting terminology for the various distinctions that now appeared. The result was that before very long definite norms were established for determining under exactly what circumstances obstacles to matrimonial consent on the part of the intellect and will were present to a degree sufficient to vitiate the consensual act of the will and invalidate the marriage.

§ 1. *The Decree of Gratian*

Gratian's work, appearing around the year 1142,[105] was an at-

[100] *Ad consulta Bulgarorum*, c. 3—Mansi, XV, 403; Jaffé, *Regesta*, 2123; *MPL*, 119, 980; Hefele, *Conciliengeschichte*, IV, 347; cf. c. 2, C. XXVII, q. 2.

[101] Esmein, *Mariage en Droit Canonique*, I, 106-107; De Smet, *Betrothment and Marriage*, I, 61.

[102] Cappello, *De Matrimonio*, n. 577; Wernz-Vidal, *Jus Matrimoniale*, p. 39, note 68; p. 546, note 11; Freisen, *Canonisches Eherecht*, pp. XXVIII-XXXIV.

[103] C. 3, X, *de sponsa duorum*, IV, 4. Cf. Esmein, *Mariage en Droit Canonique*, I, 140.

[104] Cf. Kelly, "Roman Law," *Catholic Encyclopedia*, IX, 88; Sohm, *The Institutes*, pp. 135-138.

[105] Friedberg, *Corpus Juris Canonici*, Prolegom., IX; Schulte, *Geschichte*, I, 48.

tempt to remedy the confused disorder of ten centuries of ecclesiastical legislation. He considered the question of marriage in the second part of the Decree, *Causa XXVII* to *Causa XXXVI*. The treatment of matrimonial consent is found in *Causa XXVII* under the second question where, after giving the arguments for and against the *copula* theory, he decided in favor of it.[106]

As far as marriage contracted under the influence of coercion is concerned, Gratian devoted no special section to its study. The matter of abduction and violence in general is considered separately.[107] Coercion and moral compulsion, however, are discussed as part of the thirty-first *Causa*. The Magister proposes the following case: A man committed adultery with another's wife. When the latter's husband died, the partners in the crime were married. A daughter born of this union was promised in marriage by the father, but she refused her consent to the union. When he gave her in marriage to another, the one to whom she had been first promised sought to obtain her for himself. Thereupon Gratian questions: (a) whether partners in adultery can marry; (b) whether a daughter who refuses to give consent can be given in marriage; (c) whether after her father's promise she can be given to another.

It is in the second question therefore that Gratian deals with matrimonial coercion and constraint. He answers by stating definitely that no one should be compelled to marry and refers to the commentary of St. Ambrose on the words of the Apostle: "A woman is bound by the law as long as her husband liveth; but if her husband die, she is at liberty: let her marry to whom she will; only in the Lord."[108] A widow, according to St. Ambrose, should marry one whom she thinks compatible with herself in all things. She must enjoy this liberty because a marriage contracted unwillingly is wont to have unfortunate consequences. Provided she marry "in the Lord," she is to be free in her choice.[109] It is particularly noteworthy that, whereas St. Paul's words were addressed to widows, and St. Ambrose also seems to have had only such in

[106] De Smet, *Betrothment and Marriage,* n. 97; Esmein, *Mariage en Droit Canonique,* I, 119-125.

[107] Cc. 1-3, C. XXXVI, q. 1; cc. 1-11, C. XXXVI, q. 2.

[108] I Cor. 7:39.

[109] *Dictum Gratiani* ad C. XXXI, q. 2.

mind, Gratian nevertheless uses them in reference to a daughter who is unwilling to marry the man selected by her father. Hence it appears that the same liberty once enjoyed only by widows was now extended to any woman regardless of her status.

As proof for his assertion Gratian offers various authoritative decrees which have been already discussed. A girl is not compelled to contract a marriage to which she is opposed, despite the oath or promise made by her father. The judgment of Urban II in the case of Jordan is authority for this conclusion.[110] Following is a *palea* containing the communication of Hormisdas in which he distinguishes the marriage of an adult son from that of one not as yet of age.[111] Furthermore, according to the reply given by Urban to Sancho, those who are to become of one body must also be of one mind.[112] Finally, the letter of instruction given by Nicholas I to his representatives is cited.[113]

Having established his first proposition by these authorities, Gratian concludes: *His auctoritatibus evidenter ostenditur, quod nisi libera voluntate nulla est copulanda alicui.* The expression *libera voluntate* is little less than extraordinary for Gratian's era. In none of the documentary evidence which he cites, nor in any authoritative pronunciations which heretofore have come to notice, whether of Councils or Popes, has this phraseology been employed. What is more, there seems to be no reason for attributing the origin of the idea to Gratian as being unheard of before his time. It is true that his conclusion is of purely private value. Still, as a canonist well versed in the letter and spirit of ecclesiastical legislation, a fact demonstrated by his work, he must have been guided in his personal views and deductions by the juridical customs and practices of his time.

Hence, Gratian's conclusion may safely be accepted as arguing well for an existing ecclesiastical discipline which demanded some kind of freedom of consent, or at least lack of open dissent, for the legitimate conclusion of the marriage contract. It must have been based on the same laws to which Urban II had reference when he

[110] C. 1, C. XXXI, q. 2.
[111] C. 2, C. XXXI, q. 2.
[112] C. 3, C. XXXI, q. 2.
[113] C. 4, C. XXXI, q. 2.

spoke of the *canonum et legum auctoritas*. Nevertheless, it appears too bold a conclusion to presume that the author of the Decree comprehended the notion of matrimonial freedom or liberty of consent in the same clear fashion as canonists of later ages.

The real canonical development and treatment of the influence of fear on the marriage contract occurred only in the post-Gratian period.[114] Even then there seems to have been much confusion and contradiction involved in the principles of *raptus* on one side, and on the other those governing *vis et metus* as a matrimonial impediment. This, however, can in general be ascribed to a difference of terminology which underwent many changes before acquiring the stabilized form of the present day.[115] It is beyond dispute that Gratian's definite treatment of the matter of coercion relative to marriage became the foundation for numerous illuminating remarks and comments concerning the question as made by the earliest glossators and canonists.[116]

§ 2. *The Decretals of Gregory IX*

When the study of moral compulsion and fear relative to marriage as contained in the Decretals of Gregory IX has been completed, little of importance will remain to be written concerning the historical development in ecclesiastical legislation of this impediment to matrimonial consent. In this authoritative compilation the law on matrimonial coercion received so clear and accurate a determination that the legislation of the Church thereafter remained substantially the same. With the exception of a few points which were somewhat doubtful, it has found its way practically unchanged into the present codification of Canon Law.[117]

When Gregory IX (1227-1243) commissioned Raymund of Pennaforte to make a collection of the legislation enacted since the appearance of the *Decretum Gratiani,* his purpose was to have a uniform compilation convenient for the use of ecclesiastical courts and schools. This authentic collection, promulgated on September 5,

[114] Freisen, *Canonisches Eherecht,* p. 262.
[115] Cf. Wernz-Vidal, *Jus Matrimoniale,* n. 498.
[116] Cf. Freisen, *Canonisches Eherecht, Vorrede,* p. VI; 262-264.
[117] Ayrinhac, *Marriage Legislation,* n. 205.

1234, was to be employed in the study and practice of Church legislation, and as a law-text each and every chapter in its dispositive part was to enjoy full juridical value. In a word, the collection was to be received as *the* Code of Canon Law for the universal church.[118] These observations indicate the authority of that particular legislation in the Decretals concerning marriage contracted under the influence of violence and fear.

The remarkable clarity and precision of the legislation is due in great measure to the efforts of the Popes. When consulted on problems having to do with compulsory marriage, they offered solutions with principles of ecclesiastical jurisprudence which were then recognized. The first definite legislation was enacted by Alexander III (1159-1181) whose rules of action, as incorporated in the Decretals, remain for all time the classic norms concerning the influence of fear on the essential consent required for valid marriage.[119] The decisions of this Pontiff as well as those of certain of his successors [120] give excellent testimony to the law and procedure of their day.

In the Decretals it is expressly stated that the consent of the parties concludes marriage.[121] Innocent III especially brought out this point very clearly. When the Bishop of Arles inquired of him whether deaf-mutes could validly contract marriage, he replied that they could validly do so, as long as they were not restricted by any other impediments. Consent alone suffices for marriage and where this cannot be given in words, it can be indicated by means of satisfactory signs.[122]

Writing to the Bishop of Vercelles, Innocent permits him to declare null and void the marriage of a woman contracted with a man who was mentally unbalanced, because consent could not be validly given in such a case.[123] In answer to the difficulty as to how an immaterial thing like matrimony could be contracted by

[118] Const. "Rex Pacificus"—Friedberg, *Corpus Juris Canonici,* II, 2-3; Augustine, *Commentary,* I, 37.

[119] Triebs, *Kanonisches Eherecht,* III, 502.

[120] Lucius III (1181-85), Urban III (1185-87), Clement III (1187-91), Celestine III (1191-98). Innocent III (1198-1216), Honorius III (1216-27).

[121] C. 1, X, *de spons. et matr.,* IV, 1.

[122] C. 23, X, *de spons. et matr.,* IV, 1.

[123] C. 24, X, *de spons. et matr.,* IV, 1.

words alone, the same Pope responds that marriage is concluded indeed by the legitimate consent of a man and woman; words, however, are required as evidence of the internal act of the will, or at least signs which are equivalent to words and indicative of consent.[124]

Nevertheless, not any kind of consent will effect a valid marriage. The act of the will must be free and uninfluenced. This is not verified when fear and compulsion are present because under such circumstances the person gives his consent to what as a matter of fact he has no liking or desire for. This decision, made by Alexander III, is the classical foundation for the entire teaching of the Church concerning the invalidity of marriage contracted under the influence of violence and fear. It reads as follows:

> As there is no consent where fear or force intervenes, it is necessary that where consent of someone is required the matter of fear must be excluded. Marriage, however, is contracted only by consent and when concerning it there is question, it must enjoy full freedom and security. Wherefore the mind of the one in question must be investigated in order that a person may not through fear say that he is pleased with what he hates, and the sad consequences follow which are wont to come from marriages entered into against one's will.[125]

Hence, according to the same Pope, marriage contracted because of compulsion is *ipso jure* null and void. This disposition resulted from a case where the parents gave their daughter to a man against her express will. She had to submit, but remained stubborn in her opposition to the man and would have nothing to do with him. At last he deserted her and married another woman, and the girl another man. Alexander decided that if the girl was separated by the ecclesiastical court from the man to whom she had been given by her parents, the second man was to consider her as his lawful wife.[126]

That forced matrimonial consent is invalid is also demonstrated by a decision of Clement III. A marriage entered into because of coercion and constraint is subsequently made valid by the willing

[124] C. 25, X, *de spons. et matr.*, IV, 1.
[125] C. 14, X, *de spons. et matr.*, IV, 1.
[126] C. 13, X, *de spons. et matr.*, IV, 1.

cohabitation of the parties.[127] The declaration of convalidation would mean nothing if the marriage were not null and void from the beginning. Moreover, no matter what the age of the parties concerned, they are not bound by the contract agreed to out of fear or undue influence.[128] If a girl already espoused to one party is unwilling to wait until the latter attains the age required for marriage, she cannot be compelled to wait but may contract with another, provided she has not cohabited with the other.[129]

Although matrimonial consent extorted through fear is invalid, not every kind of fear has this vitiating effect since there is a difference between fear and fear.[130] Alexander III determined the norm to be followed. Similarly as in Roman law,[131] *metus qui posset in virum constantem cadere* alone is sufficient to render marriage null and void.[132] Honorius III likewise decided that only this kind of fear is to be considered in determining the validity of a compulsory marriage.[133] Alexander insinuates when fear attains such a degree in his disposition of the case of a man who had been confined in prison and chains until he consented to marry a certain woman.[134] Furthermore, it cannot be doubted that the general principles of violence and fear, as found in the first book of the Decretals,[135] also had their application in the matter of marriage.

While a marriage contracted under the influence of coercion and fear was null and void, it could subsequently become valid by giving consent.[136] Apparently, consent had not to be given expressly but could be interpreted from the actions of the coerced party. Thus it seems that in a certain case, the willing cohabitation of the parties, extending over a year and a half, was considered equivalent to a ratification of consent.[137]

[127] C. 21, X, *de spons. et matr.*, IV, 1.
[128] C. 9, X, *de despons. impub.*, IV, 2.
[129] C. 11, X, *de despons. impub.*, IV, 2.
[130] C. 6, X, *de spons. et matr.*, IV, 1.
[131] Dig. 4, 2, 7.
[132] C. 15, X, *de spons. et matr.*, IV, 1.
[133] C. 28, X, *de spons. et matr.*, IV, 1.
[134] C. 2, X, *de eo, qui duxit*, IV, 7.
[135] Cc. 1-7, X, *de his, quae vi metusve*, I, 40.
[136] C. 21, X, *de spons. et matr.*, IV, 1; c. 9, X, *de despons. impub.*, IV, 2.
[137] C. 21, X, *de spons. et matr.*, IV, 1.

Those, however, who had been compelled to marry were not permitted to separate and marry again unless the nullity of the first union had been verified and so declared by competent ecclesiastical authority.[138] That there existed such a recognized mode of procedure is evident from the decisions of the Popes in the cases submitted to them for a solution. Such expressions as *hujus rei veritate plenius comperta, rei veritatem diligenter inquiras, rei veritate diligenter inquisita et cognita,* occur in almost all of their communications. The same can be argued from the declaration of Honorius III that a woman should not be believed when she denies that she freely consented to marry and the man proves the contrary; it is different if she proves that she gave consent because of such fear as might constrain a steadfast and resolute person.[139] Evidence of a like nature is furnished by a letter of Clement III in which he reviews the case of a girl who, after living several years with her husband, *contra matrimonium proclamavit* on grounds of coercion and constraint.[140]

Such in brief outline is the legislation of the Decretals concerning the effect of fear and moral compulsion on matrimonial consent. It is true that no special title was assigned to this subject and it is more or less scattered throughout the fourth book. Still it must be admitted that the law is stated with an exactness and precision surpassing any previous legislation and definitely establishing the meaning and content of the invalidating statute. Consent is sufficient to conclude the matrimonial contract but it must be free and uninfluenced. Compulsion and fear are possible factors that may vitiate the consent which is essential. Fear only then renders a marriage null and void when it is of such a nature as would affect a firm and prudent person. Regardless of the nature of fear, however, the marriage may be convalidated by subsequent consent, whether actual or implicit. Finally, re-marriage is permitted only after a declaration of nullity has been given by the proper authority upon investigation of the case. Making use of these authoritative pronunciations as fundamental principles underlying the entire mat-

[138] C. 13, X, *de spons. et matr.*, IV, 1.
[139] C. 28, X, *de spons. et matr.*, IV. 1.
[140] C. 4, X, *qui matr. accus. poss.*, IV, 18.

ter, canonists and theologians of succeeding ages were enabled to build up their many elaborate systems of legal reasoning and juridical commentary on the subject of matrimonial consent extorted under the influence of coercion and fear.

§ 3. *The Council of Trent*

Following the legislation of the Decretals, historico-canonical sources reveal no further authentic enactments on the matter of the forced marriage contract until the dispositions of the Council of Trent (1545-1563) are encountered.[141] The later additions to the *Corpus Juris Canonici* maintain silence in the matter. The evolution continued, it is true, in the work of canonists and theologians. But the progress was one of systematic method in treating the question rather than the formation of new principles for determining the value of coerced consent. Just as from that time on the history of matrimonial discipline assumed a new character, consisting more in methods of practice and procedure than the enactment of new and direct legislation, so also new illumination and enlightenment is to be sought from these sources.[142]

In accordance with the character of all its work, the legislation of the Council of Trent concerning the liberty of the matrimonial contract was reformatory. Two important enactments were made which were destined to guarantee a full and complete liberty of consent for marriage. One of these dispositions, by far the more important, was the creation of a new impediment, that of abduction, which had been known to ancient ecclesiastical legislation but which had little by little disappeared until it vanished almost entirely.[143]

All through the ages of its evolution, during its development from particular and penal expression to its universal generalization, *vis et metus* had never been wholly free from a confused relation with the impediment of *raptus*. Tridentine legislation now formulated abduction as a strict impediment of ecclesiastical law. To enter into any detailed discussion concerning the matter is not within

[141] Wernz-Vidal, *Jus Matrimoniale*, n. 498; Knecht, *Katholisches Eherecht*, p. 568.

[142] Freisen, *Canonisches Eherecht*, *Vorrede*, pp. VII; 273.

[143] Esmein, *Mariage en Droit Canonique*, II, 249.

the scope of this study. It is sufficient to indicate that the main point of the law was to declare that between the abductor and the woman abducted there could be no valid marriage as long as she remained in his power.[143a] The establishment of this impediment protected the freedom of marriage inasmuch as it demanded liberty of place or station for the parties to the contract. Moreover, by bringing out in sharp distinction what constitutes *raptus,* it likewise determined to some extent what was to be understood by *vis et metus.* Freisen's [144] opinion that this decree is not to be referred to *raptus* but considered as a further safeguard of matrimonial consent does not seem tenable. Reliable authorities [145] hold opposite views and the discipline of the present Code of Canon Law enumerates abduction as defined by the Tridentine decree among the matrimonial impediments proper and lists violence and fear as defects of consent.[146]

The second enactment of importancc to this study was a decree condemning temporal lords and magistrates who violated the liberty of marriage by compelling subjects constituted under their authority to marry. This abuse, particularly in France, had become so widespread that it challenged the attention of the Fathers of the Council. Secular princes and judges by means of formal orders compelled their subjects to contract marriages, prompted many times by greed for worldly emoluments or pecuniary advantages. Evidence has already been furnished how early Gallic councils prohibited such an unjust exercise of power by sovereigns and rulers and how even in feudal times this kind of compulsion and constraint was condemned. As time passed and the feudal system lost its political force and ascendancy, these reprehensible practices gradually ceased. But with the reappearance of absolute sovereignty in the kingdoms of Europe, royal authority again asserted its right to marry subjects as it saw fit. Marriages were arranged which were more to the interests of others rather than for the good of the parties concerned.

143a Conc. Trid., sess. XXIV, *de ref. matrim.,* c. 6; Esmein, *Mariage en Droit Canonique,* II, 254-255.

144 *Canonisches Eherecht,* pp. 272-273.

145 Cappello, *De Matrimonio,* n. 476; Vlaming, *Praelectiones Juris Matrimonii,* 308-309; Wernz-Vidal, *Jus Matrimoniale,* n. 498.

146 *Codex Juris Canonici,* cc. 1074, 1087.

The instrument which generally served this purpose was the *lettre de cachet,* a royal or municipal document ordering parents to give their children in marriage to certain determined persons.[147]

No greater abuse could have existed to deprive the matrimonial contract of its rightful freedom. The arrangement of marriage without the least consideration or solicitude for the wishes of the parties, let alone their parents or guardians, was a flagrant violation of justice. The Council of Trent, accordingly, dealt with this abuse stringently and summarily in these terms:

> Worldly aims and covetousness frequently so blind the eyes of temporal lords and magistrates that they use threats and penalties to compel men and women residing in their jurisdiction, especially if they are rich or have the prospect of a great inheritance, to contract marriages against their own will with persons chosen by such temporal lords and magistrates themselves. Wherefore, since it is in the last degree nefarious to violate the liberty of marriage, and that such wrong should be done by those from whom justice is to be expected, the holy Synod commands all men, of whatever rank, dignity, or condition they may be, and under pain of anathema which they shall incur *ipso facto,* to use no constraint direct or indirect, by which persons shall be deprived of freedom in contracting marriages.[148]

So straightforward a condemnation of any interference with the liberty of marriage is the expected action of an institution which has so consistently defended the freedom of the individual. No more decisive prohibition and censure could have been promulgated by the Church to demonstrate to what extent she would go to assure marriage the freedom of choice and consent so essential to its nature. Esmein[149] observes that the prohibition of the Council was ineffective, as were various civil ordinances concerning the abuse, and that the practice continued to be customary in France until the Revolution. The fact nevertheless remains that the Tridentine legislation is, from the historical viewpoint, another link in the long chain of evidence tending to show that the Church was

[147] Cf. Esmein, *Mariage en Droit Canonique,* II, 255-258.
[148] Conc. Trid., sess. XXIV, *de ref. matrim.,* c. 9.
[149] *Mariage en Droit Canonique,* II, 258.

ever ready to protect the liberty of marriage and was never found wanting when appropriate legislative measures were necessary to guarantee that freedom. Such legislation could not have been enacted had it not been the *vigens Ecclesiae disciplina* that parties to a marriage must enter into the relationship of their own free choice and without force or pressure from external agencies influencing their decision.

The Tridentine excommunication enjoined upon magistrates and temporal princes who interfered in any way with the liberty of marriage was not abrogated by the Constitution of Pius IX [150] but remained as a censure *nemini reservata* until the appearance of the present codification of Canon law.[151] The ambitus of the penalty was variously stated by canonists,[152] although as a penal law it required a strict interpretation. Direct interference was understood to be that affecting the parties themselves; indirect, that applied to parents, guardians, etc. Temporal lords and magistrates in the exercise of their public jurisdiction over those subject to them were comprehended, not however emperors, kings, ecclesiastical superiors, or persons enjoying merely private authority, as parents and others, even though the latter should abuse the powers they possessed. To incur the censure coercion had to be exercised for the purpose of marriage with a determined person. Marriage had to be forced on the person, mere prevention of marriage was not covered by the penalty.[153]

§ 4. *Ecclesiastical Jurisprudence*

The present historical study would appear incomplete without a word of reference to the vast system of ecclesiastical jurisprudence that has resulted from the ecclesiastical law invalidating marriage

[150] Const. "Apostolicae Sedis," 12 Oct. 1869—*Fontes*, n. 552.

[151] Wernz, *Jus Matrimoniale*, n. 271.

[152] Cf. Sanchez, *De Matrimonii Sacramento*, lib. II. disp. XXVII; lib. IV, disp. XXII; St. Alphonsus, *Theologia Moralis*, lib. VI, n. 849; Bucceroni, *Comment. in Const. Apost. Sed.*, n. 89; Pennachi, *Comment. in Const. Apost. Sed.*, II, 257; Feije, *De Impedimentis et Dispensationibus Matrimonialibus*, n. 144; Gasparri, *De Matrimonio*, n. 957; Wernz, *Jus Matrimoniale*, n. 271; Hollweck, *Kirchliches Strafgesetz*, p. 260; Hinschius, *Kirchenrecht*, V, 767; *Nouvelle Revue Théologique*, XV, 552.

[153] Gasparri, *De Matrimonio*, n. 957; Wernz, *Jus Matrimoniale*, n. 271.

contracted under the influence of violence and fear. Just as the *lex orandi* is appealed to as a norm of faith, so also what may be termed the *lex procedendi* goes on record as one more piece of historical evidence testifying to the traditional stand of the Church in regard to matrimonial freedom. Although strict canonical legislation in the matter had come to an end with the law of the Decretals, the Church continued to exercise its jurisdiction over vitiated matrimonial consent in the attention that was given to cases appealed on grounds of violence and fear before her competent tribunals. Numerous decisions of the Sacred Congregation of the Council[154] and of the Roman Rota, of greater importance perhaps for discovering the mind of the Church and for giving a correct interpretation of her law, are invaluable as historical testimony to her unceasing endeavor to safeguard the liberty of marriage through the centuries.

Certain instructions were likewise issued by the Holy See to regulate the practice and procedure employed in the trial and judgment of marriages attacked because of the influence of fear and coercion.[155] These all serve to indicate the mind of the Church on marriages contracted through fear.

Article III.—General Conclusions

The historical study of canonical legislation concerning matrimonial consent vitiated by violence and fear reveals one outstanding fact: the meagre evidence available for clearly delineating the evolution and development of the existing law of the Church. Reason for this phenomenon may be found in the fluctuating character of the problem itself. It is not a question of positive legislation obligating the faithful to the performance of some duty, but rather of how the Church met and coped with factors which were entirely opposed to the essential security of marriage. The sacrament of

[154] Cf. *Thesaurus Resolut. S. Cong. Conc. passim;* Richter, *Canones et Decreta Concilii Tridentini,* pp. 238-244, nn. 71-82; Pallottini. v. *Matrimonium quoad Impedimentum Dirimens Vis et Metus,* § XIX, nn. 1-203.

[155] Cf. S. C. S. Inquis., *Instructio ad Episc. Rit. Orient.,* 20 Jun. 1883, nn. 35-39—*ASS,* XVIII, (1885), 356-359; S. C. de Prop. Fid., *Instructio pro Foed. Stat. Amer. Ordin.,* a. 1883, § § 36-40—*ASS,* XVIII (1885), 379-381; *Collectanea,* II, 1587; *Concilii Plenarii Baltimorensis III,* pp. 271-274.

matrimony had been confided to her care and it was not long before she noted how existing secular laws and notions were at marked variance with her own teachings.[156]

Although the legal existence of the Church was not officially recognized until after the Edict of Milan in 313,[157] her competence in matrimonial matters became more and more pronounced with each new legislative act.[158] In all of her legislation her conduct was guided by the conception of Christian marriage as an indissoluble contract that must be freely concluded. Once that is done, however, it is irrevocable and must be adhered to as long as one of the parties survives. Hence the Church was faced with the alternative of either declaring that force and fear had absolutely no effect on the contract or that it had an invalidating effect. The first could not be adopted since even according to natural law a forced contract is contestible. Neither could the second alternative be followed absolutely or without some qualification. Consequently, ecclesiastical law had to determine the exact conditions under which violence and fear would invalidate matrimonial consent.

The evolution of this determination naturally depended upon the existing conditions which the Church encountered in each age and country. In the early centuries, when her boundaries practically coincided with those of the Roman Empire, scarcely any ecclesiastical law can be found dealing directly with violence or coercion, or even abduction. When the Church spread, however, and received into her fold the barbarian peoples of the north, their practices of forcing marriage called forth appropriate legislation prohibiting and anathematizing abduction and every kind of physical violence. As these nations, under the beneficent direction of the Church, advanced in culture and refinement, the use of violence gradually fell into abeyance. The effect on canonical legislation was a decreasing necessity for laws proscribing abduction and all that it entailed. Now, however, the Church was confronted with a new species of infringement of matrimonial liberty. This was

[156] Cf. St. Jerome, *Epist. ad Oceanum*, 77—*Corp. Script. Eccles. Latin.*, 55, 39; St. Augustine, *De Nuptiis et Concupiscentiis*, I, c. 10—*Corp. Script. Eccles. Latin.*, 42, 222.

[157] Funk, *Manual of Church History*, I, 117.

[158] Duchesne, *Early History of the Church*, II, 517.

the abuse of compelling marriage by the unlawful use of authority, punishment, threats, etc. To legislate against this injustice was much more difficult because of its illusive nature and intangible character. Hence it is not strange that, instead of finding direct law pertaining to such cases of forced marriage, historical silence shrouds the entire matter. Still, in the utter absence of positive legislation, the authoritative declarations and decisions referred to above are unintelligible, unless they are viewed as undeniable evidence of a well-defined ecclesiastical principle that freedom is required for the validity of matrimonial consent. When these fragments were officially incorporated into the authentic collection of Gregory IX, they supplied for the universal Church the equivalent of a statute law in place of the former customary or common law. From this time onward, no positive change occurred in the legislation and the whole question resolved itself into one of the *praxis Ecclesiae.*

Any objection to the general nature of the legislation cannot be reasonably sustained. Despite this characteristic it served to uphold the liberty of marriage and to disapprove of and condemn any action that violated matrimonial freedom. Sight must not be lost of the fact that ecclesiastical legislation, emanating as it does from the authority established by Christ in His society, was not a finished product from the beginning, but rather a gradual growth, each phase of which was dictated by the ecclesiastical wisdom of the time. In the early Christian centuries the Church lived largely on tradition and custom, and such written laws as existed were not originally universal laws, but local or provincial statutes, to which later a broader obligation was added through the express or tacit approbation of legitimate authority.[159]

Furthermore, the legislation in question is none the less impressive because of its indefiniteness. In the first place, many centuries had to pass before Canon Law arrived at a clear and coherent conception of the doctrine regarding violence and fear. For the longest time it is found expressed in its most rudimentary form, in contrast to laws of more urgent demand which were clarified into

[159] Cf. Besson, "Collections of Ancient Canons," *Catholic Encyclopedia*, III, 281.

definite legal formulae at comparatively early dates.[160] Secondly, to interpret the laws treating of abduction or violence as referring to the ecclesiastical impediment of *raptus* is neither historically nor canonically correct, since abduction became an ecclesiastical impediment only at a much later date.[161] Canonical science was as yet in too embryonic a stage for making the distinctions of subsequent ages between physical violence and moral compulsion, freedom of consent and freedom of place. Finally, circumstances and conditions of the various times and peoples, subscribed to as far as was consistent by ecclesiastical legislators and superiors, prevented the true position of the Church from emerging into more definite legislation. As regards the absence of any law expressly stating the nullity of extorted matrimonial consent, it appears a safe conclusion to state that the dictates of the natural law together with the *jus consuetudinarium* regulated the matter.[162]

Coming down to the present day, an ecclesiastical norm has resulted to the effect that marriage is invalid when it is entered because of violence or grave fear, caused by an external agent, unjustly, to free himself from which one is compelled to choose marriage; on the other hand, no other fear, even though it would give cause to the contract, entails the nullity of marriage. This is the law in force at present in the universal Church. It remains now to be interpreted in order to discover its full significance and content.

[160] Freisen, *Canonisches Eherecht,* p. 259.

[161] Cappello, *De Matrimonio,* n. 476; Augustine, *Commentary,* V, 193.

[162] Wernz-Vidal, *Jus Matrimoniale,* n. 498. Cf. c. 22, C. XXII, q. 4.

PART III

CANONICAL EXPOSITION

CHAPTER V

GENERAL STUDY OF THE LAW OF INVALIDITY

Canon 1087.—§ 1. Invalidum quoque est matrimonium initum ob vim vel metum gravem ab extrinseco et injuste incussum, a quo ut quis se liberet, eligere cogatur matrimonium.

§ 2. Nullus alius metus, etiamsi det causam contractui matrimonii nullitatem secumfert.

In this brief canon is embodied the present legislation of the Church concerning matrimonial consent vitiated by violence and fear. The law expressly declares that marriage is null and void when it is contracted because of violence or grave fear, caused by an external agent, unjustly, to free himself from which, one is compelled to choose marriage. No other fear, however, even if it would give cause to the contract, entails the nullity of marriage.

That the Church is not content with any kind of consent and declares invalid a marriage unless consent is free and uninfluenced may appear to be a very stringent measure. But imperative reasons are not lacking to justify the law. Freedom of will is demanded for every legal transaction involving the transfer of rights and the acceptance of obligations. The more important the transaction and the more responsible the obligations, so much the greater in proportion must be the liberty of choice and freedom of action. No transaction approaches in meaning and importance the matrimonial contract, whose obligations are not only severe but binding until death severs the marital bond. Reason alone suggests that no individual should be bound by these obligations unless he freely decides to accept them. To surround this choice with the fullest possible liberty, the Church refuses to sanction as valid a marriage where consent is not voluntarily given but is the result of undue influence and constraint.[1]

[1] Triebs, *Kanonisches Eherecht*, III, 502.

Furthermore, the unhappy experience of the Church has been that marriage due to force and compulsion results in most unfortunate consequences, a fact recognized in some of the earliest definite legislation concerning this matter.[2] To enumerate but a few, the really disastrous are to the good of the offspring and the observance of conjugal fidelity. On account of his antipathy and aversion to the union, the coerced party will generally refuse to coöperate for the procreation of children. The undesired relationship easily exposes the parties to the danger of adultery, inasmuch as they refuse to honor their mutual rights and obligations.[3]

To say the least, therefore, it is expedient that the matrimonial contract be assured as much liberty as is humanly possible. If a compulsory marriage were valid, neither the individual nor the human race would be protected from the injury of its unhappy results. Consequently, the only reasonable measure is that adopted by ecclesiastical law in declaring the union null and void.[4] The reasons advanced by St. Thomas [5] to account for the law are similarly founded and reducible to these grounds.

The nature of canon 1087 is such that, when the conditions enumerated are verified, the act of matrimonial consent becomes automatically ineffective to produce the juridical effects which would ordinarily follow from valid consent. The four conditions of the law are absolutely necessary if fear is to invalidate marriage, but at the same time they suffice.[6] Although in the external forum the invalidity of the contract will not be recognized until it has been so declared by due process of law, the marriage is nevertheless null and void from the beginning. This will readily be admitted in the hypothesis of physical violence or fear so intense as to exclude deliberation. But even in the case of moral compulsion inducing a grave fear, circumstances under which consent is possible, the marriage is null and void from the beginning because consent, vitiated as the

[2] C. 14, X, *de spons. et matr.*, IV, 1.

[3] Schmalzgrueber, *Jus Ecclesiasticum Universum*, lib. IV, tit. I, n. 386; Ballerini-Palmieri, *Opus Theologicum Morale*, VI, tr. X, n. 1115.

[4] Schmalzgrueber, *Jus Ecclesiasticum Universum*, lib. IV, tit. I, n. 394.

[5] *Summa Theologica*, Suppl. q. 47, a. 3.

[6] Payen, *De Matrimonio*, II, 1681; Triebs, *Kanonisches Eherecht*, III, 503, 516.

law requires, acts similarly as a diriment impediment.[7] It is not as though the marriage existed as valid until the judicial declaration that the obstacle vitiating consent really existed, upon which the union becomes null and void. In accordance with ecclesiastical law, marriage must be either valid from the beginning or null and void from the beginning: *semel conjux semper conjux.* As in all cases of nullity, however, the marriage is recognized as valid in the external forum as long as the contrary has not been proven and a declaration of nullity granted.

A point which requires special emphasis is that even though the coerced party *truly* consents to the marriage, the contract is nevertheless null and void if the conditions of the law are fulfilled. Too frequently it is thought that marriage, contracted under the influence of grave fear, is valid if the passive subject gives a true consent.[8] This is a false notion. The Church does not invalidate the forced marriage on the presumption of either denial of internal consent or simulation thereof.[9] The contract would then be null and void on other grounds.[10] A true consent is admitted but one whose voluntariness is diminished under the influence of grave fear. The Church deems such consent insufficient to constitute a valid marriage and, in order to protect the liberty of the institution, declares it juridically ineffective.[11]

Furthermore, to have this invalidating effect on matrimonial consent, fear must continue to the very moment of and exist at the time of the actual celebration of the marriage, because only then and not before is the act of consent required for the essence of matri-

[7] Cf. S. R. R., *Nullit. Matrim.*, 7 Mar. 1922—*Decisiones*, XIV (1922), dec. VI, n. 2: "unde impedimentum dirimens matrimonium quod impedimentum metus audit."

[8] Cf. Payen, *De Matrimonio*, II, p. 78, note 1.

[9] Cf. S. R. R., *Nullit. Matrim.*, 12 Jul. 1922—*Decisiones*, XIV, (1922), dec. XXIV, n. 2; S. R. R., *Nullit. Matrim.*, 29 Jul. 1922—*Decisiones*, XIV (1922), dec. XXV, n. 2; S. R. R., *Causa Transylvanien.*, 1 Maii, 1912—*Decisiones*, IV (1912), dec. XVIII, n. 4.

[10] *Codex Juris Canonici*, cc. 1081, § 1; 1086, § 2.

[11] St. Thomas, *Summa Theologica*, Suppl., q. 47, a. 3; Sanchez, *De Matrimonii Sacramento*, lib. IV, disp. XII, n. 18; Pirhing, *Jus Canonicum*, lib. IV, tit. I, n. 100; Schmalzgrueber, *Jus Ecclesiasticum Universum*, lib. IV, tit. I, n. 392; Ballerini-Palmieri, *Opus Theologicum Morale*, VI, tr. X, nn. 1115-1116; Wernz, *Jus Matrimoniale*, p. 395, note 29.

mony to be given. If fear, which previously affected a person, is removed or dispelled before the celebration, it cannot be said to influence consent and the marriage is valid.[12] Should the party, however, deny interior consent or simulate it, the marriage is clearly invalid, but not on grounds of moral compulsion and fear.[13] The exact condition under which the party suffering undue influence gave consent must be determined in the internal forum from the declaration of the penitent, in the external forum from the various circumstances offered as evidence.[14] But once fear has been inflicted for the purpose of compelling marriage, it is considered to persevere also in the actual celebration. Therefore the contract is presumed to have been entered under force until the contrary is proven.[15]

Marriage contracted under the influence of grave fear is invalid in both the internal and external forums. St. Thomas [16] mentions the prevalence of an opinion that marriage could be valid before God, but invalid in the eyes of the Church. This opinion must be rejected for several reasons. It supposes an opposition between the forum of conscience and the ecclesiastical forum, an altogether impossible assumption from the nature of the matter. A marriage objectively invalid must be such in both forums. While the invalidity, however, may be evident in the internal forum, as long as it is not juridically proven, validity is presumed in the external forum. The opinion likewise falsely regards the impediment in the external forum as being based on the presumption that no true consent is

[12] Cappello, *De Matrimonio,* n. 608; Gougnard, *De Matrimonio,* p. 169; Payen, *De Matrimonio,* II, n. 1686; De Smet, *Betrothment and Marriage,* n. 539. Cf. S. R. R., *Nullit. Matrim.,* 27 Aug. 1912—*Decisiones,* IV, (1912), dec. XXXVIII, n. 7; S. R. R., *Nullit. Matrim.,* 1 Aug. 1913—*Decisiones,* V (1913), dec. XLII, n. 13; S. R. R., *Causa Nicien.,* 30 Dec. 1915—*Decisiones,* VII (1915), dec. XLII, n. 5; S. R. R., *Nullit. Matrim.,* 2 Jul. 1918—*Decisiones,* X (1918), dec. VIII, n. 17; S. R. R., *Nullit. Matrim.,* 8 Mar. 1919—*Decisiones,* XI (1919), dec. VII, (fear influenced the coerced party not only at the time of the civil celebration but continued to exist up to the moment of the religious ceremony); S. R. R., *Causa Parisien.,* 31 Jan. 1922—*Decisiones,* XIV (1922), dec. III, n. 4.

[13] Cf. S. R. R., *Nullit. Matrim.,* 9 Jun. 1911—*Decisiones,* III (1911), dec. XXII.

[14] Gasparri, *De Matrimonio,* n. 929.

[15] Cappello, *De Matrimonio,* n. 608. Cf. S. R. R., *Nullit. Matrim.,* 15 Feb. 1919—*Decisiones,* XI (1919), dec. II, n. 6.

[16] *Summa Theologica,* Suppl., q. 47, a. 3.

given. As pointed out above, the law does not presume a fictitious or simulated consent but renders a truly existing consent juridically ineffective.[17]

The law of invalidity affects both parties, similarly as when a diriment impediment exists on one side only.[18] The nature of the matrimonial contract requires mutual consent. Consequently, it cannot be concluded by parties, one of whom freely consents, the other consenting only because of some external pressure brought to bear against him. The nullity of the marriage, however, is in favor of the party suffering the coercion and only indirectly affects the other, since his consent alone is not sufficient to establish the contract.[19]

Formerly canonists argued whether it was necessary for a person to be forced to contract marriage with a definite individual, or whether compulsion to marriage in general sufficed.[20] From the very general terms of canon 1087, § 1, it is now certain that undue influence need be exercised for the purpose of marriage in general.[21] Besides, the motives of the law, the injury inflicted and unhappy consequences, remain the same, whether a person is unjustly coerced to contract marriage with some choice of persons or whether he is forced to marry a determined party. For marriage a mere elective consent cannot suffice, when one consents only under compulsion to the choice itself.[22]

The law of canon 1087 is prohibiting as well as invalidating.[23] Reverence for the sanctity of the sacrament of matrimony imposes a serious obligation to avoid exposing it to the danger of invalidity

[17] Schmalzgrueber, *Jus Ecclesiasticum Universum*, lib. IV, tit. I, nn. 408-410; Ballerini-Palmieri, *Opus Theologicum Morale*, VI, tr. X, n. 1116; Wernz-Vidal, *Jus Matrimoniale*, p. 588, note 28. Cf. c. 2, X, *de eo, qui duxit*, IV, 7.

[18] *Codex Juris Canonici*, c. 1036, § 3.

[19] Gasparri, *De Matrimonio*, n. 930.

[20] Sanchez, *De Matrimonii Sacramento*, lib. IV, disp. XII, n. 20; Schmalzgrueber, *Jus Ecclesiasticum Universum*, lib. IV, tit. I, nn. 395-396; Pirhing, *Jus Canonicum*, lib. IV, tit. I, n. 103.

[21] Vlaming, *Praelectiones Juris Matrimonii*, n. 539; Chelodi, *Jus Matrimoniale*, n. 119; Gougnard, *De Matrimonio*, p. 169; Cappello, *De Matrimonio*, n. 606; Payen, *De Matrimonio*, II, n. 1686; Knecht, *Katholisches Eherecht*, p. 576, note 6.

[22] Gasparri, *De Matrimonio*, n. 931.

[23] Cf. Maroto, *Institutiones*, I, n. 225; Michiels, *Normae Generales*, I, 271.

by contracting it through compulsion. While the celebration is unlawful, ignorance or good faith may easily excuse the parties from moral guilt. If the marriage is unavoidable and the parties are aware of its nullity, they must have the intention of not consummating the union. To enter the contract without this intention is a grievous sin. Where the coerced party has the firm intention of avoiding all conjugal acts or, because of ignorance or good faith, lacks the intention, he commits no sin whether consent is simulated or really elicited under the influence of fear.[24]

It is evident that all acts which are forbidden to the unmarried are likewise unlawful to parties whose marriage is null and void on account of grave and unjustly inflicted fear. Considering the matter objectively, the party who has been coerced should sooner suffer death than permit or consent to any conjugal practices. Still, passive resistance in the face of threats of violence or actual force is admitted as possible and lawful. Furthermore, good faith or invincible ignorance will readily excuse from sin similarly as in the actual celebration of the marriage.[25]

The excommunication which the Council of Trent [26] decreed against all temporal lords and magistrates who directly or indirectly compelled their subjects or others to marry is no longer in force. This is certain from the rule of canon 6, n. 5 that former ecclesiastical penalties of which no mention is made in the Code are abolished.[27] Although the censure has been abrogated, there is no reason why one might not be declared by particular law.[28] Should conditions become such as to demand it, ecclesiastical superiors can legitimately establish a penal sanction for the punishment of those who violate the liberty of marriage.[29]

It is beyond dispute that all who make use of grave and unjust

[24] Gasparri, *De Matrimonio,* nn. 910, 923; Cappello, *De Matrimonio,* n. 613.

[25] Lehmkuhl, *Theologia Moralis,* II, n. 968; Pruemmer, *Manuale Theologiae Moralis,* III, n. 799; Gasparri, *De Matrimonio,* n. 932; Payen, *De Matrimonio,* II, p. 86, note 1.

[26] Conc. Trident., sess., XXIV, *de ref. matrim.,* c. 9.

[27] Cappello, *De Matrimonio,* n. 612; Triebs, *Kanonisches Eherecht,* III, 515; Knecht, *Katholisches Eherecht,* p. 582; De Smet, *Betrothment and Marriage,* n. 541.

[28] Pruemmer, *Manuale Theologiae Moralis,* III, n. 800.

[29] Cf. *Codex Juris Canonici,* c. 2222, § 1; Gasparri, *De Matrimonio,* n. 928.

fear to compel others to marry sin grievously against both justice and charity. The same is to be said of the person who knowingly contracts marriage with one who is the victim of coercion and constraint. The guilt may be only venial when the fear inspired is unjust but not of a grave nature. Occasionally, however, the culpability will be grievous, especially if fear becomes the real cause of the contract and serious consequences follow. Under certain circumstances the use of coercive measures may be justified. But the action can then offend against charity and prudence. Hence, one who has inflicted a just fear is not always free of all blame.[30]

In concluding this chapter it may not be amiss to refer to another point of ecclesiastical discipline concerning compulsory marriage. The brief historical study has clearly demonstrated that the Church has ever insisted upon the liberty of marriage and has refused her sanction to any that has not been entered into knowingly and willingly by both parties. To extend protection to each individual contract, Canon Law prescribes that the parties be interrogated on their freedom of consent, or willingness to marry, in the pre-nuptial investigation. The woman in particular should be examined on this point, since she is more liable to undue influence and duress.[31]

It is to be regretted that even in the present day, when marriage must ordinarily be contracted in the presence of a priest and two witnesses, matrimonial freedom is so wantonly violated. The Church can only defend the liberty of marriage through her representatives, particularly pastors or those designated to assist at the nuptial celebration. Neglect on their part to ascertain whether consent is being freely given cannot be too severely condemned. Frequently they are the only ones to whom the distressed party can turn for assistance. Consequently, this angle of the examination before marriage is of the greatest importance and failure to give it due consideration must be accounted as a flagrant violation of an ecclesiastical law intended for the best interests of souls.

When there are cogent reasons for believing that external pressure or influence has been exercised on one or the other of the con-

[30] Gasparri, *De Matrimonio,* n. 928; Cappello, *De Matrimonio,* n. 613.

[31] *Codex Juris Canonici,* c. 1020, § 2: "Tum sponsum tum sponsam etiam seorsum et caute interroget . . . an consensum libere, praesertim mulier, praestent. . . ."

tracting parties, the priest should not hesitate about supporting them against parents or those responsible for the situation.[32] He is certainly obliged to refuse his assistance at the marriage, unless the party who suffers the fear is ready and willing publicly to deny consent in the actual celebration.[33]

[32] Ayrinhac, *Marriage Legislation*, n. 36.
[33] Payen, *De Matrimonio*, II, n. 1687.

CHAPTER VI

DETAILED ANALYSIS OF CANON 1087

SINCE the ecclesiastical law as described in the preceding chapter directly concerns the invalidity of so important a transaction as marriage, which has the nature of both a sacrament and a contract, it must be strictly verified before it can have application in any particular case. The conditions made by the law must be morally certain before a marriage can be definitely declared null and void. To establish this moral conviction, the meaning and content of the law must be fully appreciated. This knowledge is best acquired by making a detailed analysis of each of its elements. These will now be examined under the headings of physical violence, moral compulsion and fear, and the exclusive character of the law.

ARTICLE I.—ABSOLUTE VIOLENCE

There seems to be no sound basis for asserting that the case of absolute violence is not contemplated by canon 1087.[1] The law expressly states: *ob vim vel metum.* The disjunctive *vel* excludes the use of the terms as correlatives, *vis et metus,* or as synonyms, *vis seu metus.*[2] Whether or not the law as formulated includes the case of marriage contracted because of such violence, some pertinent remarks to be made in this connection offer sufficient reason for treating of it here.

The earlier study of the nature of absolute violence revealed it to be such that it excluded all possibility of a human act. An action performed because of it is merely an *actus hominis* with no moral or juridical value whatsoever. Where it is employed in relation to marriage, it certainly invalidates the contract since the constitutive element of consent is entirely lacking. The physical force in no way moves the party suffering it to give a valid matri-

[1] Cf. Payen, *De Matrimonio,* II, n. 1678; De Smet, *Betrothment and Marriage,* n. 534; Schoensteiner, *Kirchliches Eherecht,* p. 65.

[2] Triebs, *Kanonisches Eherecht,* III, 503.

monial consent. It may affect his physical body by compelling him, for instance, to enter the church, or it may wrest some external manifestation of consent from him, such as a forced nod of the head or extension of the hand to the bride. These signs of consent may be given externally, but the will itself fully dissents and the celebration is purely external.[3] Although instances may be rare, it is not entirely impossible for absolute force to be used to effect the celebration of marriage. While it is beyond doubt that the internal consent of the will cannot suffer violence, still certain external expressions of matrimonial consent can be forced and thus give the appearance of marriage.

Matrimonial consent must ordinarily be expressed by words and the use of equivalent signs is forbidden to the contracting parties when they are capable of speech.[4] But if one or both of the parties are naturally incapable of speech, as in the case of mutes or those suffering from defective utterance, or if speech is impossible because of some very grievous illness,[5] then equivalent signs, such as nodding of the head, pressure of the hand, placing the ring on the finger, etc., may be used to manifest internal consent.[6] Should a sign of this kind be absolutely forced, valid matrimonial consent is not given and the marriage is clearly null and void. A mere physico-motor action of the body, to which the will is positively opposed, cannot effect a change of juridic status. Even in the hypothesis that the party actually gives an internal consent when the sign is wrested from him by physical force, the marriage would be invalid. That sign expresses valid consent when it is voluntarily given by the party, not however when it is the result of physical violence. Hence, in the above hypothesis, interior consent is not externally manifested in a way required for the validity of marriage.[7] Exception might be made of received national customs and circumstances according to which an external stimulus is used to se-

[3] Cappello, *De Matrimonio,* n. 605; Gougnard, *De Matrimonio,* p. 165; Payen, *De Matrimonio,* II, n. 1678.

[4] *Codex Juris Canonici,* c. 1088, § 2.

[5] Cappello, *De Matrimonio,* n. 617.

[6] Cf. S. C. S. Off., 22 Aug. 1860—*Collectanea,* I, n. 1201; *Fontes,* n. 964.

[7] Gasparri, *De Matrimonio,* n. 926.

cure a sign deemed sufficiently indicative of true internal consent.[8]

Again, the celebration of marriage by proxy is valid if done in accordance with the rules laid down by the Code.[9] Should one of the parties, however, be physically forced to sign the mandate, the marriage is evidently null and void.[10] Likewise, physical force and absolute defect of consent is to be presumed if a person is induced under hypnotic influence to contract a marriage to which he was opposed in his conscious state.[11] More especially the element of violence is likely to be found in the compulsory marriages of those but recently converted from heathenism. Pagan customs and traditions regarding the rights of parents and superiors to compel children and subjects to marry, even though physical force must be employed to effect the celebration, not infrequently would seem to cause the invalidity of a marriage as much on grounds of physical violence as moral compulsion and fear.[12]

Under this head may also be mentioned the case where fear or trepidation is so intensely paralyzing as to upset the mental balance completely. Deliberation and volition are impossible and marriage is chosen almost instinctively in order to avoid some immediately threatening evil. As an example, take the situation, impossible as it seems, in which a man with drawn revolver threatens a girl with immediate death unless she marries him *hic et nunc*, and the girl, completely overcome with terror and fright, utters words of consent. This action falls into the category of those acts termed *actus primo primi*: it is performed by one having the use of reason but so suddenly that it is antecedent to any operation of the intellect and will. Consent is completely lacking and the action is plainly involuntary. Marriage contracted under these circumstances is certainly null and void.[13]

While this case may become equivalent to that of absolute vio-

[8] Cf. S. C. de Prop. Fid., 4 Feb. 1664—*Collectanea*, n. 1416.

[9] *Codex Juris Canonici*, cc. 1088, § 1, 1089.

[10] Gougnard, *De Matrimonio*, p. 165, note 1.

[11] Knecht, *Katholisches Eherecht*, p. 577, note 4; Triebs, *Kanonisches Eherecht*, III, 500.

[12] Cf. S. R. R., *Causa Vicariat. Apost. Taikon*, 16 Jan. 1913—*AAS*, V (1913), 253-261.

[13] Gasparri, *De Matrimonio*, n. 927; Chelodi, *Jus Matrimoniale*, n. 118.

lence, especially when external force plays a part, it may be noted that the present legislation, in canon 103, § 2 as well as in canon 1087, § 1, fails to mention this exception. To include it in the *nullus alius metus* of canon 1087, § 2 would be absurd, if for no other reason than that the canon deals with defective consent. But a presumption of defective consent, i.e., a *voluntarium secundum quid,* cannot be sustained once fear takes away all deliberation. It is true that such a total destruction of liberty as described would be difficult to prove unless some external force were also present. Nevertheless, should that condition be demonstrated, the principle of canon 88, § 3 might be analagously applied. This would classify one who so acts with those who lack full use of reason.[14]

Article II.—Moral Compulsion and Fear

Canon 1087, § 1 proceeds further to state that marriage is null and void *ob metum.* The Church, however, does not deal lightly with this matter. The declaration of Alexander III[15] that fear differs from fear clearly indicates that not every kind of fear has an invalidating effect. As a general principle it may be held that fear which renders other contracts liable to rescission invalidates the matrimonial contract.[16] More specifically ecclesiastical law decrees that four conditions must be strictly verified if a marriage is to be invalid *ex capite metus.* These four conditions, moreover, must be collectively existent in each particular case and must be established in the external forum with at least moral certainty to justify a declaration of nullity.[17] According to the exact requirements of the law fear to invalidate marriage must be (1) grave, (2) from without, (3) unjustly inflicted, (4) compelling marriage. The juridical content of these terms will now be analyzed in detail.

§ 1. *Grave Fear*

The first condition necessary that fear invalidate marriage is that it be grave. Slight fear, as will be seen, does not render a

[14] Cf. Bouuaert, "De Metus Influxu,"—*Jus Pontificium,* III (1926), 107.

[15] C. 6, X, *de spons. et matr.,* IV, 1.

[16] Schmalzgrueber, *Jus Ecclesiasticum Universum,* lib. IV, tit. I, n. 390; Gasparri, *De Matrimonio,* n. 938.

[17] Triebs, *Kanonisches Eherecht,* III, 503.

marriage invalid. What constitutes grave fear, however, is difficult to define in theory as well as in practice. Hence in cases dealing with the nullity of marriage, much of the difficulty involved frequently hinges on the question as to whether fear is grave or not.[18] For the sake of clarity, grave fear in general will first be discussed, then absolutely grave fear, finally relatively grave fear.

In general that fear is grave which, in accordance with the condition of a person, greatly diminishes his matrimonial freedom. It is such that it can move the one who suffers it, although otherwise a firm and prudent person, from his intention of not contracting marriage.[19] In a word, it is the ***metus cadens in virum constantem*** of Roman law [20] and the law of the Decretals,[21] whether viewed absolutely or relatively, because this expression is in the nature of a juridical axiom that is true of any fear intimidating any firm and prudent man or woman.[22]

St. Thomas [23] with customary precision explains this classical phrase which finds no place in the present legislation. Fear befalling anyone means that he is compelled by reason of it. One is compelled by fear when, in order to avoid the thing feared, he chooses that which otherwise he would not elect. In this situation the ***vir constans*** is distinguished from the opposite type in two ways. The first is with regard to the quality or intensity of the evil feared. The resolute person, correctly reasoning as to what must be done or avoided, knows that the lesser evil or the greater good is always to be chosen. Consequently, he is acted upon by fear of a greater evil to sustain a lesser, but he is not forced to suffer a greater evil to avoid a lesser. With the imprudent and unsteadfast person the case is different. Fear compels him to choose a greater evil, e.g., he will commit sin to avoid corporal punishment. In the second place, the ***vir constans*** is distinguished by his estimation of the

[18] Payen, *De Matrimonio,* II, n. 1682.

[19] Schmalzgrueber, *Jus Ecclesiasticum Universum,* lib. I, tit. XL, n. 2.

[20] Dig. 4, 2, 1, 6.

[21] Cc. 15, 18, X, *de spons. et matr.,* IV, 1.

[22] Sanchez, *De Matrimonii Sacramento,* lib. IV, disp. III, nn. 3-4; Gasparri, *De Matrimonio,* n. 939; Wernz-Vidal, *Jus Matrimoniale,* n. 496. Sometimes the expression *cadens in virum constantem* is used only of absolutely grave fear. Cf. Cappello, *De Matrimonio,* n. 604.

[23] IV *Sent.,* dist. 29, q. 1, a. 2.

imminence or immediate nearness of the evil or danger. He is prevailed upon to act only from a strong probability that the evil impends, whereas the slightest probability will incite the other to action. The resolute and firm person faces his fears undauntedly. He does so, however, not because he is fearless, but because his sound and prudent judgment does not permit him to fear what he should not, nor when or where it is unnecessary.

Although the law of the Code merely states *metus gravis,* the distinctions of canonists as well as the decisions of the Roman Rota make it clear that fear may be absolutely or relatively grave for the invalidation of marriage. Absolutely grave fear is that which befalls or is experienced by any person and can efficaciously compel him to choose marriage.[24]

For the existence of absolutely grave fear certain conditions are required: (a) the evil which is feared must be grave in itself and not merely in the estimation of the person fearing; (b) this evil must certainly, or at least with great probability, threaten the person; (c) the one causing the fear must have it in his power to execute his threats; (d) the author of the fear must be in the habit of carrying out his intentions; (e) the person fearing must be unable in any way to escape the evil feared.[25] The last three conditions may be conveniently reduced to the second since they are only further consequences derived from it.[26]

According to the first condition, the evil which is feared must in itself be of great consequence and not merely in the estimation of the person fearing, for it is not the nature of the *vir constans* to fear what is of little import.[27] This means that the evil must be grave in its objective reality. It is not enough that it be grave in comparison to some lesser evil. Grave fear may be accepted in the wide sense to mean fear of any evil whatsoever, even the slightest evil,

[24] Santi, *Praelectiones Juris Canonici,* lib. IV, tit. I, n. 142; Cappello, *De Matrimonio,* n. 604; Farrugia, *De Matrimonio,* n. 29; Vlaming, *Praelectiones Juris Matrimonii,* n. 539; Payen, *De Matrimonio,* II, n. 1682; Augustine, *Commentary,* V, 246; Knecht, *Katholisches Eherecht,* p. 569; Triebs, *Kanonisches Eherecht,* III, 503-504.

[25] Sanchez, *De Matrimonii Sacramento,* lib. IV, disp. I, nn. 10-24; Ojetti, *Commentarium,* II, 149.

[26] Reiffenstuel, *Jus Canonicum Universum,* lib. I, tit. XL, n. 19.

[27] Sanchez, *De Matrimonii Sacramento,* lib. IV, disp. I, n. 10.

but still great in comparison with another evil. But the *raison d'être* of the law, which refers fear to contracts and permits their rescission or declares their nullity when contracted under its influence, demands that the fear proceed from an objectively grave evil. The law regards only fear of such an evil as interfering with that completely free exercise of the will required for assuming burdensome contractual obligations. An evil trivial in nature will not ordinarily produce a trepidation of mind which impedes deliberation or curtails volitional liberty. Hence it cannot, objectively viewed, be called grave in the sense that it efficaciously vitiates consent or produces an action juridically deficient of its proper effects.[28] Neither can a fictitious fear, which is the result of pure imagination and without objective cause or reality, be termed juridically grave. This is merely a *metus vani hominis,* an "empty" fear. Just as under Roman law such fear did not enjoy the protection of the praetor's edict,[29] so also it receives no consideration from ecclesiastical law.[30]

Certain evils are regarded by the law to be absolutely grave in their objective reality inasmuch as they are capable of mentally upsetting or intimidating anyone. Enumerated among such evils are death, corporal abuse, violation and mutilation, privation of freedom, imprisonment, banishment, or exile, withdrawal of the means of livelihood or subsistence, loss of an entire fortune, the greater part of it, or even a considerable portion, disinheritance, disownment or expulsion from the parental home, continued ill-treatment as manifested by blows, insults, privation of nourishment, confinement, etc., damage to honor, good name, reputation, and excommunication.[31]

Although these evils are considered the source of an absolutely grave fear, it is advisable to append a few observations concerning them. The fear of death or bodily mutilation is always grave. This

[28] Sanchez, *De Matrimonii Sacramento,* lib. IV, disp. I, nn. 11-13.

[29] Dig. 4, 2, 6.

[30] Sanchez, *De Matrimonii Sacramento,* lib. IV, disp. I, n. 14; Triebs, *Kanonisches Eherecht,* III, 503.

[31] Sanchez, *De Matrimonii Sacramento,* lib. IV, disp. V, nn. 1-29; Reiffenstuel, *Jus Canonicum Universum,* lib. I, tit. XL, n. 19; St. Alphonsus, *Theologia Moralis,* lib. VI, n. 1048; Gasparri, *De Matrimonio,* n. 941; Kutschker, *Eherecht,* IV, 193; Schoepf, *Katholisches Kirchenrecht,* IV, 68; Knecht, *Katholisches Eherecht,* pp. 569-570; Triebs, *Kanonisches Eherecht,* III, 503.

is also generally true where death is threatened by a gun or other weapon, even though the one threatening does not actually flourish it, or later puts it away.[82] The word "generally" is used advisedly because the nature of the author and the victim of the fear must be given consideration in such cases.[83] Thus, in one instance the Roman Rota was of the opinion that threats of shooting might not constitute grave fear for a man who later had the courage to serve his country in time of war and had been exposed to shell-fire.[84] Ordinarily, however, force of arms may be said to produce a grave fear.

The evil of imprisonment demands some consideration. Absolutely speaking, imprisonment is a grave evil, but it may not be such in every place, to every person alike, or under all circumstances. In order that the fear of prison may invalidate a compulsory marriage, it must be clearly proved that the hardship of imprisonment, viewed physically or morally, or both, constitutes a really grave and present evil for the person forced by fear of it to contract marriage. The duration of the term as well as the nature of the imprisonment calls for attention. Again, a man convicted of a wrong which entails the privation of his liberty may suffer thereby certain disabilities which ostracize him from his friends and deprive him upon his release of the means of respectable support. On the other hand, that which is a source of permanent disgrace and serious loss for one person may hardly affect the social status of one who has no office of competency or trust, no public standing, no especial claim to honorable consideration. It must of course be remembered that the civil law usually proportions the penalty to the injury of which the culprit is proved guilty. Therefore the average citizen simply gets his just deserts for having caused a scandal already made public to a degree by the trial. Hence imprisonment for a known offence might not

[82] Sanchez, *De Matrimonii Sacramento*, lib. IV, disp. V, nn. 4-5.

[83] Cf. e.g., S. R. R., *Causa Massilien.*, 26 Maii, 1913—*Decisiones*, V (1913), dec. 29, n. 16; S. R. R., *Causa Calatanisiaden.*, 28 Jul. 1916—*Decisiones*, VIII (1916), dec. XXI, nn. 7, 9; S. R. R., *Causa Montereyen. Angelorum*, 21 Dec. 1917—*Decisiones*, IX (1917), dec. XXX, n. 4.

[84] S. R. R., *Nullit. Matrim.*, 7 Aug. 1922—*Decisiones*, XIV (1922), dec. XXVIII, n. 10.

constitute a grave fear unless there be exceptions as indicated above.[35]

Physical violation and dishonor inspires a grave fear both for men and women. As far as the latter are concerned, this is to be held not only with regard to virgins or widows, but also those who have been guilty of an immoral life. Although the texts of the law and the authors would seem to refer only to the former class, they speak rather of the more frequent case without intending to restrict it to that class alone. It is true that a presumption against the gravity of fear due to a threat of *stuprum* will exist in the case of one who is immoral. But this will yield to contrary evidence because even for such a one the evil in question under certain circumstances can induce a grave fear the same as for a virtuous person.[36]

Loss of reputation or injury to dignity induce a grave fear especially when a person enjoys a good standing among his fellowmen and the author of the threats is one who would not hesitate to calumniate or detract the person. The same is to be said of infamy or disgrace, whether of law or fact. While these evils of themselves cannot be said to be sufficient to nullify marriage, it is evident that, in view of personal qualities and characteristics, they may be the source of real hardships and serve to influence consent.[37]

The penalty of excommunication constitutes a grave fear if it is unjust and cannot be easily avoided. An instance would be a censure inflicted in violation of canon 1017 § 3. If the penalty is just, it has the nature of a medicinal remedy. Should the delinquent refuse to abide by it, he has no one to blame but himself. If it can be easily avoided or lifted, e.g., by appeal to the proper authority, the fear it engenders cannot be termed grave. But when it is unjust and difficult of removal, even though it does not bind in the forum of conscience, still in the external forum it becomes the cause of grave inconveniences and perhaps injurious consequences. It must be accounted therefore as an evil inspiring grave fear for every one, if not in itself at least in its effects.[38]

[35] Cf. *AER,* XVIII (1898), 531-532.

[36] Sanchez, *De Matrimonii Sacramento,* lib. IV, disp. V, n. 12.

[37] Sanchez, *De Matrimonii Sacramento,* lib. IV, disp. V, n. 16. Cf. S. R. R., *Nullit. Matrim.*, 9 Apr. 1915— *Decisiones,* VII (1915), dec. XV, n. 2.

[38] Sanchez, *De Matrimonii Sacramento,* lib. IV, disp. V, nn. 17-19.

The loss, privation, or confiscation of temporal goods in the form of money, property or the equivalent is an evil causing a grave fear, provided it becomes the source of real hardship.[39] The person, however, must have a *jus in re* or a *jus ad rem* to the goods, as in the case of an inheritance, or at least must have the right of not being unjustly impeded from securing them.[40] Mere *lucrum cessans* does not constitute grave fear unless one has some kind of legal claim or title.[41] Thus, if a girl has been promised an increase in her inheritance or a special fund of money in order to entice or reward her for contracting a certain marriage, her consent is valid. Not the fear of losing something to which she was entitled, but rather hope and desire for what otherwise might have been refused prompted her consent.[42] Hence a title or right to the goods must exist and if this is lacking the evil entailed in the loss cannot be said to constitute a grave fear.

It is not necessary that any of the evils above described [43] directly and immediately threaten the party who is induced to give consent. The fear will not cease to be grave if the evil threatens one akin by ties of blood, marriage, friendship, or other relationship, such as a parent, brother or sister, guardian, business associate, even one who is a domestic or employee.[44] The attempt of some authors to restrict the degree of relationship does not seem practical. No absolute rule is possible since, no matter how far removed the kinship, grave fear can always result from threats directed against one who is particularly loved, esteemed, intimate, or valued. In general it may be said that it suffices if the evil threatens persons so closely

[39] Sanchez, *De Matrimonii Sacramento,* lib. IV, disp. V, nn. 21-24.

[40] Sanchez, *De Matrimonii Sacramento,* lib. IV, disp. V, n. 28; St. Alphonsus, *Theologia Moralis,* lib. VI, n. 1048; Gasparri, *De Matrimonio,* n. 941.

[41] Knecht, *Katholisches Eherecht,* p. 569, note 6.

[42] Cf. S. R. R., *Causa Nicien.,* 31 Jul. 1915—*Decisiones,* VII (1915), dec. XXXIII, n. 17; S. R. R., *Causa Nicien.,* 30 Dec. 1915—*Decisiones,* VII (1915), dec. XLII, n. 16.

[43] The evils giving rise to reverential fear, as well as all other points pertaining to that subject, will be discussed in a special chapter.

[44] Dig. 4, 2, 8, 3; Sanchez, *De Matrimonii Sacramento,* lib. IV, disp. IV, nn. 1-11; Reiffenstuel, *Jus Canonicum Universum,* lib. I, tit. XL, n. 19; St. Alphonsus, *Theologia Moralis,* lib. VI, n. 1047; Gasparri, *De Matrimonio,* n. 941.

connected or associated as to seriously disturb the mental equilibrium of the one suffering the fear.[45] Further than this circumstances must decide in each particular case.

In this connection reference must be made to the threat of suicide, e.g., if a girl's father or suitor threatens to kill himself unless she consent to marry. Suicide *per se* is not necessarily a grave evil in relation to the one suffering the fear and consequently it cannot be said absolutely to inflict a grave fear. The person threatening suicide may not be at all loved or esteemed by the other. Moreover, the sincerity of his intention may be doubted, or, if sincere, his death may work no great harm or loss. Thus, if the girl refused to marry because she did not love the other and would suffer neither qualms of conscience nor injury to her good name, as would be the case, e.g., where the suicide would not be ascribed to any wrong-doing on her part but to her singular qualities, or perhaps her levity and inconstancy, it is doubtful in such a hypothesis if suicide would be the source of grave fear.[46]

Per accidens, however, it may become a grave evil. Under certain circumstances it can cause a fear that is really grave as e.g., a threat from the father of a girl who is young and impressionable, or deeply conscientious and religious.[47] Thus, if a person's suicide should bring discredit to one holding a public office, or entail disgrace in the eyes of the people due to a suspicion of seduction or deception, or invite the vengeance and hatred of those who could not be escaped, threats of suicide may then be taken as inducing a grave fear.[48]

In the presence of any of the evils above described, a presumption exists for the fact of grave fear. This is not, however, a *praesumptio juris et de jure.*[49] Consequently, when the contrary is demonstrated, even one of the evils enumerated will not render a

[45] Feije, *De Impedimentis et Dispensationibus Matrimonialibus*, n. 132.

[46] Cf. S. R. R., *Nullit. Matrim.*, 18 Oct. 1922—*Decisiones,* XIV (1922), dec. XXXV, nn. 14-15.

[47] Knecht, *Katholisches Eherecht*, p. 570, note 8.

[48] Cf. S. R. R., *Nullit. Matrim.*, 31 Mar. 1922—*Decisiones,* XIV (1922), dec. IX, n. 9; S. R. R., *Causa Southwarcen.*, 29 Jul. 1926—*AAS,* XVIII (1926), 501-506.

[49] Schoepf, *Katholisches Kirchenrecht*, IV, 68, note 13.

marriage invalid. In such instances the evil, objectively grave, is the cause of a subjectively slight fear.[50]

The evils mentioned are not given *modo taxativo,* i.e., they are not to be understood as excluding all other evils. They are rather norms or standards whereby the gravity of other possible evils may be estimated.[51] The complexity and depravity of human nature makes it impossible to list all of them and hence the matter is left to the prudence of the judge in any particular case.[52] Thus the Roman Rota decided in a certain case that the actual privation of the sacraments was, for one who was daily accustomed to receive them, an evil inducing a fear sufficiently grave to invalidate the matrimonial consent given under its influence.[53]

The second condition required for the existence of an absolutely grave fear is that the evil be morally certain to eventuate, or at least threaten with great probability. Even though a serious evil is in question, it cannot give origin to an action-compelling fear unless the person fearing has at least a soundly probable conviction that the evil will befall.[54] Fear will move to action only upon a prudent and probable estimation that the evil will be suffered unless action is taken. Slight probability of the evil eventuating will not induce a fear grave enough to derange the operations of the intellect and will or interfere with judgment and choice. Probability of its imminence without actual infliction of the evil will suffice, however, since, were the latter necessary, it would no longer be a question of fear but of positive loss or injury.[55]

The strength and soundness of the conviction that the evil will be suffered unless marriage is contracted results from the various circumstances declared in the three final conditions given above for the constitution of grave fear. The agent inducing the fear must have it in his power to inflict the evil and must be in the

[50] Gasparri, *De Matrimonio,* n. 941.

[51] Heiss, *De Matrimonio,* p. 99.

[52] Sanchez, *De Matrimonii Sacramento,* lib. IV, disp. V, n. 2.

[53] S. R. R., *Causa Vic. Apostol. Nyanzae Septentr.,* 10 Maii, 1918—*Decisiones,* X (1918), dec. V, n. 5; Sec. Inst., 13 Maii, 1919—*Decisiones,* XI (1919), dec. XI, n. 21.

[54] Gasparri, *De Matrimonio,* n. 944; Payen, *De Matrimonio,* II, n. 1682; Triebs, *Kanonisches Eherecht,* III, 503.

[55] Sanchez, *De Matrimonii Sacramento,* lib. IV, disp. I, nn. 15-16.

habit of carrying out his threats.[56] A person will not be seriously disturbed by the threats of one who is incapable of executing them, e.g., when they are made by an aged, feeble or helpless person against one who is young or able to protect himself. Actual possibility is not necessary, however; a reasonable probability of the agent's capacity and intention suffices, even though the threats cannot materialize for reasons unknown to the intended victim. The menacing talk of one who is not in the habit of fulfilling his word cannot be regarded as inducing a grave fear. The threats of those who are readily provoked to anger but just as readily conciliated, or of those who are given to loquacity and idle boasting are for the most part empty and powerless to produce a serious mental perturbation. Thus, if a father should be in the habit of threatening suicide or disinheritance whenever things go contrary to his wishes or his children offend him, the same threats when made in connection with consent to marriage do not necessarily cause a grave fear.[57]

St. Alphonsus[58] objects to a too strict interpretation of this notion. In his opinion an evil can be feared from one who with serious intent and purpose threatens another. Moreover, a single threat would seem sufficient, provided the agent's usual *modus agendi* was to proceed injuriously against all who contradict his will, if not in the same way threatened, at least in just as violent a fashion.[59] In practice, however, all the circumstances must be diligently investigated. Threats, for instance, made in the heat of passion and afterwards retracted by words or letter of apology cannot be said to give rise to grave fear,[60] much less a single or occasional threat made by one whose nature is not consistent with such a procedure.[61]

[56] Gasparri, *De Matrimonio,* n. 944; Feije, *De Impedimentis et Dispensationibus Matrimonialibus,* n. 131; Farrugia, *De Matrimonio,* n. 29.

[57] Sanchez, *De Matrimonii Sacramento,* lib. IV, disp. I, nn. 19-20.

[58] *Theologia Moralis,* lib. VI, n. 1047.

[59] Sanchez, *De Matrimonii Sacramento,* lib. IV, disp. I, nn. 21-22.

[60] Cf. S. R. R., *Nullit. Matrim.,* 24 Mar. 1922—*Decisiones,* XIV (1922), dec. VIII, n. 9.

[61] An excellent illustration of these points is found in S. R. R., *Causa Montereyen. Angelorum,* 21 Dec. 1917—*Decisiones,* IX (1917), dec. XXX, 315-327.

The final circumstance tending to create an absolutely grave fear is the inability of the person fearing to escape the evil threatened. Impossibility of easily resisting the author of the threats or of avoiding the evil makes for a strong probable conviction that the danger really impends and consequently induces a grave fear.[62] Hence even though the evil threatened is serious, the gravity of fear is lessened if means are present to avoid it. *Scienti et volenti non fit injuria.*[63]

Among such means may be mentioned: making known the situation of coercion to a parent (supposing his absence), relative, friend, pastor or other reliable person and invoking their assistance in counteracting the plans of the author of the compulsion; actually leaving the scene or parental home, especially if the person suffering the fear is of age and trained to make his way in the world; making use of every opportunity to show resistance and displeasure for the intended marriage. Failure to make use of these means leads to a strong presumption that matrimonial consent was given more willingly than appears under the circumstances and was not the result of a grave fear.[64] While, however, the person suffering the fear must seek help, he is not held to do what is impossible or known to be useless.[65] Thus, circumstances may be such that even flight to another city may not avail to escape the threats which are made.[66] or it becomes impossible because of a public position

[62] Sanchez, *De Matrimonii Sacramento,* lib. IV, disp. I, n. 24; Feije, *De Impedimentis et Dispensationibus Matrimonialibus,* n. 131; Gasparri, *De Matrimonio,* n. 944.

[63] *Reg.* 27, R. J. in VI°.

[64] Cf. e.g., S. R. R., *Causa Massilien,* 26 Maii, 1913—*Decisiones,* V (1913), dec. XXIX, n. 18; S. R. R., *Nullit. Matrim.,* 1 Aug. 1913—*Decisiones,* V (1913), dec. XLII, nn. 14-16; S. R. R., *Nullit. Matrim.,* 29 Nov. 1913—*Decisiones,* V (1913), dec. L, nn. 28-29; S. R. R., *Causa Mediolanen.,* 17 Aug. 1916—*Decisiones,* VIII (1916), dec. XXVII, nn. 29-30; S. R. R., *Causa Parisien.,* 31 Jan. 1922—*Decisiones,* XIV (1922), dec. III, n. 8; S. R. R., *Nullit. Matrim.,* 18 Oct. 1922—*Decisiones,* XIV (1922), dec. XXXV, n. 8; S. R. R., *Nullit. Matrim.,* 24 Mar. 1922—*Decisiones,* XIV (1922), dec. VIII, n. 10.

[65] S. R. R., *Nullit. Matrim.,* 15 Feb. 1919—*Decisiones,* XI (1919), dec. II, nn. 5-6.

[66] S. R. R., *Nullit. Matrim.,* 28 Jan. 1918—*Decisiones,* X (1918) dec. II, n. 8.

which is held in the community.[67] The necessity, therefore, of examining the facts in each particular case requires no emphasis.

Word remains to be said concerning the proximity of the evil which impends. The evil or danger, according to the definition of fear, must be of the present *(instans)* or immediate future. This is fully necessary to constitute an absolutely grave fear, for an evil which is remote creates only a slight mental trepidation. Even though the evil is grave in itself, it cannot be considered grave in respect to marriage when it threatens in the distant future, because various ways may be counted upon to present themselves for its avoidance.[68] Nevertheless, as Sanchez[69] observes, if it should become clear that a grave evil, which will probably eventuate some time after *(multo post tempore)*, cannot be avoided except by entering the present contract, the fear must be judged as grave. An instance of this would be where a girl was told she would certainly be disinherited unless she acquiesced to her parents' wishes in the matter of her marriage.

Whenever, accordingly, the above conditions are found to exist, an absolutely grave fear sufficient to invalidate matrimonial consent is verified. But it is evident from the very nature of fear as well as from what has already been said, that it is affected by various mental modifications and consequently is conditioned to a large extent by personal qualities and characteristics. Hence the necessity for considering relatively grave fear.

Fear is said to be relatively grave when it moves to action some men or women whereas it will not affect others. Relative to the person suffering it, it is that fear which, considering the nature of the threats and the adjuncts of their author and victim, is really equal to extorting matrimonial consent. The gravity of this fear, accordingly, will especially depend upon the physical, mental, and moral qualities and characteristics of the persons involved.[70] Precisely

[67] S. R. R., *Nullit. Matrim.*, 31 Mar. 1922—*Decisiones,* XIV (1922), dec. IX, n. 12.

[68] Reiffenstuel, *Jus Canonicum Universum,* lib. I, tit. XL, n. 19; Santi, *Praelectiones Juris Canonici,* lib. IV, tit. I, n. 142; Gasparri, *De Matrimonio,* n. 944; Payen, *De Matrimonio,* II, n. 1682.

[69] *De Matrimonii Sacramento,* lib. IV, disp. I, n. 16.

[70] Payen, *De Matrimonio,* II, n. 1682; Triebs, *Kanonisches Eherecht,* III,

because of these personal and subjective elements it becomes impossible to set down a general principle or common rule for the constitution of relatively grave fear. Each particular case must be judged on the evidence submitted.

Attention must be given to the person who inflicts the fear. It is beyond doubt that his nature and character, his habitual *modus agendi,* the authority which he possesses, and other circumstances are of great weight for determining the influence of his threats upon the other's will. Consequently, among the points to be investigated the following may be emphasized: the power or authority he enjoys over the person suffering the fear; the reasons and motives for his action; his dispositions and habits; how he is accustomed to exercise his authority; whether he is naturally inclined to anger and violence; whether he readily executes his threats and carries out determined plans; whether he is so obdurate and obstinate as to brook no opposition or suffer no contradiction.[71]

The greatest consideration must be given to the person who has suffered the fear in order to establish its relative gravity. The circumstances tending to constitute it from his viewpoint are too numerous to attempt their mention. They can most easily be classified as those relating to sex, age, health, natural disposition, training, education, relation to the author of the fear, attitude toward the person he was compelled to marry, and any other facts or conditions which will act as presumptions and serve to give moral certitude that fear was relatively grave.[72]

The stress given to the personal and subjective qualities of the author and victim of coercion does not mean that the objective

503-504; Augustine, *Commentary,* V, 246; S. R. R., *Causa Gravinen.,* 2 Jul. 1918—*AAS,* XI (1919), 194; S. R. R., *Causa Parisien,* 12 Jun. 1919—*Decisiones,* XI (1919), dec. XI, n. 2; S. R. R., *Nullit. Matrim.,* 26 Jul. 1919—*Decisiones,* XI (1919), dec. XV, n. 2.

[71] S. C. S. Inquis., *Instructio ad Episc. Orient.,* 20 Jun. 1883 n. 36—*ASS,* XVIII (1885), 357; S. C. de Prop. Fid., *Instructio pro Foed. Stat. Amer. Ordin.,* a. 1883, § 37—*ASS,* XVIII (1885), 379; De Becker, *De Sponsalibus et Matrimonio,* p. 63; Triebs, *Kanonisches Eherecht,* III, 504, 515-516; Knecht, *Katholisches Eherecht,* p. 570.

[72] *Instructio ad Episc. Orient.,* n. 37; *Instructio pro Foed. Stat. Amer. Ordin.,* §§ 37, 38; Santi, *Praelectiones Juris Matrimonii,* lib. IV, tit. I, n. 142; Heiss, *De Matrimonio,* p. 98; Farrugia, *De Matrimonio,* n. 29; Payen, *De Matrimonio,* II, n. 1682; Triebs, *Kanonisches Eherecht,* III, 504.

gravity of the evil is to be entirely disregarded. While the relative gravity of fear does not depend so much upon the objective gravity of the evil as upon the characteristics of the persons inflicting and suffering it,[73] an empty fear of a purely imaginary evil or one of a trivial nature cannot be construed as causing a relatively grave fear.[74] Nevertheless, the same strict conditions of objective gravity and sound probability are not required for it as for an absolutely grave fear. What incites one person to action, may not move another; what is truly an object of fear to a woman, may not affect the average man; an evil may be grave for this particular girl but trivial for other women; finally, evils slight in themselves can collectively constitute a grave evil for a certain person.[75]

Thus, bodily injury or ill-treatment which is sustained by one may be of little consequence to another. Infamy and contumely, of little import to a private person or one of lower condition, may become intolerable and grievously harmful to one of noble rank, or of some prominence and held in high esteem. The loss of a certain sum of money may mean nothing to a wealthy person but may be a source of grave inconvenience or actual hardship for a poor individual. Imprisonment for a few months or years would be of little significance to a man who had many times previously been incarcerated for wrong-doing. Feelings of shame and disgrace consequent upon such imprisonment may be, apart from any physical suffering, a reason far outweighing the gravest fear sufficient to invalidate marriage, especially in the case of one who has never been similarly punished. Confinement in a convent may not necessarily be hard to bear for a girl who prefers solitude and is disposed to the pursuit of a retired life.[76]

Since no general norm can be given as to what exactly constitutes relatively grave fear, the duty of deciding whether it is qualified

[73] Sanchez, *De Matrimonii Sacramento*, lib. IV, disp. III, n. 5.

[74] Payen, *De Matrimonio*, II, n. 1682; Triebs, *Kanonisches Eherecht*, III, 503; cf. S. R. R., *Causa Lugdunen.*, 28 Jun. 1912—*AAS*, IV (1912), 647.

[75] Sanchez, *De Matrimonii Sacramento*, lib. IV, disp. III, nn. 2-4; Schmalzgrueber, *Jus Ecclesiasticum Universum*, lib. IV, tit. I, n. 431; Ballerini-Palmieri, *Opus Theologicum Morale*, VI, tr. X, n. 1123; Heiss, *De Matrimonio*, pp. 98-99.

[76] Gasparri, *De Matrimonio*, n. 941; Schoepf, *Katholisches Kirchenrecht*, IV, 67, note 11.

with the required gravity devolves upon the judge. His investigation should follow along lines indicated by the above exposition. To render an equitable judgment he must carefully weigh the evidence submitted and prudently evaluate it.[77] In this matter he can have no better rule for his guidance than that given by Gasparri,[78] and so frequently quoted with approval by the Roman Rota,[79] that the imminent evil must be grave for the particular person who fears it and that he must be convinced that this evil really threatens him.

§ 2. *External Causation*

The second condition required by ecclesiastical law for grave fear to have an invalidating effect on matrimonial consent is that it be induced *ab extrinseco*. This requirement is not difficult to understand and but little need be said concerning it. Regardless of the principle employed in distinguishing fear *ab intrinseco* from that *ab extrinseco,* canonists and moralists understand the latter, where there is question of the rescindability of contracts or the nullity of marriage, of that fear which proceeds from a free cause.[80] This free cause can be no other agent than man. He alone has it in his power to threaten another with evil or harm unless he respects his wishes or executes his will.

Although canon 1087, § 1 does not expressly state that the cause of fear must be free, still it implicitly makes this condition by further requiring that the fear be unjustly inflicted.[81] As has been

[77] Sanchez, *De Matrimonii Sacramento,* lib. IV, disp. V, n. 1; Ballerini-Palmieri, *Opus Theologicum Morale,* VI, tr. X, n. 1123; Feije, *De Impedimentis et Dispensationibus Matrimonialibus,* n. 129; Farrugia, *De Matrimonio,* n. 29.

[78] *De Matrimonio,* n. 940. Cf. Wernz-Vidal, *Jus Matrimoniale,* n. 496; Cappello, *De Matrimonio,* n. 604.

[79] Cf. e.g., S. R. R., *Nullit. Matrim.,* 28 Jan. 1918—*Decisiones,* X (1918), dec. II, n. 6; S. R. R., *Nullit. Matrim.,* 15 Feb. 1919—*Decisiones,* XI (1919), dec. II, n. 2; S. R. R., *Nullit. Matrim.,* 16 Dec. 1919—*Decisiones,* XI (1919), dec. XXII, n. 2.

[80] Sanchez, *De Matrimonii Sacramento,* lib. IV, disp. XII, n. 2; St. Alphonsus, *Theologia Moralis,* lib. VI, n. 1046; Santi, *Praelectiones Juris Canonici,* lib. IV, tit. I, n. 145; Feije, *De Impedimentis et Dispensationibus Matrimonialibus,* n. 128; Wernz-Vidal, *Jus Matrimoniale,* n. 501; Knecht, *Katholisches Eherecht,* p. 572.

[81] Vlaming, *Praelectiones Juris Matrimonii,* n. 539; Noldin, *Summa Theologiae Moralis,* III, n. 634.

seen, one purpose of the law of invalidity is to safeguard the rights of the contracting parties by voiding the marital transaction where injustice has been suffered. Unless, however, rights have been really injured, there can be no question of injury and no reason for invoking the protection of the law. But only an agent exempt from all internal necessity and endowed with independent self-determination, such as man, can be the source of an injurious act which violates the rights of another. Agents not invested with this capacity, as are necessary causes or natural events, can never be said to violate rights or act unjustly in the juridical sense. Moreover, it has been observed that the mere existence or presence of a fear arising from pure imagination, groundless worries, etc., is not sufficient to invalidate consent. The fear, howsoever grave, must have its inception in the actions or threats of another and these can conceivably proceed only from man acting as a free agent.[82]

The immediate consequence is that fear inspired by any other cause than a free agent does not work an invalidating effect on matrimonial consent. Marriage contracted under the influence of supernatural fear is certainly valid, no matter how grave the fear may be. Generally speaking, any act posited in such circumstances is neither rescindable nor invalid. Marriage in this hypothesis is not the result of external compulsion but is freely chosen as a means to consult the best interests of conscience and to avoid the greatest of evils. To say the least, a marriage contracted with this end in view is a most commendable act and any attempt to maintain its nullity is plainly absurd.[83]

Nor can it be held that supernatural fear is excited *ab extrinseco* when it is inspired not by the individual's personal reflection or meditation but by the words of a preacher or confessor. This is certainly not so, if the latter does not threaten a new evil but merely draws the attention of the person to evils designed by God to inspire fear. Fear is not thus properly caused but the mind is simply made more conscious of the evils by having them recalled, even though

[82] Triebs, *Kanonisches Eherecht,* III, 505.

[83] Santi, *Praelectiones Juris Canonici,* lib. IV, tit. I, n. 145; Gasparri, *De Matrimonio,* n. 946; Blat, *Commentarium,* III, n. 486

the danger, for instance, of eternal damnation, should be somewhat exaggerated.[84]

The only possible exception might be in the hypothesis where a person conspired to force a certain marriage by deliberately employing supernatural arguments to extort the consent of the unwilling party, especially should the latter be of a deeply religious nature or of tender conscience. Here the fear is freely caused similarly as when one makes use of another's illness to urge him to perform some action. This supernatural fear is specious and in reality unjust.[85] Practically, however, an instance of this kind seems improbable where marriage is concerned. Other coercive measures will in all likelihood accompany the act of compulsion and evidence of their use will sufficiently demonstrate the causation of fear *ab extrinseco.*

Marriage which is contracted through a natural fear, whether it proceeds from a necessary cause, as virulent disease, fatal injuries, illness, poor health, or from a natural event, as fire, earthquake, shipwreck, or other catastrophe, is valid. Fear induced by these or similar causes is of no account before the law. The impossibility of such a cause ever acting unjustly is evident from what has been stated above. Since no injustice is involved in a marriage contracted under its influence, this fear cannot invalidate matrimonial consent.[86]

Intrinsic fear does not infringe upon a person's liberty nor violate matrimonial freedom. The individual is not compelled by another's will but determines himself. As it is expressed in Roman law, *metum sibi infert.*[87] Inasmuch as justice is based on the distinction of one person from another, he cannot work an injustice properly so-called upon himself.[88] He may "do harm" to himself in choosing marriage but in the face of untoward circumstances he acts reasonably. He voluntarily elects that alternative with no one urging him to do so in order to avoid an evil or danger that threatens.

[84] Cf. Jombart, "De Ingressu ex Metu," *Periodica,* XII (1923), (55)-(56).

[85] Cf. Vermeersch, "De Metu ab Intrinseco vel Extrinseco," *Periodica,* XVII (1928), 143*.

[86] Schmalzgrueber, *Jus Ecclesiasticum Universum,* lib. IV, tit. I, n. 388; Feije, *De Impedimentis et Dispensationibus Matrimonialibus,* n. 128; Cappello, *De Matrimonio,* n. 606; Noldin, *Summa Theologiae Moralis,* III, n. 634.

[87] Dig. 4, 2, 2, 1.

[88] St. Thomas, *Summa Theologica,* 2, 2, q. 58, a. 2.

Any involuntariness in his choice cannot be attributed to another, but has its occasion in a combination of objective facts and subjective conditions beyond his or anyone else's control.[89] Finally, only that fear is qualified to nullify marriage which renders other contracts voidable. Since fear of an intrinsic nature has no effect upon the latter, *a fortiori* it can not invalidate the matrimonial contract.[90]

In accordance with these principles, valid consent is given in the following instances: the marriage of a man to his concubine or mistress from fear of God's judgment, to escape eternal damnation, or for peace of conscience; the marriage of a girl to a wealthy man in order to avoid a life of poverty or to assure a position of affluence in the social world; the marriage of one in a state of ill health on the advice of his physician that it will be beneficial to him; the marriage of a girl who feared the anger of her father and the inconveniences that might result therefrom, without the parent having inflicted such fear by any positive act; the marriage of one who seduced a girl due to fear inspired not by actual threats but by thoughts of the disgrace that may be incurred or the vengeance that may follow upon his act; marriage contracted in a time of panic, calamity, or disastrous event.[91] In these and similar cases, fear is not unjustly caused by a free human agent and the contracting parties sustain no injury. They merely choose the marital state as a means to attain what is sometimes a greater good, notwithstanding the fact that if circumstances were otherwise they would not marry. If disastrous consequences result, they have no one but themselves to blame. Since the law is intended only to protect against injustice, it can have no application where marriage is contracted because of this kind of fear.

The question may arise as to the validity of marriage contracted through the influence of fear inspired from without but with a mixture of intrinsic fear. The possibility of such a case is not too re-

[89] Sanchez, *De Matrimonii Sacramento,* lib. IV, disp. XII, n. 3; Reiffenstuel, *Jus Canonicum Universum,* lib. IV, tit. I, n. 326; Santi, *Praelectiones Juris Canonici,* lib. IV, tit. I, n. 145; Blat, *Commentarium,* III, n. 486.

[90] Schmalzgrueber, *Jus Ecclesiasticum Universum,* lib. IV, tit. I, n. 388; Reiffenstuel, *Jus Canonicum Universum,* lib. I, tit. XL, n. 26; Gasparri, *De Matrimonio,* n. 947.

[91] Sanchez, *De Matrimonii Sacramento,* lib. IV, disp. XII, nn. 4-5; Gasparri, *De Matrimonio,* n. 947; Gougnard, *De Matrimonio,* p. 167; Farrugia, *De Matrimonio,* n. 29; De Smet, *Betrothment and Marriage,* II, 54, note 3.

mote to warrant consideration. A seducer is approached by the girl's relatives and threatened with death unless he marries her. He steadfastly refuses to accede to their wishes and in the dispute which follows is seriously wounded. In grave danger of death, he marries the girl, as much, it seems, from the fear of death and to ease his conscience as from the threats actually executed against him. Marriage contracted under these circumstances is invalid because of the external causation of the force. Prescinding from any injustice in the matter, matrimonial consent is defective the moment it is extorted by force of arms, for instance, by a drawn revolver, even though the weapon is not actually used or is later put aside.[92] *A fortiori*, when threats have been executed to the extent of inflicting mortal injury, consent given under such circumstances should be viewed as due more to the unjust action of the author of the threats than to internal causes. The records show a case of this kind in which a decision was rendered in favor of nullity.[93]

A problem requiring solution under the head of external causation is whether grave fear inflicted by an insane person will invalidate marriage. The case is not entirely impossible or improbable. Such a situation may especially occur where one is under the authority of a chronic paranoiac suffering from impairment of the intellect and systematized delusions of power, grandeur, etc.

Although authors say nothing expressly concerning this question, the various juridical principles that come into play would seem to lead to the conclusion that grave fear induced by a person of the type described does not invalidate matrimonial consent. In the first place, the actual gravity of the fear inflicted may be doubted. Investigation must be made to ascertain whether means could and should have been taken to avoid the marriage by appealing for aid or placing the fear-inspiring agent in an asylum. Admitting, however, the gravity of the fear, the law further demands that it be inflicted by a free cause, that is, by man endowed with a free will. Fear from any other cause is either from within or is assimilated to that species as far as its juridic effects are concerned. Moreover, the

[92] Sanchez, *De Matrimonii Sacramento*, lib. IV, disp. V, n. 5.

[93] S. C. C., Jul. 13, Sept. 22, 1725—Richter, *Canones et Decreta Concilii Tridentini*, n. 82, pp. 243-244.

actions of one suffering from insanity are not human acts *(actus humani)* but acts of man *(actus hominis)*. As such, they must be accounted as proceeding from a natural cause. Consequently the fear inflicted should be viewed as *ab intrinseco* or equivalent to it. Finally, the injustice of the action may be disputed.[94] Injury can be done only by acts which are human and free. Those not so qualified, even though they have man for their author, can never be just or unjust. For these reasons fear caused by an insane person cannot be said, at least certainly, to invalidate a marriage contracted under its influence.[95]

Further difficulties are encountered where the person suffering from insanity has lucid intervals or is otherwise of sound mental condition except for an abnormal obsession in the matter of marriage. An illustration of the latter instance would be a father who is afflicted with a monomania in regard to the marriages of his children. The difficulty to be settled is whether in the particular case of marriage he is to be reckoned as equivalent to a necessary cause on account of his mental affliction, or whether because of his otherwise healthy mentality he is to be judged as being a free agent. Reason might be found for classifying a person of this type with those characterized by outbursts of violent anger, inordinate ambition, excessive greed, etc. No one denies that coercion exercised by such will, under the required conditions, nullify matrimonial consent. Payen [96] is of the opinion that a marriage due to grave fear induced by a

[94] It may be pointed out that formal injustice is not required for the nullity of marriage. The Roman Rota has made it clear in several of its decisions that material injustice, or coercion without malicious intent, is sufficient for invalidity. Cf. e.g., S. R. R., *Causa Veszprimien.*, 2 Jun. 1911—*AAS*, IV (1912), 115: "Quod si pater in metu inferendo bonum sive filiorum sive parentum intendat, optima potest esse sua intentio coram Deo et hominibus; sed metus, quatenus laedit libertatem filiorum in matrimonio contrahendo, vulnerat eorum jus et fit injustus, et hinc causa nullitatis matrimonii, si sit gravis." S. R. R., *Causa Vicariat. Apost. Ce-Li Central.*, 10 Feb. 1917—*Decisiones*, IX (1917), dec. III, n. 8: "Parum enim refert, si mater animo filiam cogere intendebat; nam error inferentis metum a peccato excusare potest, sed objectivam injustitiam metus non aufert."

[95] Cf. Bernardini, "De Metu ab Amente Incusso in Ordine ad Matrimonium,"—*Apollinaris*, III (1930), 454-455; Haring, "Zwang zum Eheabschluss durch Einen Irrsinnigen"—*LQS*, LXXXIV (1931), 151-152.

[96] *De Matrimonio* II, p. 82, note 1.

person suffering from so unusual a mental condition is invalid. Because of the doubt which exists, however, the silence of authors concerning it, and the fact that no known precedent has been established, singular cases of this kind should be referred to the Holy See.

While the source of fear must be a free agent, his identity is of no immediate consequence. It may be the individual who wishes to contract the marriage or a third person espousing his cause: a parent, relative, or friend, whether in a private, public, or official capacity. Nor does it make any difference if the latter acts with or without the previous knowledge, wish or command of either of the contracting parties.[97] The law declares nullity not so much in reproach of the fear-inducing agent as in favor of the liberty of marriage and the rights of the coerced party. Injury is done no matter by whom the fear is inflicted, whether by one of the contracting parties or a third person. Moreover, other contracts are voidable, irrespective of the cause of the fear, as long as it is a free agent. The same principle holds in regard to marriage.[98]

While the condition of extrinsic causation as set forth by canon 1087, § 1 is not difficult to understand, it must not be dismissed lightly or taken for granted in any particular case. Care must be exercised to determine whether the alleged fear, presuming its existence and gravity have been demonstrated, really proceeds from a free extrinsic cause. It is possible for the evil which threatens to be involved in the objective circumstances of the situation and marriage in a certain sense is imperative if other evils are to be avoided. Thus, even where grave threats have been proven, they may be merely the occasion of matrimonial consent, whereas its formal reason or cause may be a guilty conscience recognizing obligations it is bound to fulfill.[99] Should circumstances of this kind derive their coercive force independently of a free will, the gravest

[97] Pichler, *Jus Canonicum,* lib. IV, tit. I, n. 109; De Becker, *De Sponsalibus et Matrimonio,* p. 64; Cappello, *De Matrimonio,* n. 606; Knecht, *Katholisches Eherecht,* p. 572.

[98] Reiffenstuel, *Jus Canonicum Universum,* lib. IV, tit. I, n. 326; Schmalzgrueber, *Jus Ecclesiasticum Universum,* lib. IV, tit. I, n. 392.

[99] Cf. S. R. R., *Nullit. Matrim.,* 24 Mar. 1922—*Decisiones,* XIV (1922), dec. VIII, n. 11.

degree of fear will not vitiate consent or invalidate the marital pact.[100]

§ 3. *Unjust Infliction*

It is not sufficient for the moral compulsion and fear which induce a person to give matrimonial consent to be of a grave character and proceed from an external agent. The law furthermore requires that it be a *metus injuste incussus.* The coercion employed must be unjustly brought to bear upon the party who gives reluctant consent and inflict upon him a real injury. If injury is not done in the strict sense, if it is not objectively real but merely a subjective belief or persuasion, the ecclesiastical law of nullity does not apply and the marriage is valid.[101]

The exact significance of this requisite is often but obscurely understood, owing in no small measure to the brevity and confusion with which it is treated. To determine in any particular case if fear has been unjustly inflicted, investigation must be made to ascertain whether the party who alleges compulsion and constraint has suffered any violation of his rights. As a guide in this matter two fundamental principles should be borne in mind. Real injury is not inflicted by one who legitimately possesses a right and lawfully exercises it,[102] nor is real injustice suffered by one who lacks a strict right. Secondly, not every morally wrong action violates justice: it may merely offend against the virtue of charity.[103]

When the question is raised as to when fear is justly or unjustly inflicted relative to marriage both the active agent and the passive subject must be considered. As Schmalzgrueber[104] expresses it, in order that fear be justly inflicted it is not sufficient that the one who suffers it has placed a just cause: the one who inflicts it must also have a right to do so. Hence the injustice may be considered in regard to the one who suffers the constraint either because he has come into the fear-situation through no fault of his own and has

100 S. R. R., *Nullit. Matrim.*, Nov. 29, 1913—*Decisiones,* V (1913), dec. L, n. 3.

101 Triebs, *Kanonisches Eherecht,* III, 505.

102 Cf. Dig. 50, 17, 155: "non videtur vim facere, qui jure suo utitur."

103 Wernz-Vidal, *Jus Matrimoniale,* p. 587, note 24.

104 *Jus Ecclesiasticum Universum,* lib. IV, tit. I, n. 392.

given the active agent no cause or reason for the employment of coercive measures, or because he has suffered the fear in an unjust manner.[105] Again, the injustice may be regarded from the viewpoint of the one who inflicts it, either because he does not possess the right of threatening an evil for the purpose of compelling marriage, or at least exceeds the limits of his power, or because he does not observe the proper mode in its infliction.[106]

Hence, to justify coercion and compulsion with respect to marriage, the passive agent must have placed a cause entailing a moral obligation to marry, or to choose between marriage and some alternative, and the force or constraint should proceed from one, either a public official in the due exercise of his office or a private person in certain cases, who has the right to employ such measures.[107] On the contrary, fear is unjustly inflicted as often as the person suffering it is under no moral obligation to marry, or even to choose between marriage and some other obligation, should that alternative be provided, and the compelling agent does not enjoy the right of using coercive measures for its exaction.[108]

For the purpose of clarifying the foregoing general determinations of just and unjust infliction of fear, canonists make the useful distinctions between ***metus juste vel injuste incussus quoad substantiam*** and ***metus juste vel injuste incussus quoad modum.*** Fear is justly inflicted ***quoad substantiam*** if the evil is due in justice, that is, an evil which one deserves for a just reason or cause and by which one is in justice deprived of some good. Fear is justly inflicted ***quoad modum*** if a just evil is threatened in a just way, that is, in accordance with the established legal formalities of competence, rules of procedure, imposition of penalties, etc. Fear is unjustly inflicted ***quoad substantiam*** if the evil is unjust, that is, an evil which one deserves for no just reason or cause and by which one is deprived, without any or at least without strict right, of a good due to him.

[105] Knecht, *Katholisches Eherecht,* p. 570.

[106] Blat, *Commentarium,* III, n. 486.

[107] Schmalzgrueber, *Jus Ecclesiasticum Universum,* lib. IV, tit. I, n. 389; Feije, *De Impedimentis et Dispensationibus Matrimonialibus,* n. 133; Smith, *Marriage Process,* n. 157; Petrovits, *Church Law on Matrimony,* n. 422.

[108] Ballerini-Palmieri, *Opus Theologicum Morale,* I, tr. I, n. 129; VI, tr. X, n. 1127; De Becker, *De Sponsalibus et Matrimonio,* p. 64; De Smet, *Betrothment and Marriage,* n. 538.

Fear is unjustly inflicted *quoad modum* if the evil is just but is threatened in an unjust manner, that is, not in compliance with the formalities of the law.[109]

From these distinctions it follows that fear, in general or in relation to marriage, is justly inflicted when the evil feared is just from every angle both *quoad substantiam* and *quoad modum.* Such would be the case of a just penalty as punishment for an offense really committed, inflicted by a competent judge in accordance with all the formalities of law. Fear is unjustly inflicted when the evil feared is for some reason or other unjust: *quoad substantiam,* if the evil is due under no condition whatsoever, e.g., a penalty threatened for an offense which has not been committed, or if the offense has been committed, but that particular penalty is in no way deserved; unjust *quoad modum,* if the offense has been committed and the penalty threatened is just, but not from that particular person or in that particular fashion, e.g., a penalty inflicted by an incompetent judge or without observance of legal formalities; unjust *quoad substantiam* and *quoad modum* from a combination of these circumstances.[110]

Since just or unjust infliction of fear *quoad substantiam* in relation to marriage implies the presence or absence of an obligation to marry, and just or unjust infliction of fear *quoad modum* refers to the means employed to enforce that obligation, it is advisable for avoiding confusion to discuss briefly these notions before attempting to discover the validity of marriage contracted under the influence of one or the other.

The expression *quoad substantiam* has reference to the cause or reason on account of which fear is inflicted to compel marriage. If a just cause exists to compel marriage, the evil threatened for that purpose engenders a fear justly inflicted *quoad substantiam;* in its absence, the fear will be unjustly inflicted *quoad substantiam.* The only cause or reason, however, which can justify the infliction of fear is an obligation to marry. Consequently, if the one who suffers fear

[109] Payen, *De Matrimonio,* II, n. 1685; Wernz-Vidal, *Jus Matrimoniale,* n. 501; cf. Rossi, "De Consensu Matrimoniali," n. 110—*Analecta Ecclesiastica,* II, (1911), 73.

[110] Gasparri, *De Matrimonio,* n. 948; Maroto, *Institutiones,* I, n. 397; Cappello, *De Matrimonio,* n. 604.

is obliged on the basis of some law to contract the marriage in question and refuses to fulfill that obligation, he suffers no injustice or injury upon being held to its fulfillment through threats of grave evil made by the rightful claimant or party. If, however, one is compelled to contract marriage through threats of grave evil in the absence of a legal or just obligation to that effect, he suffers a grave injustice and the coercion employed is applied unjustly *quoad substantiam.*[111]

According to ecclesiastical law, an obligation to contract marriage may arise either *ex contractu* or *ex delicto.* The former obligation is consequent to a promise of marriage made strictly in accordance with the formalities prescribed by the law of the Church.[112] In virtue of this formal engagement, the parties are bound by a grave obligation to marry within a time left to their own prudent judgment.[113] This obligation is exclusive and absolute. Hence were evil threatened to enforce it, the fear caused thereby would be just *quoad substantiam.*[114]

The obligation to contract marriage *ex delicto* is incurred by one who is guilty of the offense known to canonists and moralists as *stuprum.* This is to be understood in the sense of acquiring carnal knowledge of a woman against her will, whether by physical violence or moral means, e.g., fraudulently seducing her with the promise of marriage, persuasions, threats, etc., makes no difference. Added to the malice of fornication is that of the injustice suffered by the woman who is thus overcome.[115] In the eyes of the Church the obligation to marry which arises *ex delicto* is not absolute but conditional. The delinquent has the option of marrying the girl or making a financial settlement, according to the axiom: *duc aut*

[111] Triebs, *Kanonisches Eherecht,* III, 505.

[112] *Codex Juris Canonici,* c. 1017, §§ 1, 2.

[113] Cappello, *De Matrimonio,* n. 107; Wernz-Vidal, *Jus Matrimoniale,* n. 93; Farrugia, *De Matrimonio,* n. 40; Chelodi, *Jus Matrimoniale,* n. 18; Cerato, *Matrimonium,* 6, n. 4; Knecht, *Katholisches Eherecht,* pp. 154-155; Ayrinhac, *Marriage Legislation,* n. 27.

[114] Triebs, *Kanonisches Eherecht,* III, 512.

[115] Pirhing, *Jus Canonicum,* lib. V, tit. XVI, n. 37; Sanchez, *De Matrimonii Sacramento,* lib. VII, disp. XIV, n. 1; Laymann, *Theologia Moralis,* lib. III, tr. 3, c. 13, n. 1; Lehmkuhl, *Theologia Moralis,* I, n. 1048; cf. c. 2, C. XXXVI, q. 1.

dota.[116] Consequently, should the man guilty of such an offense be threatened with a grave evil in order to compel him to marry the girl, fear is unjustly inflicted *quoad substantiam* because he is not exclusively obliged to contract marriage.

Finally, the obligation may arise *ex contractu et delicto.* This occurs when a formal engagement or a real promise of marriage made possible the seduction. In the opinion of authors this obligation is also absolute and cannot be fulfilled by a payment of damages. Nevertheless, they admit that an exception may be made when there are good reasons for excusing from it, e.g., mutual aversion of the parties, danger of scandal, probable unhappy consequences, etc.[117]

The term *quoad modum* relates to the means employed to enforce the obligation to marry. Although the fear inflicted may be just *quoad substantiam,* still the one thus constrained to fulfill his obligation may suffer injustice on account of the measures taken to attain that end. Formerly under ecclesiastical law the possibility of doing injury in this fashion was great. Up to the appearance of the present codification, the obligation to contract marriage *ex contractu* was enforceable by means of various punishments,[118] as well as by taking action in the external forum,[119] even to the extent of having censures imposed with the object of exacting marriage from the party who had unlawfully withdrawn from the engagement.[120]

According to the existing discipline,[121] however, one party no longer has the right to force the other through an ecclesiastical tri-

[116] Lugo, *De Justitia et Jure,* disp. XII, nn. 15-22; St. Alphonsus, *Theologia Moralis,* lib. III, nn. 642-650; Noldin, *Summa Theologiae Moralis,* II, n. 469; Genicot, *Institutiones Theologiae Moralis,* I, n. 568; De Smet, *Betrothment and Marriage,* I, 16, note 2; cf. *Collationes Brugenses,* II (1897), 617-619.

[117] Pirhing, *Jus Canonicum,* lib. V, tit. XVI, n. 54; D'Annibale, *Summula Theologiae Moralis,* III, 521; Gasparri, *De Matrimonio,* n. 98; Triebs, *Kanonisches Eherecht,* III, 506.

[118] Cc. 46, 47, 51, C. XXVII, q. 2; cc. 22, 31, X, *de spons. et matr.,* IV, 1; cf. Sanchez, *De Matrimonii Sacramento,* lib. I, disp. XXVII; Gasparri, *De Matrimonio,* n. 122; Ballerini-Palmieri, *Opus Theologicum Morale,* VI, tr. X, nn. 131-141.

[119] Cc. 10, 17, X, *de spons. et matr.,* IV, 1; c. 25, X, *de jurejurando,* II, 24; cf. Feije, *De Impedimentis et Dispensationibus Matrimonialibus,* n. 554.

[120] C. 10, X, *de spons. et matr.,* IV, 1; cf. Bangen, *De Sponsalibus et Matrimonio,* I, 58-59.

[121] *Codex Juris Canonici,* c. 1017, § 3.

bunal to keep his promise of marriage.[122] This does not mean that the Code denies the existence of a grave obligation to marry. It rather takes it for granted, otherwise it would not give it the attention which it does in canon 1017.[123] Neither does the present law allow an action to compel marriage where the obligation arises *ex delicto* or *ex contractu et ex delicto*.[124] In all these cases, though the obligation exists in the internal forum, the only action permissible is that to recover damages if any have been suffered. Today, accordingly, the injury *quoad modum* can only be inflicted, as far as ecclesiastical law is concerned, by threatening an evil which the juridical order gives no right whatsoever to inflict. One who has no right to inflict an evil also lacks the right to threaten it.

This brief exposition of the Church's stand relative to incurring the obligation to marry and the enforcement thereof would suffice for the present study were it not for another angle to the problem. Occasionally it happens that the obligation to contract marriage is imposed by civil authority in apparent contradiction to ecclesiastical law with the result that the party so compelled seems to suffer injustice. The difficulty is not encountered in the case of breach of promise of marriage. A civil court will rarely if ever compel marriage on these grounds but simply allow a suit for possible damages sustained. The conflict between ecclesiastical and civil law usually occurs when a secular judge imposes the alternative of marriage or imprisonment on a man who has had criminal knowledge of a woman either against her will or by seducing her with the prospect of marriage. The case where a previous consent had been given and where the law only secures the outward ratification of a past clandestine marriage is not here contemplated.

In this hypothesis of marriage contracted under compulsion of a civil judge, the proved guilt of the accused party must not be identified with the justice of the sentence which condemns him either to go to prison or to marry the party whom he has wronged. According to what has been previously stated, in order that fear may be

[122] Cf. Cappello, *De Matrimonio*, n. 109; Wernz-Vidal, *Jus Matrimoniale*, n. 93; Triebs, *Kanonisches Eherecht*, I, 107-109; Augustine, *Commentary*, V, 44.

[123] Woywod, *Practical Commentary*, I, n. 985.

[124] Triebs, *Kanonisches Eherecht*, III, 507.

said to influence a person justly, it is not sufficient that he be guilty or that by his delinquent conduct he may have brought the penalty upon himself. It is also necessary that the penalty be of just proportion to the wrong done, and that it be imposed by a person having a just right to do so. In the case under consideration, it may be questioned whether or not a judge, placing the alternative of imprisonment or marriage, does not exercise his power at the expense of his right. In other words, the difficulty to be settled is whether injustice is done by a judge who under threat of imprisonment exacts marriage absolutely to the exclusion of the alternative of financial payment admitted by ecclesiastical law under such circumstances.[125]

As has been pointed out above, authors commonly teach that one who is guilty of the offense described can be forced under threat of some punishment to repair the damage by marrying the girl or making a financial settlement. The obligation to contract marriage should not be absolutely imposed. In other words, the delinquent should be given the choice of marriage or payment or punishment. Such is the principle which has governed the practice of the Church and her jurisprudence, especially as manifested in the decisions of the Roman Rota.[126]

According to the same authorities, however, this general rule admits of exceptions, particularly since it was not always in force. In the earliest days the seducer was under obligation to marry the girl he had wronged. He was not given the choice of a money payment, most likely because this could not repair the essential damage which had been done.[127] But the disastrous results consequent to forced marriages of this kind made necessary a different disposition in the matter. In order to provide better for the security of marriage, the custom gradually was introduced of imposing upon the seducer the alternative of marrying the girl or endowing her.[128]

[125] Cf. *AER,* XVIII (1898), 532-533.

[126] Cf. e.g., S. R. R., *Imped. ad Matrim.,* 22 Jan. 1911—*Decisiones,* III (1911), dec. IV, nn. 11-15; S. R. R., *Imped. ad Matrim. et Damn.,* 31 Aug. 1912—*Decisiones,* IV (1912), dec. XXXVII, n. 5; S. R. R., *Imped. et Damn.,* 1 Aug. 1913—*Decisiones,* V (1913), dec. XLI, n. 4.

[127] Triebs, *Kanonisches Eherecht,* III, 506.

[128] Pirhing, *Jus Canonicum,* lib. V, tit. XVI, n. 41; Engel, *Collegium Universi Juris Canonici,* lib. V, tit. XVI, n. 10.

Justification for this practice was found in the prescription of the Mosaic law [129] which eventually was transferred *verbatim* into the ecclesiastical code.[130]

Furthermore, crimes of this nature were formerly under the jurisdiction of the Church. The offender had the choice of marriage or settlement, unless he preferred to undergo a punishment in proportion to the crime. This was usually excommunication or confinement in a monastery. By common interpretation these penalties were also inflicted upon a seducer who refused to marry but at the same time could make no financial reparation on the principle: *qui non habet in aere, luat in corpore.*[131]

The offense in question, however, pertains to both forums and consequently disposition of it can be made by civil authority. Since its restriction is to the best interests of the common good,[132] its punishment under prevalent conditions is left almost universally to a secular judge.[133] For this reason if the wisdom of the legislator or the prudence of the judge should deem it necessary for the welfare of society, the alternative of paying damages can be withdrawn and the obligation to marry imposed absolutely.[134] Even though this procedure is at variance with that of ecclesiastical law, no injustice will be done if the one accused is really guilty of the offense.[135] The sentence will not be unjust *quoad substantiam* because the alternative of paying damages is only of custom and does not pertain to the essence of the matter. Inasmuch as the commonweal must look to its welfare, it will not be unjust *quoad modum.*[136]

In treating of marriage contracted under compulsion of a civil magistrate, authors generally refer to certain laws found in North

[129] Exodus, 22: 16-17.

[130] C. 1, X, *de adult. et stup.*, V, 16: "Si seduxerit quis virginem nondum desponsatam, dormieritque cum eo, dotabit eam et habebit (eam) uxorem. Si vero pater virginis dare noluerit, reddet pecuniam juxta modum dotis, quam virgines accipere consueverunt."

[131] Engel, *Collegium Universi Juris Canonici,* lib. V, tit. XVI, n. 11.

[132] Pontius, *De Sacramento Matrimonii,* lib. IV, c. XIX, n. 2; St. Alphonsus, *Theologia Moralis,* lib. III, n. 641.

[133] Engel, *Collegium Universi Juris Canonici,* lib. V, tit. XVI, n. 13.

[134] Cf. S. R. R., *Nullit. Matrim.,* 9 Jun. 1911—*Decisiones,* III (1911), dec. XXII, n. 5.

[135] Gasparri, *De Matrimonio,* n. 949.

[136] D'Annibale, *Summula Theologiae Moralis,* III, n. 445, note 19.

America which condemn a man to prison with no possibility of release until he takes the woman he has wronged for his wife. This is not an exact statement of the issue. In the United States legislation having any connection with this matter is usually found in the form of Seduction and Bastardy statutes. Diverse as are the laws of the various jurisdictions, none of them, as far as can be ascertained, oblige to marriage absolutely under penalty of imprisonment. The guilty party is ordinarily given the option of marrying the woman he has wronged, supposing she is willing, or making a money settlement to repair as far as possible the damage or to provide for the off-spring that has or will be born. In the event that neither of these conditions is fulfilled, the law may permit a penalty of imprisonment to be inflicted where the action taken, as on a paternity charge, is criminal.

Where such laws as these are in force, it would appear that a secular judge commits an injustice by absolutely imposing marriage or the alternative of going to prison. Imprisonment is admittedly a grave evil and to inflict it for refusal to marry would seem to constitute grave and unjust coercion. In the first place, however, authorities are not lacking who assert the right of the judge to inflict the alternative of imprisonment or marriage.[137] In the second place it must be remembered that the duty of the judge is to apply the existing law with prudence, discretion and equity. Hence, if he has sound reason for withdrawing the alternative of paying damages, where this is provided for by the law, he cannot be accused of injustice. Such a consideration might be the fact that the delinquent lacks the resources to make the financial settlement justly decreed by the court.[138] This action cannot be construed as unjust since in reality it is the offender's own inability which deprives him of the alternative of payment. He inflicts the fear on himself after having placed a cause from which he knew the evil of imprisonment was due. *Qui non habet in aere, luat in corpore* applies equally in this situation. The action of the judge, therefore, at least apart

[137] Santi, *Praelectiones Juris Canonici,* lib. IV, tit. I, n. 146; De Becker, *De Sponsalibus et Matrimonio,* p. 64; Genicot, *Institutiones Theologiae Moralis,* II, n. 463; Kutschker, *Eherecht,* IV, 202; *AER,* XVIII (1898), 533.

[138] Cf. S. R. R., *Nullit. Matrim.,* 9 Jun. 1911—*Decisiones,* III (1911), dec. XXII, n. 7.

from exceptional cases, cannot be viewed as an injustice and the fear arising therefrom cannot be termed unjust coercion or duress.

The distinctions concerning the just or unjust infliction of fear *quoad substantiam* and *quoad modum,* as is evident, find application in this matter. If the accused is really guilty of the offense and a just penalty has been inflicted in accordance with all the formalities of the law, the fear thereby caused is justly inflicted *quoad substantiam* and *quoad modum.* Where none of these conditions are fulfilled, the opposite is true. Where the offense has not been committed but the required legal proceedings have been observed, the fear is unjust *quoad substantiam* though just *quoad modum.* Should the offense have been actually committed but the coercion exercised is not in conformity with the prescriptions of the law, the fear is justly inflicted *quoad substantiam* and unjustly *quoad modum.* It should also be noted that, while the judge may have the right to punish a delinquent, he can do so in no other way than that sanctioned by the law. He is not permitted to decree a punishment substantially different and more grievous than that provided by the statutes, e.g., death in place of imprisonment, or a longer term than is commonly meted out, or a financial settlement entirely out of proportion to the merits of a case. Should he proceed in this fashion, he would act unjustly, not indeed *quoad modum,* supposing his competence, but *quoad substantiam* by decreeing a penalty beyond that justly due to the offense.[139]

While public authorities in the due exercise of their official duties have a right to use coercion in the manner described, it cannot be denied that private persons, e.g., parents, relatives, etc., can also employ it under certain circumstances.[140] This must be done, however, in accordance with the laws of justice. As far as concerns the urging or enforcing of an obligation by the threatening or infliction of penalties, private persons, not even one who has suffered the injury, have no competence. The obligation to repair any injury arises only, in the external forum at least, when it has been juridi-

[139] Cf. Gasparri, *De Matrimonio,* n. 948.

[140] De Becker, *De Sponsalibus et Matrimonio,* p. 64; Smith, *Marriage Process,* nn. 157, 160.

cally proven before a competent judge. Consequently in the present case the right of enforcement belongs only to the proper authority after the matter has been fully investigated and the offender duly convicted. The party suffering the injury or his agent can, however, urge the obligation of reparation by inducing fear of a penalty stated by the law itself, to be decided and inflicted by a competent judge according to the prescriptions of the law. In other words, he may give the delinquent the choice of marriage or payment of damages or legal proceedings. Fear will then be just *quoad modum,* because the person has a right to appeal to the law and therefore has a right to threaten to do so. But if he threatens the punishment provided by the law and intends to inflict it himself, the fear is unjust *quoad modum* since the offender would be coerced and condemned without a competent judge or proper judicial investigation. Finally, if a penalty such as death or grave bodily harm is threatened, the fear inflicted would be unjust *quoad substantiam* for the same reasons given above: the punishment would exceed that merited by the offense in the eyes of the law.[141]

Brief though this explanation of the obligation to contract marriage and its enforcement necessarily is, it will serve the purpose of the present study. The distinctions given make it at once apparent that through combination four possibilities arise with regard to the just or unjust infliction of fear with the object of compelling matrimonial consent: (*a*) *metus juste incussus et quoad substantiam et quoad modum;* (*b*) *metus injuste incussus et quoad substantiam et quoad modum;* (*c*) *metus injuste incussus quoad substantiam, juste quoad modum;* (*d*) *metus juste incussus quoad substantiam, injuste quoad modum.* An attempt will now be made to ascertain the effect of fear on the validity of marriage in each hypothesis.

(a) Canonists are unanimous in upholding the validity of marriage due to fear justly inflicted in every respect.[142] The evil which is feared can by strict right be inflicted both in regard to its substance and its mode. A just cause exists for inspiring fear and this

[141] Cf. S. R. R., *Nullit. Matrim.,* 8 Jul. 1919—*Decisiones,* XI (1919), dec. XIII, n. 5.

[142] Sanchez, *De Matrimonii Sacramento,* lib. IV, disp. XIII, n. 3; Pirhing, *Jus Canonicum,* lib. IV, tit. I, n. 104; Schmalzgrueber, *Jus Ecclesiasticum Uni-*

is done in accordance with the requirements of the law. The one who inflicts it has a right to do so in order to secure a matrimonial consent which he can exact.[143] Consequently no injustice is done to the party who is thus coerced. The law of invalidity is designed to protect one whose right of matrimonial freedom has been unlawfully violated. Where no injury is done, however, there is no reason for the law extending its protection.[144]

Whenever evil is threatened to compel an action due in justice, the fear caused thereby is considered as proceeding from the law and the nature of the offense. But the law itself cannot be presumed to invalidate marriage and the fear is rather from within than from without. Within the person himself is found the reason for fearing. Some previous fact or deed warrants the use of coercive measures. He has no one to blame, accordingly, but his own reprehensible conduct which justifies the compulsion.[145] Furthermore, over and above the reason that other contracts are not invalidated by a justly inflicted fear, perhaps the most conclusive of all is that the Church neither has nor could declare marriage null and void on such grounds.[146]

Hence, if a father, under threat of instituting legal proceedings, gives his daughter's seducer the choice of marrying her or providing a proportionate financial consideration; if a girl, after having become pregnant through fraudulent seduction, threatens to reveal her condition in order to vindicate her rights; if a judge, in the exercise of his official capacity and according to the existing law, after due legal

versum, lib. IV, tit. I, n. 389; Lugo, *De Justitia et Jure,* disp. XXII, n. 158; St. Alphonsus, *Theologia Moralis,* lib. VI, n. 1049; Reiffenstuel, *Jus Canonicum Universum,* lib. IV, tit. I, n. 329; Santi, *Praelectiones Juris Canonici,* lib. IV, tit. I, n. 146; Gasparri, *De Matrimonio,* n. 949; D'Annibale, *Summula Theologiae Moralis,* III, n. 445; Wernz, *Jus Matrimoniale,* n. 265; Genicot, *Institutiones Theologiae Moralis,* II, n. 463; Farrugia, *De Matrimonio,* n. 30.

143 Cappello, *De Matrimonio,* n. 604; Maroto, *Institutiones,* I, n. 397.

144 Gasparri, *De Matrimonio,* n. 949; Rossi, "De Consensu Matrimoniali," n. 111—*Analecta Ecclesiastica,* II (1911), 73.

145 Sanchez, *De Matrimonii Sacramento,* lib. IV, disp. XIII, n. 3; Santi, *Praelectiones Juris Canonici,* lib. IV, tit. I, n. 146; Smith, *Marriage Process,* n. 157.

146 Reiffenstuel, *Jus Canonicum Universum,* lib. I, tit. XL, n. 27; Schmalzgrueber, *Jus Ecclesiasticum Universum,* lib. IV, tit. I, n. 390; Gasparri *De Matrimonio,* n. 949.

process compels the guilty party under the foregoing circumstances to contract marriage under penalty of imprisonment,—in all these instances fear is justly inflicted in all respects and the marriage contracted under its influence is valid. A just cause exists for the infliction of fear and the persons have a right to the line of action followed. *Juris executio non habet injuriam.*[147]

(b) If marriage is certainly valid where fear is in every respect justly inflicted, it is as surely invalid when fear is unjustly caused both *quoad substantiam* and *quoad modum.* In this hypothesis the formal reason for the ecclesiastical law of invalidity is clearly verified. By nature every individual has a strict right not to be impeded in the legitimate use of his liberty. Relative to marriage a person is free to marry or not to marry, free to marry one of his own choice. Unless his right of freedom has been forfeited by reason of some previous act, he is manifestly injured when he is forced to contract marriage through moral compulsion and constraint. Real injustice is done every time matrimonial liberty is unlawfully interfered with by another. Consequently the condition of *metus injuste incussus* is certainly fulfilled and a marriage which is the result of such undue influence, *ceteris paribus,* is undoubtedly null and void. *Quae contra jus fiunt debent utique pro infectis haberi.*[148]

Where, for instance, the parents or relatives threaten to shoot or do great bodily harm to a girl's seducer unless he marries her, an unjust fear *quoad substantiam* and *quoad modum* is brought to bear upon him. Granting the existence of an obligation to marry, it is not absolute but conditional. He has the alternative of choice between marriage or payment of damages. Since the former is imposed under penalty of death, it is unjust *quoad substantiam.* It is also unjust *quoad modum.* A private person has no right on his own authority to exact an obligation, especially where there may be possible doubts as to its existence. Justice in the matter must be sought with the intervention of legitimate authority according to the prescribed

[147] Vlaming, *Praelectiones Juris Matrimonii,* n. 539; Farrugia, *De Matrimonio,* n. 29; Pruemmer, *Manuale Theologiae Moralis,* III, n. 795; De Smet, *Betrothment and Marriage,* n. 538; Smith, *Marriage Process,* nn. 159-160; Schoepf, *Katholisches Kirchenrecht,* IV, 69.

[148] *Reg.* 64, R. J., in VI°.

formalities of the law. Consequently the marriage contracted in this or a similar situation is null and void.[149]

(c) No less is marriage invalid when fear is unjustly inflicted *quoad substantiam* but justly *quoad modum.* An illustration is the case of a man who after due process of law is compelled by a competent judge to contract marriage under the threat of imprisonment although he is entirely innocent of the criminal charge brought against him; or again, a man threatened with legal procedure by a father on charges of seducing his daughter when, as a matter of fact, the one so accused is under no obligation to marry, either because he is not in the least guilty or, admitting the offense, because it is mutual and both parties are equally to blame.[150]

Though the measures adopted to enforce the obligation may be just, the same fundamental injustice as in the previous case is suffered by the party who is thus coerced. He is under no obligation to marry, either absolutely or conditionally. The fact that the formalities of law are observed does not remove the injury sustained by him. Sanchez [151] seems to hold that marriage contracted under these circumstances is valid. This opinion, however, must be rejected. While the fear in the manner of its causation is according to the laws of justice, it is inflicted only on the presumption that an objective cause justifies it. When evidence reveals that no obligation to contract marriage existed, the presumption falls to the ground and with it any action based on it. The infliction is materially just, but formally or substantially unjust. Since the real injury suffered in

[149] D'Annibale, *Summula Theologiae Moralis,* III, n. 445; Genicot, *Institutiones Theologiae Moralis,* II, n. 463; Farrugia, *De Matrimonio,* n. 29; Bangen, *De Sponsalibus et Matrimonio,* II, 95-96; Smith, *Marriage Process,* n. 160; cf. S. C. C., *Causa Vigilien.,* 13 Jul., 17 Sept. 1725—Richter, *Canones et Decreta Concilii Tridentini,* n. 82, pp. 243-244; S. R. R., *Nullit. Matrim.,* 28 Jan. 1918—*Decisiones,* X (1918), dec. II, n. 10; *Sec. Inst.,* 8 Jul. 1919—*Decisiones,* XI (1919), dec. XIII, n. 5.

[150] Cf. S. R. R., *Nullit. Matrim.,* 31 Mar. 1922—*Decisiones,* XIV (1922), dec. IX, 78-82. A declaration of nullity on grounds of coercion was granted to a man who had been compelled to marry upon threats being made by the girl that she would reveal him as having fraudulently seduced her. While the mode of compulsion might be termed just, real cause was lacking to justify its infliction. Evidence showed that he had given no promise of marriage and that both were equally guilty of the sinful relationship.

[151] *De Matrimonii Sacramento,* lib. IV, disp. XIII, n. 8.

being compelled to marry remains, justice requires that the rights of the party so coerced be vindicated. This can only be attained by the nullity of the marriage.[152]

(d) When it comes to deciding the validity of marriage contracted under the influence of fear justly inflicted *quoad substantiam* but unjustly *quoad modum,* no unanimity of opinion is found among authors. Examples of this situation are e.g., the case of a man actually guilty of a criminal offense but urged to the fulfillment of his obligation by threats of punishment equivalent to that fixed by the law but inflicted by the girl's father; or that of a seducer compelled to marry the girl or make financial reparation after due judicial investigation but conducted by an incompetent judge; or that of a delinquent really guilty of the offense on account of which he is forced to marry by a competent judge but who appears innocent on the face of the evidence brought against him. In all these instances an obligation really exists and therefore the infliction of fear to urge its fulfillment is substantially just. But the manner of its infliction is unjust either because the formalities of the law are not observed or because of incompetence on the part of those enforcing the obligation. The question is whether marriage contracted under the influence of such an unjust fear is valid.

Previous to the Code two opinions were held relative to the validity of marriage due to fear of this kind. According to one the marriage was valid. The injustice of coercion employed for the purpose of extorting matrimonial consent was to be estimated from the substantial truth in the matter. Since objectively a just cause was had to warrant the use of coercive measures, the fear was justly inflicted regardless of any injustice in the *way* the fear was inflicted. Failure to observe the due legal formalities was injurious to the law, not however to the person who suffered the compulsion.[153] Moreover, other contracts entered because of such fear were valid in both the internal and external forum and did not admit of rescission. Con-

[152] Pontius, *De Sacramento Matrimonii,* lib. IV, cap. XIX, n. 11; St. Alphonsus, *Theologia Moralis,* lib. VI, n. 1052; D'Annibale, *Summula Theologiae Moralis,* III, n. 445; Gasparri, *De Matrimonio,* n. 953; Rossi, "De Consensu Matrimoniali," n. 119—*Analecta Ecclesiastica,* III (1911), 106.

[153] D'Annibale, *Summula Theologiae Moralis,* III, n. 445, note 19.

sequently, for even greater reasons the matrimonial contract should be valid.[154]

Opposed to this position was the opinion that the marriage was invalid when fear was unjustly inflicted *quoad modum* though just *quoad substantiam*.[155] The reason for this contention was that not only was injustice done by one who exacted that to which he had no right, e.g., marriage, but also by one who, admitting that he is justified in compelling marriage, does so with unjust means.[156] The law is in favor of one suffering fear in order to serve the ends of justice. Hence, if this law is not observed and fear is inflicted to the exclusion of the legal formalities, not only is the law infringed but injury is done to the person suffering the fear. Finally, in particular cases, when fear is inflicted by incompetent persons or those enjoying only private authority, it cannot be ascertained when fear is just in itself or how it can be justly inflicted. Fear is juridically just according as and in the way in which it is inflicted by the law, not however according as and in the way in which it is inflicted by one not empowered by the law to inflict it.[157] In attempts to strengthen their opinions, both sides referred to the older canonists but their failure to make clear distinctions and the resulting confusion and obscurity led to no more definite conclusion in the matter.[158]

With the appearance of the existing ecclesiastical legislation as formulated in canon 1087, the controversy has not ceased though there seems to be even less reason now for its continuation.[159] Those who hold to the validity of marriage when fear is unjust only with regard to the manner in which it is inflicted apparently take no notice

[154] Gasparri, *De Matrimonio,* n. 950.

[155] Wernz, *Jus Matrimoniale,* n. 265; De Becker, *De Sponsalibus et Matrimonio,* p. 64; Feije, *De Impedimentis et Dispensationibus Matrimonialibus,* n. 133; Santi, *Praelectiones Juris Canonici,* lib. IV, tit. I, n. 146.

[156] Wernz, *Jus Matrimoniale,* p. 393, note 23.

[157] Rossi, "De Consensu Matrimoniali", n. 112—*Analecta Ecclesiastica,* II (1911), 73-74.

[158] Cf. Sanchez, *De Matrimonii Sacramento,* lib. IV, disp. VIII, n. 9; disp. XIII, n. 8; Pontius, *De Sacramento Matrimonii,* lib. IV, cap. XIX, n. 11; Lessius, *De Justitia et Jure,* lib. II, cap. XVII, n. 43; Pichler, *Jus Canonicum,* lib. I, tit. XL, n. 2; Lugo, *De Justitia et Jure,* disp. XXII, n. 157; St. Alphonsus, *Theologia Moralis,* lib. VI, n. 1052.

[159] Payen, *De Matrimonio,* II, n. 1685.

of the new law and appeal to the reasons of the pre-Code canonists to substantiate their claims.[160] While the more probable opinion before the Code may have been that maintaining the validity of the marriage,[161] authors as a rule now seem to favor the extension of the law of invalidity to the case where fear is unjust only *quoad modum.*[162]

The weight of the arguments formerly offered in support of this opinion is considerably increased by the terminology of the present law. Before the codification the usual expression for designating the element of injustice in fear was *metus injustus.* Now, however, the law speaks of *metus injuste incussus.* While at first sight the two phrases—*metus injustus* and *metus injuste incussus*—may seem to convey the same meaning, analysis leads to a different conclusion. The word *injustus,* after the nature of any adjective, qualifies the noun *metus* and defines an attribute essential to it if it is to invalidate marriage. Consequently it refers to *metus in se,* i.e., in its substantial entity, and signifies, strictly speaking, *metus injustus quoad substantiam.* By a rigid interpretation it cannot be understood to embrace the notion of the manner in which fear is inflicted.

On the other hand, the term *metus injuste incussus* has a more comprehensive connotation. The use of the adjectival adverb *injuste* qualifying the adjective *incussus* directly considers the injustice in the infliction of fear. It does not limit the injustice to the fear itself but, prescinding from the fact whether this is just or unjust in its essence, attends only to the injustice of its causation. Certainly no one will deny that fear is unjustly inflicted if the evil threatened is in no way due or if no reason is had for inducing it. But it is also unjustly inflicted when the means employed or the method pursued is not in accord with the dictates of justice. Hence the present law

160 Genicot, *Institutiones Theologiae Moralis,* II, n. 463; Maroto, *Institutiones,* I, n. 339; Tanquerey, *Synopsis Theologiae Moralis,* I, n. 941; De Smet, *Betrothment and Marriage,* n. 538.

161 Ayrinhac, *Marriage Legislation,* n. 207.

162 Cappello, *De Matrimonio,* n. 606; Chelodi, *Jus Matrimoniale,* n. 119; Cerato, *Matrimonium,* n. 83; Wernz-Vidal, *Jus Matrimoniale,* n. 501; Payen, *De Matrimonio,* II, n. 1685; Vlaming, *Praelectiones Juris Matrimonii,* n. 539; Blat, *Commentarium,* III, n. 486; Vromant, *De Matrimonio,* n. 190; Vermeersch-Creusen, *Epitome,* II, n. 376; Triebs, *Kanonisches Eherecht,* III, 508, 512; Knecht, *Katholisches Eherecht,* p. 571.

contemplates the injustice in the causation of fear, regardless of whether it be *quoad substantiam* or *quoad modum.* Unless this is admitted, the use of the modal adverb *injuste* cannot be satisfactorily explained. As it stands in the law it signifies not what kind of fear is inflicted but precisely how this is done.[163]

The argument based on the word *injuste* cannot be characterized as mere verbal quibbling and therefore lightly dismissed. In the first place, ecclesiastical laws are to be interpreted according to the proper meaning of the terms of the law.[164] On this principle, in view of the reasons given above, the law of invalidity must be understood to include the case where marriage is due to fear unjust only *quoad modum.* The law itself does not distinguish and consequently no distinction should be made.[165]

Furthermore, where the validity of so sacred a transaction as marriage is in question, confusing terminology would especially be avoided. It would be preposterous to suppose that the legislator was unaware of the former controverted point and equally as absurd to assume that he did not give it earnest consideration. If the invalidity of marriage due to coercion was meant to apply only to a *metus injustus quoad substantiam,* this would have been stated definitely and not by terms making for equivocation or ambiguity. Consequently the adverb *injuste* must have been used advisedly with the object of putting an end to the existing doubt.[166]

Finally, confirmation for the opinion that canon 1087 has application when the fear extorting matrimonial consent is unjust only in its mode of infliction may be derived from another source. Canon 18 further directs that, if the meaning of any term in the Code remains doubtful after due consideration has been given to its proper sense, recourse must be had to the purpose of the law and the intention of the legislator. The law invalidating marriage on account of grave and unjustly inflicted fear is designed to safeguard matrimonial freedom and protect the individual against any injurious infringement of his rights in the matter. The question to be decided,

[163] Cappello, *De Matrimonio,* n. 606; Chelodi, *Jus Matrimoniale,* n. 120.

[164] *Codex Juris Canonici,* c. 18.

[165] Triebs, *Kanonisches Eherecht,* III, 508.

[166] Vromant, *De Matrimonio,* n. 190; Chelodi, *Jus Matrimoniale,* n. 119.

accordingly, is whether the legislator considered a fear inflicted unjustly *quoad modum* to be an undue interference with the liberty of marriage and, as such, a factor invalidating matrimonial consent given under its influence. An affirmative answer appears to be demanded from a careful study of the innovation made by the Code concerning a formal engagement or betrothal. No longer can action be taken to force marriage on the party who has unlawfully withdrawn from the agreement—suit for damages is alone permitted.[167] While authors generally state that the Church made the change in order to conform as far as possible to those civil laws which admit only a suit for damages sustained by a breach of promise of marriage, they assert that the real reason was her wish to protect marriage against every kind of undue influence.[168] In other words, the legislator viewed with disfavor any coercion *quoad modum* to compel marriage even though the obligation to contract existed. This seems sufficient reason for concluding that the intention of the legislator, if he was to be consistent, was to include a fear unjust only *quoad modum* within the scope of canon 1087.[169]

It is evident, of course, that until a decisive interpretation of the Holy See clears away the doubt, no marriage can be declared null and void on grounds of fear unjustly inflicted *quoad modum.* This must be particularly noted with regard to marriage contracted under compulsion of a civil judge. Some canonists [170] maintain that the latter has no right to offer the guilty man only the alternatives between marriage and prison, since he should also be given the opportunity of compensating the woman by a financial settlement. From this they argue that the action of the judge is unjust *in modo* and therefore invalidates the marriage. Nevertheless, as long as the law

[167] *Codex Juris Canonici,* c. 1017, § 3.

[168] Cappello, *De Matrimonio,* n. 109; Cerato, *Matrimonium,* n. 6, 7.

[169] With apparently but one exception, nothing definite can be gleaned from ecclesiastical jurisprudence in this connection. Speaking of the fear which invalidates matrimonial consent, it is stated in one decision of the Roman Rota: "(metus) injuste incussus a parte personae sive publicae sive privatae, sive quoad substantiam sive quoad modum saltem, cum nemo jus habeat neque ad rem injustam neque ad usum mediorum injustorum." Cf. S. R. R., *Nullit. Matrim.,* 9 Jan. 1922—*Decisiones,* XIV (1922), dec. I, n. 3.

[170] Vermeersch, *Theologia Moralis,* III, n. 789; Woywod, *Practical Commentary,* I, n. 1085; cf. *AER,* XLVIII (1913), 181-188.

remains doubtful, a declaration of nullity could never be granted on these grounds.

Neither can a marriage of this kind be declared invalid on the plea that whenever a judge compels matrimonial consent the coercion employed redounds to that inflicted unjustly *quoad substantiam.*[171] Whatever is to be said of the weight of the reasons offered to support the opinion that fear induced by a court sentence is justly inflicted, it must be termed at least probable on account of the extrinsic authority of the authors who favor it.[172] Hence, wherever such laws are in force and the judge applies them, the fear inflicted cannot be termed *certainly* unjust. Judgment must be rendered, accordingly, in favor of the validity of marriage.[173] In very exceptional cases, in which injustice is clearly proven along lines suggested by this study, as e.g., where a man who is wholly innocent of the charges brought against him is convicted after due process of law on purely circumstantial evidence or false testimony, a sentence in favor of nullity might be granted.

§ 4. *Matrimonial Correlation*

Moral coercion and fear as explained in the foregoing pages must be correlated to marriage if it is to have the invalidating force attributed to it by the law. Because the marital state is in the nature of a *servitus perpetua,*[174] the Church seeks to protect it from all undue influence. But not any kind of grave and unjustly inflicted fear will suffice. It must be referred at least in some way to

[171] Payen, *De Matrimonio,* II, n. 1685.

[172] Gasparri, *De Matrimonio,* n. 949; D'Annibale, *Summula Theologiae Moralis,* III, 445, note 19; Santi, *Praelectiones Juris Canonici,* lib. IV, tit. I, n. 146; Genicot, *Institutiones Theologiae Moralis,* II, n. 463; Farrugia, *De Matrimonio,* n. 30; Blat, *Commentarium,* III, n. 486; Petrovits, *Church Law on Matrimony,* n. 428.

[173] S. R. R., *Nullit. Matrim.,* 9 Jun. 1911—*Decisiones,* III (1911), dec. XXII, n. 6. In these marriages a declaration of nullity may be possible on grounds other than violence and fear, e.g., absolute want of consent or its simulation. In certain circumstances there may be place for a dispensation *super rato et non consummato,* e.g., if the parties who married under these conditions separated immediately after the ceremony and never cohabited.

[174] St. Thomas, *Summa Theologica,* Suppl., q. 47, a. 6.

marriage because matrimonial consent is not *stricto jure* coerced unless the compulsion affects the consent itself.[175]

Canon 1087 expresses this essential condition by the words: *a quo ut quis se liberet, eligere cogatur matrimonium.* The paraphrase given by Blat [176] serves somewhat to clarify the issue: *a quo praedeterminato metu ut quis se liberet, vel ut cesset causa extrinseca ab incutiendo illo, unica via sit ei eligere, eo quod cogatur, matrimonium celebrandum.* Hence that fear invalidates matrimonial consent which compels the contracting party to choose marriage in order to free himself from the grave and unjustly threatened evil.[177]

Even when fear is grave and unjustly inflicted, a marriage contracted under its influence is not necessarily invalid. If the evil which threatened could have been avoided in any other way than by giving consent, the law of invalidity will not apply. Thus, for instance, the marriage forced by the judgment of a civil court on a man who is innocent of any wrongdoing will not be invalid if, through pride or obstinacy, he refuses to produce witnesses whose testimony would clear him of the charge. The marriage of a young woman contracted under fear of expulsion from home might not be invalid if she had means of obtaining suitable lodging among relatives or friends and failed to avail herself of the opportunity. The same might be said if she were in position to support herself in a respectable manner, or if she omitted to offer resistance to the author of the coercion, or neglected to enlist the aid of relatives or friends. In all these cases the fear inflicted is not such that marriage is the only means to be freed of it.

It is evident, therefore, that some correlation must exist between the evil threatened, the fear thereby inspired, and the marriage contracted under its influence. The mere fact of fear on one hand and the celebration of marriage on the other does not prove that marriage was due to fear or that fear was its cause. Fear-inducing threats which are made to prevent or discourage one marriage will

[175] S. R. R., *Nullit. Matrim.*, 12 Jul. 1922—*Decisiones,* XIV (1922), dec. XXIV, n. 2.

[176] *Commentarium,* III, n. 486.

[177] Cappello, *De Matrimonio,* n. 606.

not invalidate the consent given to another, unless it is evident that the latter had to be contracted in order to be rid of the fear.[178]

Again, if a person should make use of persuasions and exhortations to overcome resistance not to marriage, which of itself is not repugnant, but with the object of defeating opposition to conjugal duties and obligations which the person begins to fear, coercion is not verified according to the terms of the law.[179] Hence, in any particular case evidence must prove conclusively that the party who alleges coercion had no other means of freeing himself from the imminent evil than the marriage. This will at the same time clearly demonstrate that fear alone was the motive of marriage and that consent thereto was elicited only under the influence of compulsion.[180]

Although the words of canon 1087 seem to indicate plainly enough what is required by this fourth condition, some commentators on the Code insist on reading into the law a point which was formerly a source of much agitation but which now seems to be of purely historical interest. Reference is made to the old controversy as to whether fear directly induced to extort matrimonial consent is required or whether fear inspired for some other purpose will invalidate a marriage contracted under its influence. In order to evaluate the opinions held today, a brief discussion of the former dispute will be of assistance.

Canonists before the Code distinguished between fear directly induced to compel marriage and fear indirectly having that effect. The former *(metus consultus)* was inflicted for the one purpose of extorting matrimonial consent, as e.g., when a father threatened to kill his daughter's seducer unless he married her. The latter *(metus inconsultus)* was caused with an object other than marriage in view, e.g., if a father threatened to kill his daughter's seducer because of his criminal action but with no intention of forcing him to marry

[178] Cf. S. R. R., *Nullit. Matrim.*, 23 Maii, 1912—*Decisiones,* IV (1912), dec. XXI, 250-261; S. R. R., *Causa Nicien.*, 15 Mar. 1915—*Decisiones,* VII (1915), dec. X, n. 5.

[179] Cf. S. R. R., *Nullit. Matrim.*, 14 Aug. 1922—*Decisiones,* XIV (1922), dec. XXXII, n. 12.

[180] Triebs, *Kanonisches Eherecht,* III, 508.

her.[181] On the basis of this distinction the question was raised whether marriage was invalid when contracted under circumstances exemplified in the second instance, or whether it was necessary that fear be directly intended to force marriage.

A few weighty authorities [182] maintained that even though fear were not inspired directly to extort matrimonial consent, nevertheless, if the fear was grave and unjustly inflicted, marriage contracted under its influence was null and void. Among other reasons advanced to support this contention, it was alleged that Alexander III[183] demands full liberty from unjust fear in one who contracts marriage. The Pontiff does not distinguish between fear directly or indirectly tending to compel consent because the same unhappy consequences are to be expected whenever marriage is the result of grave and unjustly inflicted fear. Moreover, the reason for invalidating such a marriage is the injustice suffered by the innocent party. This injury, however, is equally done whether one directly forces another to marry or is the indirect cause of the contract.[184]

Besides, any contract entered because of grave fear unjustly inflicted, even though the purpose is not to extort consent, is rescindable because the one inducing the fear is the reason for the consent being given. If the active agent had not brought pressure to bear on the other by means of threats, consent would not have been given. Consequently, since his action is the source of injustice, he is responsible for all the injury which follows from it. He is bound to rescind the contract and make amends to the injured party for all his losses. If unjust fear in this hypothesis suffices to make voidable other contracts, it should certainly have force to render marriage null and void.[185] Schmalzgrueber [186] likewise draws an *a pari* argument from the law of the Decretals [187] which invalidates

[181] Sanchez, *De Matrimonii Sacramento,* lib. IV, disp. XII, n. 2; Gasparri, *De Matrimonio,* n. 951.

[182] Schmalzgrueber, *Jus Ecclesiasticum Universum,* lib. IV, tit. I, nn. 398-401; Lugo, *De Justitia et Jure,* disp. XXII, nn. 175-180; Ballerini-Palmieri, *Opus Theologicum Morale,* n. 1130.

[183] C. 14, X, *de spons. et matr.,* IV, 1.

[184] Schmalzgrueber, *Jus Ecclesiasticum Universum,* lib. IV, tit. I, n. 399.

[185] Lugo, *De Justitia et Jure,* disp. XXII, n. 176.

[186] *Jus Ecclesiasticum Universum,* lib. IV, tit. I, n. 399.

[187] C. 1, X, *de his quae vi metusve,* I, 40.

religious profession because of fear inspired for a purpose other than that of forcing the act.

Despite the fact that these arguments were not easy of refutation, especially if the natural law was considered the source of invalidity,[188] the more probable and commonly received opinion before the Code was that fear had to be inflicted *ad extorquendum consensum matrimonialem.*[189] The reasons given for this position were no less convincing. If natural law is regarded as the source of invalidity, then it would have to be proven that the liberty which this law requires for matrimonial consent is lacking when fear is inflicted for some purpose other than marriage.[190] Should ecclesiastical law, especially that found in the Decretals, be considered the origin of the nullity, its general tenor seems to justify the interpretation that force and fear must be inflicted *ad extorquendum consensum.*[191]

With the exception of one canon in the Decretals,[192] the others having reference to the impediment of fear [193] speak of fear directed to extort matrimonial consent.[194] The canon excepted, which is general in tone and which is used by Schmalzgrueber as the basis of his argument for the opposite opinion, gives a broad description of the liberty necessary for marriage. It does not declare that fear inflicted to extort some other act interferes with matrimonial liberty. In fact, granting that the words of the text are general, they seem clearly to refer to matrimonial consent. This is evident from the decision that the woman who was to give her consent to marriage

[188] Gasparri, *De Matrimonio,* n. 952.

[189] Sanchez, *De Matrimonii Sacramento,* lib. IV, disp. XII, n. 3; Reiffenstuel, *Jus Canonicum Universum,* lib. I, tit. XL, n. 28; lib. IV, tit. I, n. 328; Lega, *De Judiciis Ecclesiasticis,* I, n. 262; Feije, *De Impedimentis et Dispensationibus Matrimonialibus,* n. 134; Santi, *Praelectiones Juris Canonici,* lib. IV, tit. I, n. 148; Gasparri, *De Matrimonio,* n. 952; Wernz, *Jus Matrimoniale,* n. 265; Pichler, *Jus Canonicum,* lib. IV, tit. I, n. 112; De Becker, *De Sponsalibus et Matrimonio,* p. 64; St. Alphonsus, *Theologia Moralis,* lib. VI, n. 1049. Cf. Wyszynski, "Utrum Metus Indirecte Incussus Dirimere Possit Matrimonium", *Jus Pontificium,* III (1930), 193-200; II (1931), 42-51.

[190] Lega, *De Judiciis Ecclesiasticis,* I, p. 296, note 1.

[191] Cf. Woywod, *Practical Commentary,* I, n. 1086.

[192] C. 14, X, *de spons. et matr.,* IV, 1.

[193] Cc. 15, 28, X, *de spons. et matr.,* IV, 1.

[194] Gasparri, *De Matrimonio,* n. 952; Wernz, *Jus Matrimoniale,* p. 394, note 25.

should be secluded in a safe place where she will be immune from those who wish to influence her choice.[195]

Secondly, the law of invalidity is a legal remedy designed to protect the innocent party against the injustice he suffers when compelled to marry. This does not mean *any* injustice but a violation of his right to matrimonial freedom.[196] Hence this injustice is done when the act of consent itself is extorted. If fear is not directed toward the act of consent, it is difficult to see where injustice is suffered in the sense in which the law refers unjust fear to matrimonial consent.[197] Consequently marriage contracted under such fear is not, in the strict sense, unjustly caused but rather has its occasion in those circumstances. No one compels the one suffering the fear to marry. He freely chooses marriage as a means to avoid the evil which threatens. Any involuntariness in the act is not intended by the fear-inducing agent but merely has its occasion in his malicious conduct.[198]

When the present law as found in canon 1087 was promulgated, the question was at once raised whether the terms employed signified a modification of the old law so as to include the case in which the one inflicting fear did not even think of extorting consent to marriage although the other chose marriage as the means of avoiding the evil threatened. Not a few commentators [199] see in the words of the Code a requirement that fear be inflicted to extort matrimonial consent.

The reasons for demanding a *metus consultus* are similar to those advanced to establish the point by the old canonists. The invalidating law is intended to provide for the complete liberty of the

[195] Lega, *De Judiciis Ecclesiasticis,* I, p. 296, note 1.

[196] De Becker, *De Sponsalibus et Matrimonio,* p. 64.

[197] Lega, *De Judiciis Ecclesiasticis,* I, n. 262.

[198] Sanchez, *De Matrimonii Sacramento,* lib. IV, disp. XII, n. 3.

[199] Wernz-Vidal, *Jus Matrimoniale,* n. 501; Vlaming, *Praelectiones Juris Matrimonii,* n. 539; Ferreres, *Theologia Moralis,* n. 658; Pruemmer, *Manuale Theologiae Moralis,* III, n. 795; Genicot, *Institutiones Theologiae Moralis,* II, n. 463; Noldin, *Summa Theologiae Moralis,* III, n. 634; Tanquerey, *Synopsis Theologiae Moralis,* I, n. 942; Payen, *De Matrimonio,* II, n. 1686; Knecht, *Katholisches Eherecht,* p. 576; Linneborn, *Eherecht,* n. 290 (apparently); Leitner, *Katholisches Eherecht,* n. 99; De Smet, *Betrothment and Marriage,* n. 537; Augustine, *Commentary,* V, 246.

marriage contract. With this in view it declares a marriage null and void when grave coercion or constraint affect matrimonial consent understood in the strict sense. This occurs only when grave fear is induced precisely for the purpose of forcing a person to marry. If the fear does not aim directly at extorting marriage, coercion does not properly influence matrimonial consent.[200]

Moreover, one who is not directly compelled to marry *chooses* what is not demanded of him. In making this choice, he elects marriage as a remedy against a greater evil. Consequently, he acts rather voluntarily than under compulsion, or, granting the fact of duress and restraint, he contracts marriage rather from an intrinsic than extrinsic fear. In either case, fear does not influence consent as canon 1087 demands.[201]

The words of canon 1087 clearly intimate that a fear is required which directly affects matrimonial consent. It must force the one suffering it to contract marriage if he would be free of the evil. Fear, however, which is not caused to extort consent does not compel one to choose marriage. It is rather the occasion prompting the one under stress to determine upon marriage by a free choice. Certainly if one sees the opportunity of avoiding an evil by means of a marriage which is not demanded and accordingly chooses that avenue of escape, he is not confronted by the alternative *aut matrimonium aut malum.* Instead he freely gives himself that alternative, perhaps in preference to some other. Hence the condition of the law requiring that in order to be rid of the fear one is *forced* to choose marriage is not fulfilled.[202]

A final reason for holding that the words of the law now in force have the same meaning as the expression *ad extorquendum consensum matrimonialem* is that the Church in all her laws seeks to provide for situations which ordinarily occur. The case, however, in which fear is not inflicted to extort consent but is such that it can be removed only by marriage is rare and extraordinary.[203] Further confirmation of this opinion is found in the judicial decisions of the Roman Rota

[200] Payen, *De Matrimonio,* II, n. 1686.
[201] Vlaming, *Praelectiones Juris Matrimonii,* n. 539.
[202] Wernz-Vidal, *Jus Matrimoniale,* n. 501.
[203] Payen, *De Matrimonio,* II, n. 1686.

rendered since the promulgation of the Code. If the exact words of canon 1087 are not cited, the phrase *ad extorquendum consensum matrimonialem* is used.[204]

Asserting that the existing law introduces a modification of the old discipline, other modern canonists[205] maintain that canon 1087 does not concern itself with the reason for which fear is unjustly inflicted. Marriage will be invalid whenever it is chosen in order to be freed of the evil which threatens. The words expressing this condition do not demand either implicitly or explicitly that fear be inflicted to extort consent. It is not necessary that the active agent demand marriage as a *conditio sine qua non*. It suffices that the passive agent should have no means of escape from the evil except the choice of marriage. He must be reduced to choose marriage in order to free himself of the fear.[206]

Since no mention is made of the one inflicting the fear, his purposes or designs, the active agent is no longer considered. Consequently, it makes no difference whether the intention of the latter was to extort marriage or not. Inasmuch as the law attends only to the one suffering the fear, his intention and not that of the active agent must be considered. If the aim of the legislation is to provide for the liberty of marriage, certainty in the matter is to be deduced from the mind of the contracting party, not from the purpose of the one coercing him.[207]

This interpretation of the law does not mean that the alternative *aut matrimonium aut malum* need not exist. As a matter of fact the alternative is demanded, otherwise the person would not have been *forced* to choose marriage to avoid the evil. The law does not re-

[204] An exception is S. R. R., *Nullit Matrim.*, 9 Jan. 1922—*Decisiones*, IV (1922), dec. I, n. 3: "nihil refert, quod metus directe an indirecte influat in matrimonii consensum."

[205] Cappello, *De Matrimonio*, n. 606; Chelodi, *Jus Matrimoniale*, n. 119; Vermeersch-Creusen, *Epitome*, II, n. 376; Farrugia, *De Matrimonio*, n. 30bis; Cerato, *Matrimonium*, 83 and note d; Gougnard, *De Matrimonio*, pp. 168-169; Vromant, *De Matrimonio*, n. 190; Triebs, *Kanonisches Eherecht*, III, 509; Petrovits, *Church Law on Matrimony*, n. 424; Woywod, *Practical Commentary*, I, n. 1086.

[206] Ayrinhac, *Marriage Legislation*, n. 207; Petrovits, *Church Law on Marriage*, n. 424.

[207] Cappello, *De Matrimonio*, n. 606; Chelodi, *Jus Matrimoniale*, n. 119; Vromant, *De Matrimonio*, n. 190; Gougnard, *De Matrimonio*, p. 168.

quire, however, that the one causing the fear intends to place the passive agent in that particular situation. Whether he intended to extort matrimonial consent makes no difference as long as his conduct set up that alternative for the other.[208]

For this reason Chelodi [209] is not entirely correct in stating that marriage is forced and therefore invalid every time it is chosen under the influence of grave fear as a remedy against a graver evil. It is evident that marriage is only invalid when the above alternative exists, otherwise the word *cogatur* of the canon would have to be omitted and the text distorted to read: *a quo ut quis se liberet, eligat matrimonium.* The mere choosing of marriage in order to avoid evil is not sufficient for invalidity. If some other way of escape presents itself and marriage is elected in preference, this choice is voluntary and not forced.[210] Consequently, Cappello's [211] view must be adopted. If the fear is not inflicted to extort consent or compel marriage, it is absolutely required that the choice of marriage be the necessary, and generally the only, means of warding off the evil, either in itself or in its circumstances. (Unless this is the case, then that force which alone invalidates marriage is not verified.) If fear is not directly induced to compel matrimonial consent, the condition of the law is fulfilled only when marriage is the one and only means of escape.[212]

It is difficult to see how marriage can be said to be forced by another *(ab extrinseco)* unless the one responsible for the fear and coercion directly places the passive agent in the alternative of marriage or the evil threatened. Nevertheless the second opinion seems more favorable because of the close attention it gives to the wording of the law. The same principles apply here as in the case of *metus injuste incussus.* The Code admits that it contains some modifications of the old law. A law which agrees only in part with the former law must be interpreted according to that law in the part in which it agrees; in the part which differs, it must be interpreted according to the meaning of the words employed.[213] The meaning of the words

[208] Cf. Triebs, *Kanonisches Eherecht,* III, 509.
[209] *Jus Matrimoniale,* n. 119.
[210] Vlaming, *Praelectiones Juris Matrimonii,* n. 539.
[211] *De Matrimonio,* n. 606.
[212] Gougnard, *De Matrimonio,* p. 168.
[213] *Codex Juris Canonici,* c. 6, n. 3.

a quo ut quis se liberet eligere cogatur matrimonium seem sufficiently clear and offer no reason for introducing a difficulty, once, perhaps, of a doctrinal import but now of only historical value. Not only does the law make no distinction but its motive remains the same whether fear is directly or indirectly inflicted.[214]

Furthermore, the legislator was certainly cognizant of the old difference of opinion.[215] He might very easily have made use of the classic expression in the formulation of the law. But, in order to assure the fullest liberty and security to the matrimonial contract, he could also extend the invalidity of consent to the case of indirect infliction, not only to remove all injustice from marriage but all grave force and duress as well.[216] Therefore it is reasonably believed that the legislator intentionally chose the words employed so that they might signify not so much a fear inflicted *ad extorquendum consensum matrimonialem* as one *cogens ad matrimonium contrahendum*, regardless of the motive for its infliction. A fear which forces one to devise a means of escape is truly the cause of the means chosen and thus marriage is reasonably considered as having been contracted on account of fear.[217]

It must be confessed that little of practical importance is involved in this difference of opinion. Grave fear is almost never unjustly inflicted and such that it can be removed only by marriage without at the same time being caused to extort matrimonial consent.[218] As a rule marriage would offer no escape from unjust threats, vexations, molestations, etc., unless fear had been inspired for the purpose, directly or indirectly manifested, of forcing the person to marry.[219] According to the old law, if a doubt existed as to whether fear had

[214] Farrugia, *De Matrimonio*, n. 30bis.

[215] Lega in referring to a mention of the former controversy made in a certain Rota decision previous to the promulgation of the Code has this to say: "Ex his autem quae notantur in Decis. explicatur quare in can. 1087 in notione metus gravis praetermissa sit qualitas incussus ad extorquendum consensum ac generatim dicitur a quo ut quis se liberet cogatur eligere matrimonium"—*Coram Lega Decisiones*, p. 340, note 1.

[216] Vermeersch-Creusen, *Epitome*, II, n. 376.

[217] Gougnard, *De Matrimonio*, p. 168; Farrugia, *De Matrimonio*, n. 30bis.

[218] Vromant, *De Matrimonio*, n. 190; Vermeersch-Creusen, *Epitome*, II, n. 376.

[219] Woywod, *Practical Commentary*, I, n. 1086.

been directly or indirectly inflicted, it was presumed in the external forum of the former nature.[220] So today from the very fact that one is forced to choose marriage in order to free himself from fear, the latter is generally accounted as being precisely inflicted to compel matrimonial consent.[221] Since the opinion, however, which requires a directly inflicted fear enjoys at least extrinsic probability, a marriage in which there is any positive doubt on this point could not be declared null and void until the Holy See makes some definite declaration.[222]

Article III.—Exclusive Character of the Law

Complementing canon 1087, § 1, the legislator in § 2 has taken care to add that no other fear renders marriage null and void, even though it would give cause to the contract. Hence slight fear, though *ab extrinseco* and unjustly inflicted; fear *ab intrinseco,* no matter how serious and pressing its influence; grave fear *ab extrinseco* is justly inflicted to compel marriage; finally, grave fear, *ab extrinseco* and unjustly inflicted but where a way of escape other than marriage presented itself—in all these cases the invalidity of the marriage is not entailed.

In other words, every fear which is not qualified by the conditions of canon 1087, § 1 is excluded by the law as being juridically insufficient to impede and nullify matrimonial consent. Should one of the conditions be found wanting, the fear, even though it be the sole motivating reason for contracting the marriage, is of no juridical consequence. The marriage is valid in both forums and a declaration to the contrary is impossible. All that the law demands is that the person be willing to enter marriage and that this "will to marry," or matrimonial consent, be properly declared. How this decision is arrived at, or what motives persuaded the determination, is of no particular interest. As long as the consent itself enjoys the liberty and security demanded by the law and is not vitiated by factors

[220] Reiffenstuel, *Jus Canonicum Universum,* lib. I, tit. XL, n. 29; Gasparri, *De Matrimonio,* n. 951.

[221] Cappello, *De Matrimonio,* n. 606.

[222] Gasparri, *De Matrimonio,* n. 952; Payen, *De Matrimonio,* II, n. 1086.

which make it inefficacious to produce juridic effects, the contract it calls into existence is valid and binding.[223]

In view of what already has been said, little need be added to justify this restriction of the effects of fear within the limits assigned by the law. The Church has full power to determine to what cases her laws will apply as well as authority to interpret the natural law.[224] Nor are intrinsic arguments lacking for the limitations of the law. In all of the cases enumerated as excluded, the matrimonial contract is not afforded the protection of the Church because the fear is of such little force that it can easily be overcome and cannot be construed as unduly influencing the will *(metus levis)*, or because no injustice or injury is involved for the party suffering it *(metus ab intrinseco, metus ab extrinseco juste incussus)*, or because marriage was not the sole escape presented to the party to obtain liberation from the fear.[225] The practical application of this law of exclusion is to be seen in the frequency with which the Roman Rota refuses a declaration of nullity because, granting the existence of fear, one or the other condition required by the law fails of verification.[226]

Canon 1087, § 2 is particularly noteworthy for the words *etiamsi det causam contractui.* This express declaration settles a controversy that long existed among older canonists. It was admitted by all that marriage contracted because of slight fear was valid when the fear was merely concomitant or only the partial cause of the contract in the sense that the marriage would have been entered, even though the fear were absent. Following the opinion of some older canonists,[227] however, Lugo [228] maintained that slight fear unjustly

[223] Triebs, *Kanonisches Eherecht,* III, 514.

[224] Ayrinhac, *Marriage Legislation,* n. 207.

[225] Wernz-Vidal, *Jus Matrimoniale,* n. 499; Blat, *Commentarium,* III, n. 486; Cappello, *De Matrimonio,* n. 607.

[226] Cf. e.g., S. R. R., *Nullit. Matrim.,* 18 Feb. 1918—*Decisiones,* X (1918), dec. IV, 27-35; S. R. R., *Nullit. Matrim.,* 24 Mar. 1922—*Decisiones,* XIV (1922), dec. VIII, 70-77; S. R. R., *Causa Parisien.,* 3 Jul. 1922—*Decisiones,* XIV (1922), dec. XXII, 217-221; S. R. R., *Nullit. Matrim.,* 7 Aug. 1922—*Decisiones,* XIV (1922), dec. XXVIII, 258-263; S. R. R., *Nullit. Matrim.,* 18 Oct. 1922—*Decisiones,* XIV (1922), dec. XXXV, 321-328.

[227] Cf. Sanchez, *De Matrimonii Sacramento,* lib. IV, disp. XVII, n. 2, who mentions *Decius, Navarrus, Jacobanus, Veracruz, Manuel, Rodriguez* and *Bossius.*

[228] *De Justitia et Jure,* disp. XXII, n. 141.

inflicted for the purpose of extorting matrimonial consent invalidated the marriage in the internal forum, provided the fear was the real cause of the contract or such that in its absence the marriage would not have been contracted. In the external forum the marriage was viewed as valid because the Church presumed that consent given under the influence of slight fear was sufficiently voluntary to establish the contract.[229] The more common opinion, however, held that slight fear, even though it was the actual cause of the contract, did not entail the nullity of marriage.[230]

The difference of opinion is now definitely ended by the Code explicitly stating that no other fear, *etiamsi det causam contractui,* has an invalidating force. Slight fear, no matter what the circumstances under which it is inflicted, cannot be said *natura sua* to move the will efficaciously. It does not diminish voluntariness sufficiently to warrant its consideration as an obstacle to valid matrimonial consent. It can be overcome with little difficulty and, even if marriage results from it, the substantial goods of marriage are not endangered as with a grave fear. Besides, if slight fear, which frequently can find place in marriage, were to invalidate the contract, the appeals for nullity would be recklessly increased. The consequent harm to the indissolubility of the marital bond, the peace of family life, and the common good would in itself be reason enough for the exclusion of all fear other than that described by the law.[231] As a matter of fact, since marriage enjoys the favor of the law, any species of fear whatsoever is presumed slight until the contrary is proven.[232]

229 Cf. Farrugia, *De Matrimonio,* n. 32.

230 Sanchez, *De Matrimonii Sacramento,* lib. IV, disp. XVII, n. 4; Pirhing, *Jus Canonicum,* lib. IV, tit. I, nn. 117-118; St. Alphonsus, *Theologia Moralis,* lib. VI, n. 1055; St. Thomas, *Summa Theologica,* Suppl. q. 47, a. 3; Schmalzgrueber, *Jus Ecclesiasticum Universum,* lib. IV, tit. I, n. 387; Reiffenstuel, *Jus Canonicum Universum,* lib. I, tit. XL, n. 25; lib. IV, tit. I, n. 330; Ballerini-Palmieri, *Opus Theologicum Morale,* VI, tr. X, n. 1124; Feije, *De Impedimentis et Dispensationibus Matrimonialibus,* n. 129; Gasparri, *De Matrimonio,* n. 945; Wernz, *Jus Matrimoniale,* n. 263. Sanchez termed the opinion *probabilior,* St. Alphonsus, *communissima,* and Gasparri held it as so true and certain that the other enjoyed no real probability.

231 Cf. C. 6, X, *de his quae vi metusve,* I, 40. Wernz-Vidal, *Jus Matrimoniale,* n. 499; Cappello, *De Matrimonio,* n. 607; Farrugia, *De Matrimonio,* n. 32; Augustine, *Commentary,* V, 248-249.

232 Chelodi, *Jus Matrimoniale,* n. 120.

CHAPTER VII

REVERENTIAL FEAR

SPECIAL treatment is allotted to reverential fear because of the frequency with which the validity of marriage is impugned on these grounds. While but a single impediment of fear is sanctioned by the Code, it does not follow that the legislation completely excludes reverential fear. When this form of the defect is qualified with the conditions exacted in canon 1087 it will certainly prevent the celebration of a valid marriage.[1] Consequently, all that has been said in the preceding chapter concerning fear applies equally to reverential fear if it is to have an invalidating effect on matrimonial consent. Nevertheless, the subject merits more detailed consideration on account of the peculiar difficulties that arise in connection with it. Not the least of these is the matter of its gravity. An attempt will now be made to clarify the problem by a study of it in relation to the general law already analyzed.

ARTICLE I.—NECESSARY DISTINCTIONS

Reverential fear springs from the deferential regard which an individual under authority has for the person invested with that prerogative. Deference and respect for the known or declared wishes of parents and superiors induces children and inferiors to do or omit a thing for fear of offending or grieving them by acting contrary to their will.[2] According to this general notion, St. Alphonsus [3] defines

[1] Cf. S. R. R., *Nullit. Matrim.*, 11 Jun. 1918—*Decisiones,* X (1918), dec. VII, n. 2; S. R. R., *Nullit. Matrim.*, 2 Jul. 1918—*Decisiones,* X (1918), dec. VIII, n. 5; S. R. R., *Nullit. Matrim.*, 7 Mar. 1922—*Decisiones,* XIV (1922), dec. VI, n. 3; S. R. R., *Nullit. Matrim.*, 29 Jul. 1922—*Decisiones,* XIV (1922), dec. XXV, n. 3; S. R. R., *Nullit. Matrim.*, 30 Dec. 1922—*Decisiones,* XIV (1922) dec. XL, n. 2.

[2] Santi, *Praelectiones Juris Canonici,* lib. IV, tit. I, n. 144; D'Annibale, *Summula Theologiae Moralis,* I, n. 138, note 16; Kutschker, *Eherecht,* IV, 207; Smith, *Marriage Process,* n. 176; Augustine, *Commentary,* V, 248.

[3] *Theologia Moralis,* lib. VI, n. 1056.

reverential fear as that by which one is afraid to resist him to whom one is subject. Referred to marriage, it may be described as fear which has its source in the respect and honor owed to the superior under whose authority the contracting party is constituted and which causes him, not daring to displease or offend that person, to contract a marriage to which he is averse or opposed.[4]

Reverential fear may be distinguished according as it involves danger of none or only a slight evil, or danger of some grave evil.[5] In the former sense it is termed pure or mere reverential fear *(purus, simplex);* in the latter, qualified or mixed *(qualificatus, mixtus).*[6]

Pure reverential fear receives its influence solely from the respect which is due to parents and superiors, or, at the most, from some slight evil which a contradiction of their wishes may bring. Qualified reverential fear derives its force from additional circumstances which involve a serious evil. A conciliation of the views of authors and a comparative study of the judicial decisions of ecclesiastical tribunals leads to the adoption of the principle: Pure reverential fear *per se* is scarcely ever adequate to nullify marriage, at least in the external forum, whereas qualified reverential fear can invalidate matrimonial consent in both the internal and external forum.[7] The following articles will reveal the truth of this conclusion.

Article II.—Pure Reverential Fear

It has been stated that pure reverential fear derives its influence solely from the deference and respect which a young man or woman have for parents or superiors, with little or no danger of an evil

[4] Payen, *De Matrimonio,* II, n. 1683; Woywod, *Practical Commentary,* I, n. 1087.

[5] Cf. Rossi, "De Consensu Matrimoniali," nn. 87-89—*Analecta Ecclesiastica,* II, (1911), 67-68.

[6] Cf. S. C. C., *Causa Parisien.,* 16 Maii, 1903—*ASS,* XXXVI (1904), 87, where fear is distinguished as "metus ordinarius, si ab extraneis personis, metus reverentialis, si a parentibus vel aliis superioribus incutiatur"; the latter again is "metus reverentialis purus, si ex sola reverentia erga parentes vel alios majores concipitur," and "metus reverentialis vestitus, si aliis circumstantiis sit conjunctus."

[7] Noldin, *Summa Theologiae Moralis,* I, n. 55, III, n. 634; Payen, *De Matrimonio,* II, n. 1683.

befalling for acting contrary to their wishes. Similarly as common fear, this fear also may have its various degrees and phases. If one is merely afraid to give offense or cause sorrow to a superior, this cannot be termed fear in the strict sense but is simply reverence. It involves no evil to the person himself and fear without the threat of some evil is unintelligible.[8] The shame or embarrassment experienced in offending or grieving superiors, although an evil affecting the person, causes but a minor degree of reverential fear. Finally, the degree of reverential fear increases when the indignation or displeasure of the person in authority is dreaded. None of these degrees, however, exceed what is termed pure reverential fear.[9]

Pure reverential fear of itself is inefficacious to nullify marriage contracted under its influence. One under authority is obliged to pay proper respect and becoming honor to the one possessing authority. This relation between authority and filial piety makes a subject hesitate to do anything which might arouse the wrath of, or cause grief to, his superior. Consequently, it happens that the child or inferior will frequently do what otherwise he would not so readily do, especially where the superior has expressly manifested his wishes.[10]

Under these circumstances, however, reverential fear ordinarily has no grave influence on the formation of the will's decision to action. In the first place, reverence and fear must be properly distinguished. If this distinction is not made, the obvious absurdity results that no effective contract would be possible between superior and subject, parent and child, without danger to its validity.[11] Furthermore, even granting the presence of the element of fear in reverence, *per se* it is slight and does not seriously interfere with the will's choice. No grave evil prompts the fear and consequently its influence is so little that it cannot be said to affect the *vir constans.*

[8] Dig. 4, 2, 6; Pontius, *De Sacramento Matrimonii,* lib. IV, c. V, n. 3; D'Annibale, *Summula Theologiae Moralis,* I, n. 138, note 16.

[9] Chelodi, *Jus Matrimoniale,* n. 118; Payen, *De Matrimonio,* II, n. 1683.

[10] Triebs, *Kanonisches Eherecht,* III, 509-510; Wernz-Vidal, *Jus Matrimoniale,* n. 497.

[11] Engel, *Collegium Universi Juris Canonici,* lib. IV, tit. I, § V, n. 4; cf. S. C. C., *Causa Vasten.,* 23 Jun. 1895—*ASS,* XXVIII (1896), 400.

Unless fear attains such a degree, however, it cannot have an invalidating effect on any contract, let alone that of marriage.[12]

This is equally true of a lesser or greater degree of mere reverential fear. The confusion and shame which children suffer on account of the offense or displeasure of their parents is a slight evil.[13] Such personal embarrassment approaches an evil *ab intrinseco.* It has its origin in the person's sensitive nature and thus is self-induced: *metum sibi infert.* When, over and above the sense of guilt and confusion, the boy or girl is in apprehension of no other evil than the mere indignation or dispelasure of the parent, he cannot be said to suffer fear inspired by a grave evil. The shame and confusion suffered are not unbearable, because it is known that refusal to acquiesce to parents' wishes, e.g., in regard to a certain marriage, will not lead to any punishment or ill-treatment. The indignation or displeasure of parents will not endure, since they can easily be placated.[14] Hence it is clear that mere reverential fear, threatening, as it does, either no evil or one very trivial and remote, is *per se* slight and therefore inadequate to vitiate a matrimonial consent given under its influence.

Nevertheless, because of the psychic nature of fear, a case may occur in which pure reverential fear is subjectively grave. In a family where reverence and respect is deeply felt for elders, the filial piety of a daughter may be so profound as to make her almost scrupulously careful to avoid not only the smallest displeasure to father or mother but even the least possible sorrow. Supposing that she consents to contract a certain marriage at their suggestion rather than act contrary to their wishes, one might be prone to consider such a union null and void, at least in the internal forum. But in the external forum it receives no attention and the marriage is regarded as valid. The fear influencing consent in this hypothesis may have been subjectively grave but objectively it was wanting that grave and inevitable evil which is an essential element for even a relatively

[12] Sanchez, *De Matrimonii Sacramento,* lib. IV, disp. VI, n. 7; Reiffenstuel, *Jus Canonicum Universum,* lib. I, tit. XL, nn. 95-96.

[13] Cappello, *De Matrimonio,* n. 604; Vromant, *De Matrimonio,* n. 191.

[14] Clericatus, *De Matrimonio,* dec. XXVII, n. 22; Salmanticenses, *Cursus Theologiae Moralis,* IX, c. 9, n. 33.

grave fear. For this reason alone the law of invalidity can find no favorable application.[15]

Moreover, pure reverential fear is insufficient to impede a valid matrimonial consent because the element of injustice or injury is not verified. Parents have the right as well as the duty to impart sound advice to young and inexperienced children confronted with so important a step as marriage. They should caution them against youthful indiscretion and thoughtlessness in the matter and come to their assistance with experienced and prudent counsel.[16] On the other hand, prudence and reverence dictate that children who contemplate marriage should consult their parents, listen to their advice, and give it careful consideration. Minors in particular sin gravely if they contract marriage without the knowledge of their parents or in spite of their reasonable opposition.[17] When because of age or other circumstances children are no longer by natural right under parental authority, still the respect and reverence due to parents demands that their advice should be considered in the matter of marriage and that it should be followed as far as is reasonably possible.[18]

Parents, accordingly, who exercise their rights and fulfill their obligations are guilty of no injustice if they merely offer advice, make suggestions, or indicate the advantages conducive to the best interests of their children. Neither does a young man or woman suffer injury who follows their counsel and, out of gratitude and affection or in order to avoid giving them pain, contracts marriage in accordance with their wishes.

It is clear, therefore, that pure reverential fear of itself and as a rule does not constitute a grave fear or inflict any injustice. It may lessen to a certain extent complete freedom but its influence is regarded as too slight to cause a juridically defective consent. As long as the fear remains in its own category of being merely reverential, or at least in the lower degrees of that category, it is not an

[15] Cf. Payen, *De Matrimonio,* II, n. 1683.

[16] Knecht, *Katholisches Eherecht,* p. 572; Triebs, *Kanonisches Eherecht,* III, 510.

[17] Genicot, *Institutiones Theologiae Moralis,* II, n. 518; cf. *Codex Juris Canonici,* c. 1034.

[18] Ayrinhac, *Marriage Legislation,* n. 67; De Smet, *Betrothment and Marriage,* n. 518.

adequate cause to invalidate marriage. Matrimonial consent elicited under its influence is not vitiated sufficiently to warrant its nullification in accordance with canon 1087 and the marriage is valid in both the internal and external forum.[19]

Article III.—Qualified Reverential Fear

While reverential fear of itself cannot nullify matrimonial consent, it will have this effect when it is grave, unjustly inflicted from without, and no other means of escape is offered than the acceptance of the undesired marriage. When these conditions hold true, reverential fear ceases to be pure or simple and takes the form of what is known as qualified or mixed reverential fear.

The most difficult problem connected with reverential fear is that of its gravity. With this demonstrated, the other requirements will ordinarily not be wanting. Common fear is the apprehension of some evil which will befall in the future. Its gravity depends in large measure on whether the evil feared is serious or slight. If reverential fear includes the danger of some grave evil that threatens or can threaten from parents or superiors, the fear will certainly be such as to affect the *vir constans,* absolutely or relatively, and so become a serious obstacle to the freedom of matrimonial consent.[20] In other words, over and above personal shame and embarrassment, besides the offense and displeasure of parents, a grave evil must threaten. Mere reverential fear must be "clothed" or qualified with

[19] Sanchez, *De Matrimonii Sacramento,* lib. IV, disp. VI, n. 7; Wernz-Vidal, *Jus Matrimoniale,* n. 500; Payen, *De Matrimonio,* II, n. 1683; Triebs, *Kanonisches Eherecht,* III, 510; Knecht, *Katholisches Eherecht,* p. 573, note 3; Petrovits, *Church Law on Matrimony,* n. 417. Cf. S. R. R., *Causa Nicien.,* 31 Jul. 1915—*Decisiones,* VII (1915), dec. XXXIII, n. 3; S. R. R., *Nullit. Matrim.,* 19 Feb. 1916—*Decisiones,* VIII (1916), dec. III, n. 3; S. R. R., *Causa Parisien.,* 4 Mar. 1916—*Decisiones,* VIII (1916), dec. V, n. 2; S. R. R., *Causa Pitilianen.,* 20 Oct. 1916—*Decisiones,* VIII (1916), dec. XXIX, n. 2; S. R. R., *Causa Massilien.,* 30 Apr. 1917—*Decisiones,* IX (1917), dec. XI, n. 2; S. R. R., *Causa Lugdunen.,* 5 Jun. 1917—*Decisiones,* IX (1917), dec. XIV, n. 5; S. R. R., *Nullit. Matrim.,* 2 Jul. 1918—*Decisiones,* X (1918), dec. VIII, n. 5; S. R. R., *Nullit. Matrim.,* 11 Apr. 1922—*Decisiones,* XIV (1922), dec. XI, n. 2; S. R. R., *Nullit. Matrim.,* 30 Dec. 1922—*Decisiones,* XIV (1922), dec. XL, n. 3.

[20] Santi, *Praelectiones Juris Canonici,* lib. IV, tit. I, n. 144; Gasparri, *De Matrimonio,* n. 943; Cappello, *De Matrimonio,* n. 604.

an additional evil of a character sufficiently severe to induce the will to choose marriage in order to avoid it.

As in the case of common fear, both the objective and, for even weightier reasons, the subjective elements must be considered for the purpose of estimating the gravity of reverential fear. In regard to the first, reverential fear becomes of a grave nature, generally speaking, when parents or superiors, in order to compel a child or subject to marry, incessantly employ importunate and insistent entreaties, urgent and continuous persuasions, inconsiderate and oft-repeated exhortations; subject him to verbal abuse in the form of harsh, censorious and insulting speech, habitual reproaches, scoldings, contentions, quarrels and disputes; go so far as to threaten him with expulsion, disinheritance, confinement, disgrace, or similar evils; give unmistakable indications of a lasting and enduring indignation, anger, and contempt; or finally, actually descend to acts of physical violence in the way of corporal punishment, bodily ill-treatment, privation of nourishment, clothing, etc.[21]

When a father or mother conduct themselves in this fashion, even though the sum total of these circumstances do not occur in any particular instance, they undoubtedly embitter the child's life in the parental home. The continued torment, molestation, and vexation to which the young man or young woman is subjected create an unbearably grave situation. The verbal and moral onslaughts harass and torture the victim beyond description. It is inevitable that the child in the face of such a continual treatment is little by little morally weakened. His resistance is broken and overcome by degrees. Finally, in order to have peace and quiet with the parents, he submits to their will and contracts marriage, not with the *plena libertate* required by the law, but simply to bring an end to the oppression which he suffers.[22] The fear which decides

[21] Sanchez, *De Matrimonii Sacramento,* lib. IV, disp. VII, nn. 5-8; Cosci, *De Separatione Thori,* lib. I, cap. VIII, nn. 72-80; Pirhing, *Jus Canonicum,* lib. IV, tit. I, n. 119; Engel, *Collegium Universi Juris Canonici,* lib. IV, tit. I, § V, n. 4; Reiffenstuel, *Jus Canonicum Universum,* lib. I, tit. XL, nn. 99-101; Santi, *Praelectiones Juris Canonici,* lib. IV, tit. I, n. 143; Gasparri, *De Matrimonio,* n. 942; Wernz-Vidal, *Jus Matrimoniale,* n. 497; Vromant, *De Matrimonio,* n. 189.

[22] Triebs, *Kanonisches Eherecht,* III, 511.

his consent is the *metus reverentialis qualificatus* spoken of by canonists in contrast to *metus reverentialis simplex.*

The long list of circumstances enumerated above is not to be understood as meaning that all must be verified or exist conjointly if reverential fear is to be of sufficient gravity to vitiate matrimonial consent. Canonists are unanimous in asserting that the gravest degree of qualified reverential fear is attained when parents resort to actual violence or cruelty for the purpose of enforcing their will upon the child. Corporal abuse and inhuman treatment, blows and beatings, confinement or sequestration from friends and associates, privation of proper nourishment and suitable clothing, engender a fear that indubitably invalidates a marriage contracted under its influence.[23] As a matter of fact, when this is the case, the question is no longer one of qualified reverential fear but rather of grave, common fear.[24]

Qualified reverential fear is also accepted as grave when parents make use of threats to induce a child to accept a desired or advantageous marriage. To threaten expulsion from home, confinement in a monastery or convent, or some dark and obscure place, disinheritance, etc., produces fear in the proper sense of the term.[25] Even the threat to cut off a child with a nominal sum to prevent attacks on the last will—"pretermitting a child" as it is called and, as a general rule, permitted in the United States—is an undue interference with the freedom of matrimonial choice.[26] Where evidence shows that threats of this nature have been made, the gravity of the fear inflicted cannot be called into question,[27] and the Roman Rota has not

[23] Reiffenstuel, *Jus Canonicum Universum,* lib. I, tit. XL, n. 99; *Sanchez, De Matrimonii Sacramento,* lib. IV, disp. VI, n. 7; Knecht, *Katholisches Eherecht,* p. 573.

[24] Triebs, *Kanonisches Eherecht,* III, 511; Wernz-Vidal, *Jus Matrimoniale,* n. 497. Cf. S. C. C., *Causa Mazarien.,* 11 Dec. 1886—*ASS,* XIX (1886), 489; S. R. R., *Causa Avenionen.,* 14 Jul. 1914—*Decisiones,* VI (1914), dec. XXV, n. 2.

[25] Cf. S. R. R., *Nullit. Matrim.,* 16 Dec. 1919—*Decisiones,* XI (1919), dec. XXII, n. 3: "si timeat aliud grave malum ex. gr. exhereditationem, expulsionem e domo, metus proprie non est reverentialis."

[26] Woywod, *Practical Commentary,* I, n. 1087.

[27] Knecht, *Katholisches Eherecht,* p. 573, note 3; Payen, *De Matrimonio,* II, n. 1683.

hesitated to declare null and void marriages contracted because of its influence.[28]

A difference of opinion exists as to whether threats have to be actually made to constitute grave reverential fear.[29] It is generally admitted, however, that virtual or implicit threats involved in the circumstances will suffice.[30] If reverential fear were to be grave and invalidate marriage only when actual threats of a grave evil intervened, there would be little or no difference between it and common fear. Hence it can be grave when under the existing circumstances threats are present implicitly or equivalently so as to make the child fearful for his future safety and well-being.[31]

The particular circumstances referred to are repeated, insistent, and importunate entreaties, pleadings, and exhortations, made by a parent to induce the child to marry. In themselves these things are not sufficient to cause a grave fear. But, coming from one in authority and to whom reverence is due, they can result in severe oppression and vexation. The personal characteristics of both the author and victim of the fear require especial consideration in this case. Frequently it will be most difficult to contradict or resist one who is so grievously insistent. A soundly probable and reasonable suspicion is created that a refusal to accede to these declared wishes in regard to marriage will be productive of future grave evil or loss. Reverential fear under these conditions is grave and, if it compels marriage, the consent given is null and void.[32]

[28] Cf. e.g., S. R. R., *Causa Parisien.*, 26 Apr. 1916—*Decisiones*, VIII (1916), dec. XII, n. 4; S. R. R., *Nullit. Matrim.*, 27 Jul. 1918—*Decisiones*, X (1918), dec. XII, n. 8; S. R. R., *Causa Camenecen.*, 17 Maii, 1922—*Decisiones*, XIV (1922), dec. XVI, n. 12.

[29] Cf. Rossi, "De Consensu Matrimoniali, n. 92—*Analecta Ecclesiastica*, II (1911), 68.

[30] Sanchez, *De Matrimonii Sacramento*, lib. IV, disp. VI, n. 12; Cosci, *De Separatione Thori*, lib. III, c. IV, n. 77; Clericatus, *De Matrimonio*, dec. XXVII, n. 27. Cf. S. R. R., *Nullit. Matrim.*, 22 Jul. 1916—*Decisiones*, VIII (1916), dec. XX, n. 20; S. R. R., *Nullit Matrim.*, 18 Oct. 1922—*Decisiones*, XIV (1922), dec. XXXV, n. 3.

[31] Rossi, "De Consensu Matrimoniali," n. 93—*Analecta Ecclesiastica*, II (1911), 69.

[32] Reiffenstuel, *Jus Canonicum Universum*, lib. I, tit. XL, n. 101; Sanchez, *De Matrimonii Sacramento*, lib. IV, disp. VII, n. 7; Rossi, "De Consensu Matrimoniali," n. 101—*Analecta Ecclesiastica*, II (1911), 71-72. Cf.

Reverential fear can also be grave if a child foresees that unless he contracts the marriage planned by his parents he will incur their lasting and unending indignation, anger, contempt and abhorrence.[33] This will especially be true where the father or mother is an imperious, forceful and unbending character,[34] while the child is timid, shy, accustomed to obedience, and has a profound love for the parents. It is evident that this case differs from the mere subjectively grave fear discussed in the preceding article. Here there is question not of the mere displeasure or temporary ill-will on the part of parents who have not expressed any wishes, but of the harsh and severe indignation likely to last for a long time for refusal to bow to their declared will amounting practically to a command. That reverential fear arising out of such circumstances can be grave and efficaciously interfere with the liberty required by law for valid matrimonial consent is disclosed by recent decisions in favor of nullity granted by the Roman Rota.[35] In practice, however, strong and conclusive evidence is required to prove the gravity of reverential fear on the basis of lasting parental indignation alone, even in the case of young girls. Usually such attendant circumstances as incessant entreaties and exhortations, amounting to at least implicit threats, must be present to justify the fear being considered grave.[36]

Of vast importance in any case involving the nullity of marriage

S. R. R., *Nullit. Matrim.*, 9 Jan. 1922—*Decisiones,* XIV (1922), dec. I, n. 7; S. R. R., *Nullit. Matrim.*, 7 Mar. 1922—*Decisiones,* XIV (1922), dec. VI, n. 3; S. R. R., *Nullit. Matrim.*, 12 Jul. 1922—*Decisiones,* XIV (1922), dec. XXIV, n. 3.

33 Sanchez, *De Matrimonii Sacramento,* lib. IV, disp. VI, n. 14; Reiffenstuel, lib. III, tit. XXXI, n. 115; Cosci, *De Separatione Thori,* lib. III, c. IV, n. 87; D'Annibale, *Summula Theologiae Moralis,* I, n. 138, note 16; Wernz-Vidal, *Jus Matrimoniale,* nn. 497, 500; Knecht, *Katholisches Eherecht,* pp. 575-576. Cf. S. C. C., *Nullit. Matrim.*, 3 Feb. 1880—*ASS,* XII (1880), 408: "Sola parentis indignatio duratura meticulosae prolis libertatem ita permovet, ut consensus deficere in jure censeatur."

34 Cf. S. C. C., *Causa Mazarien.,* 11 Dec. 1886—*ASS,* XIX (1886), 489: "metum reverentialem aequivalere metui gravi . . . (si) pater sit terribilis."

35 Cf. e.g., S. R. R., *Nullit. Matrim.*, 11 Apr. 1922—*Decisiones,* XIV (1922), dec. XI, nn. 17-18; S. R. R., *Nullit. Matrim.*, 29 Jul. 1922—*Decisiones,* XIV (1922), dec. XXV, n. 9; S. R. R., *Nullit. Matrim.*, 19 Dec. 1922—*Decisiones,* XIV (1922), dec. XXXVIII, nn. 13-14.

36 Gasparri, *De Matrimonio,* n. 943; Wernz, *Jus Matrimoniale,* n. 264; Ayrinhac, *Marriage Legislation,* n. 206.

on grounds of reverential fear is the subjective element. The nature, character and personal qualities of both the author and the victim of the undue influence and constraint must be subjected to minute investigation. This is to be made along the lines suggested above in the study of relatively grave fear. The nature of the matter makes it impossible to give any definite rules. The evidence gathered, however, will determine whether a grave reverential fear existed and whether the consent to marry given under its influence was juridically deficient according to canon 1087.

What has been said concerning the gravity of reverential fear may be summarized briefly as follows: reverential fear is considered grave and invalidates marriage in two cases: (a) if, besides the displeasure and indignation of parents, some other grave evil is feared as a result of their conduct; (b) if the severe and lasting indignation of parents is feared, particularly when this is soundly probable by reason of the means employed to compel the marriage. In the former case, reverential fear sometimes ceases to be such and becomes ordinary or common fear; in the latter, fear remains in a certain sense reverential, but stands in the highest degree of that category, that of mixed or qualified fear.[37] In other words, if the offense or indignation of parents or superiors is really and properly grave in itself, which is a rare occurrence, or grave in the attendant circumstances, which frequently happens, reverential fear is grave in the sense in which the law refers it to marriage and the matrimonial consent it compels is invalid.[38] In doubt, experience makes for a presumption that it is slight. Its gravity must be clearly demonstrated in the external forum in accordance with the foregoing marks and indications.[39]

It has been observed that once the gravity of reverential fear has been established, the remaining conditions of canon 1087 will ordinarily be found to be verified. Still, they should never be overlooked by the tribunal or peremptorily dismissed. As far as the present problem is concerned, the requirement of extrinsic causation will generally be fulfilled. The source or cause of reverential fear

[37] Payen, *De Matrimonio,* II, 81, note 1.
[38] Cappello, *De Matrimonio,* n. 604.
[39] Triebs, *Kanonisches Eherecht,* III, 511.

may be any person holding authority over the child.[40] Comprehended in this notion are parents, whether natural or adoptive,[41] and all who hold the place of parents in their absence or upon their death. Among these may be mentioned an elder brother or sister in regard to a younger child,[42] grandparents, uncles and aunts, guardians, and all superiors, whether civil or ecclesiastical, who exercise authority over children, as e.g., in orphanages.

While such a relationship produces a presumption in favor of reverential fear, investigation must be made in each case whether the person attacking the marriage actually could be the victim of such an influence. It can happen that a child by reason of age or circumstances is no longer constituted under parental authority. Commands or wishes of parents mean little where such is the case and hence the presumption is against reverential fear.[43] While it is true, however, that reverential fear is more usually found in minors or those not as yet emancipated, the mere circumstance of age is not absolute.[44]

Moreover, even when evidence shows that parents or others have made use of urgent persuasions and arguments to induce a child to contract marriage, the fear may nevertheless have proceeded *ab intrinseco* rather than *ab intrinseco.* Thus e.g., if a daughter, with out reasonable suspicion founded in fact or circumstance, merely imagines that by refusing a certain marriage she will incur the indignation or displeasure of her parents, the reverential fear is *ab intrinseco.* For this reason, no matter how subjectively grave it may be, it lacks the objective gravity necessary for even reverential fear to invalidate marriage. Again, if parents simply point out the

[40] Cf. Sanchez, *De Matrimonii Sacramento,* lib. IV, disp. VI, n. 25; St. Alphonsus, *Theologia Moralis,* lib. VI, n. 1056.

[41] Cf. S. R. R., *Causa Nicien.,* 31 Jul. 1915—*AAS,* VIII (1915), 109-120. The *actrix* was an adopted child. Nullity was refused on grounds that fear was purely reverential.

[42] Cf. S. R. R., *Causa Massilien.,* 23 Jan. 1917—*Decisiones,* IX (1917), dec. II, 11-23; Sanchez, *De Matrimonii Sacramento,* lib. IV, disp. VI, n. 31.

[43] Sanchez, *De Matrimonii Sacramento,* lib. IV, disp. VI, n. 24. Cf. S. R. R., *Nullit. Matrim.,* Aug. 1, 1913—*Decisiones,* V (1913), dec. XLII, n. 12.

[44] Cf. e.g., S. R. R., *Nullit. Matrim.,* 15 Jan. 1912—*Decisiones,* IV (1912), dec. IV, 26-32; *Sec. Inst.,* 16 Maii, 1912—*op. cit.,* dec. XXII, 261-272: the *actrix,* who was twenty-eight years of age, received two decisions in favor of nullity on grounds of reverential fear.

advantages of a certain marriage, e. g., how it would relieve a distressing economic situation, and the girl, wishing to provide for their welfare as well as her own, marries in accordance with their wishes, any fear accompanying her action cannot be said *ab extrinseco* in the sense of canon 1087.[45]

Just as grave injury is the essential element from which the nullity of marriage contracted under the influence of common fear proceeds, so also grave injury must be the essential element of the nullity of marriage due to reverential fear. Hence matrimonial consent granted under the stress of reverential fear, howsoever grave, is not null and void unless other conditions exist from which the fact of grave injury may be determined. Children must be considered to have contracted marriage with grave injury as often as it is established that parents have grievously abused the natural reverence children have for them in order to compel them to marry.[46]

As has been pointed out, parents have the right to advise their children in the matter of marriage and children have the duty of considering their counsel. They are permitted to explain to children causes, founded in objective circumstances, which make marriage advisable. They may make use of persuasions and entreaties as long as they are not incessant, importunate and insistent with the result that they contain virtual threats. They may even employ moderate pressure, rebukes and chidings to urge marriage.[47]

Further than this, however, parents dare not go. They have absolutely no right to force their will upon a child in the matter of marriage.[48] When parents take advantage of their authority and

[45] Triebs, *Kanonisches Eherecht,* III, 511. Cf. S. R. R., *Causa Gallipolitana,* 16 Aug. 1917—*Decisiones,* IX (1917), dec. XXII, n. 2.

[46] Cf. S. R. R., *Nullit. Matrim.,* 7 Mar. 1922—*Decisiones,* XIV (1922), dec. VI, n. 3.

[47] Sanchez, *De Matrimonii Sacramento,* lib. IV, disp. XXII, n. 5; Triebs, *Kanonisches Eherecht,* III, 512; Knecht, *Katholisches Eherecht,* p. 572. Cf. S. R. R., *Causa Varsavien. seu Lublinen.,* 21 Jul. 1910—*Decisiones,* II (1910), dec. XXVIII, n. 8; S. R. R., *Causa Lugdunen.,* 5 Jun. 1917—*Decisiones,* IX (1917), dec. XIV, n. 5; S. R. R., *Nullit. Matrim.,* 12 Jul. 1922—*Decisiones,* XIV (1922), dec. XXIV, n. 3.

[48] Cf. S. R. R., Causa Tarvisina, 11 Mar. 1912—*AAS,* IV (1912), 504: "Nam neque ex jure divino neque ex jure ecclesiastico, filii in eligendam uxorem et filiae in eligendum conjugem, parentum voluntatem sequi tenentur."

abuse the reverential respect a child has for them in order to compel him to contract marriage, they commit an injustice and injure his rights by such molestation and vexation. For this reason the Church regards fear engendered by parental coercion and constraint as unjust and will not hesitate to declare null and void a marriage where a sufficiently grave injury has been sustained. The injustice done is not mitigated by the fact that the parent thinks he has a right to act as he does, or intends only what appears to be to the best interests of the child, e.g., to withdraw him from a life of sin or provide for his future comfort.[49] Error on the part of a parent or lack of a malicious intention may excuse from sin, but it does not remove the objective injustice of the coercion. The fear inflicted, as far as it compels the child to marry, violates his right to liberty. Hence it is, if sufficiently grave, an adequate cause for nullifying his consent.

The distinctions of *quoad substantiam* and *quoad modum* also obtain in this matter. Fear is inspired justly *quoad substantiam* when parents seek to hold to his obligation of marrying a child who has become formally engaged.[50] They inspire an unjust fear *quoad modum*, however, should they make use of an unjust means to compel him, e.g., threaten to withdraw some good which is due to him. Fear inspired for the purpose of compelling marriage where no such obligation exists is unjustly inflicted *quoad substantiam* and generally *quoad modum* also.[51]

As regards the final condition of canon 1087, it will be verified as a rule in the case of a girl who is constrained by her parents to contract a marriage of their choice. She will generally have no other way of escape from the evils which are threatened or the molestations and vexations to which she is exposed than to give her consent to the union. Relatives and friends of the family, not wishing to engage in

[49] Cf. S. R. R., *Causa Varsavien, seu Lublinen.*, 21 Jul. 1910—*Decisiones*, II (1910), dec. XXVIII, n. 8; S. R. R., *Causa Veszprimien.*, 2 Jun. 1911—*Decisiones*, III (1911), dec. XXI, n. 11; S. R. R., *Causa Vicariat. Apost. Ce-Li Central.*, 10 Feb. 1917—*Decisiones*, IX (1917), dec. III, n. 8.

[50] Cf. S. R. R., *Causa Tarvisina*, 9 Mar. 1917—*Decisiones*, IX (1917), dec. V, n. 15: "parentes, justa interveniente causa, possunt filios ad matrimonium inducere, quin ullo modo requisitam eorum laedant libertatem, et ullam in eos committant injuriam, et quin consequenter eorum matrimonium fiat irritum."

[51] Cf. Triebs, *Kanonisches Eherecht*, III, 512.

quarrels or disputes with the parents, cannot always be counted upon to come to her assistance. Where, however, the girl has been given training and education for some special career in life, by means of which she can sustain herself, the last requirement of the law may not be fulfilled. In circumstances such as these a threat, for instance, of expulsion from the parental home, cannot be construed as inducing a grave or unavoidable fear.[52] Still, other circumstances, e.g., nobility of rank, dignity of station or position in life, may make distressfully inconvenient, if not impossible, escape from the marriage in this way.[53] With a son the last condition will rarely be verified. A man can as a rule make his way through life without the assistance of his parents and consequently is not so dependent upon them as a girl might be.[54] As with common fear, accordingly, reverential fear can never be said to invalidate marriage when means are present to avoid it.

[52] Cf. e.g., S. R. R., *Causa Parisien.*, 31 Jan. 1922—*Decisiones*, XIV (1922), dec. III, n. 8. Among other things militating against the existence of grave reverential fear was the fact that the girl was a school-teacher, a position which would provide her with the necessities and comforts of life if she were expelled from her parents' home.

[53] Cf. e.g., S. R. R., *Causa Southwarcen.*, 29 Jul. 1926—*AAS*, XVIII (1926), 501-506.

[54] Cf. Triebs, *Kanonisches Eherecht*, III, 512.

CHAPTER VIII

AN UNSETTLED CONTROVERSY

On account of its important ramifications, it now becomes necessary to discuss at some length a problem which apparently defies solution. No one denies that matrimonial consent is invalid by natural law if it is extorted by absolute violence. This violence of its very nature precludes the possibility of a human act and consequently excludes consent. Likewise it is evident that marriage is null and void on the same grounds if fear is so great as to destroy the use of reason. Since the Middle Ages, however, canonists and moralists have agitated a question which remains unsettled to the present time. The controversy hinges on the point as to whether grave, unjustly inflicted fear, which does not wholly prevent consent but which nevertheless diminishes its freedom, derives its nullifying force already from the natural law or solely and entirely from ecclesiastical law. That the question is not purely theoretical is seen from the practical import it has in regard to the marriages of non-baptized persons. A further implication is the matter of dispensation.

Article I.—Natural or Ecclesiastical Law

Certain ground on which there is naught but agreement is common to the parties involved in this controversy. They agree that divine positive law does not enter into the question. The advocates of the natural law theory concede that when matrimonial consent lacks the requisite liberty, it is certainly null and void by ecclesiastical law. Those adhering to the ecclesiastical law opinion acknowledge that the natural law urges an invalidating statute but no more. Both grant that the provisions of ecclesiastical law are in perfect harmony with the dictates of the natural law.[1] The controversy, moreover, does not concern itself with an extension of the impediment by the ecclesiastical law for the purpose of assuring a more perfect degree of liberty not required by natural law,[2] similarly as

[1] Feije, *De Impedimentis et Dispensationibus Matrimonialibus,* n. 136.

[2] Cf. Payen, *De Matrimonio,* II, n. 1688.

the natural impediment of substantial error was extended by the Church to include accidental error of servile condition.[3] The dispute is restricted to the substance of the impediment: whether the nullity of matrimonial consent extorted by grave fear is so substantially and completely established by natural law that every marriage contracted under its influence is invalid independently of any further determination by civil or ecclesiastical law; or whether the nullity proceeds solely from ecclesiastical law.[4]

§ 1. *The Natural Law Theory*

The principal arguments of those authorities [5] who maintain that grave fear derives its invalidating effect from the natural law may be briefly summarized as follows:

(a) Natural law decrees that contracts entered through fear are binding but rescindable, and thereby protects the injured party by providing means for redress. The indissolubility of the matrimonial bond, however, makes impossible the application of this principle to marriage. Once a marriage is validly contracted it is irrescindable: *matrimonium semel validum semper validum.* Hence the marriage is either valid or invalid by natural law. But if it is admitted as valid, then the natural law would sanction an act from which the greatest harm would come to the common good, because there would be no way of redressing the evil. The innocent party would be forced to a perpetual and indissoluble bond necessarily entailing the irreparable injury of a life made difficult and intolerable by obligations and responsibilities which were not voluntarily assumed. On the other hand, the person guilty of inducing the fear would gain a dis-

[3] *Codex Juris Canonici,* c. 1083, § 2, n. 2.

[4] Wernz-Vidal, *Jus Matrimoniale,* n. 502.

[5] St. Thomas, *Summa Theologica,* Suppl., q. 47, a. 3; St. Alphonsus, *Theologia Moralis,* lib. VI, n. 1054; Reiffenstuel, *Jus Canonicum Universum,* lib. I, tit. XL, nn. 48-50; lib. IV, tit. I, n. 325; Lehmkuhl, *Theologia Moralis,* II, n. 965; Wernz, *Jus Matrimoniale,* n. 266; Noldin, *Summa Theologiae Moralis,* III, n. 633; Pruemmer, *Manuale Theologiae Moralis,* III, n. 795; Ballerini-Palmieri, *Opus Theologicum Morale,* VI, tr. X, nn. 110-112; 1122; Cappello, *De Matrimonio,* n. 609; Wernz-Vidal, *Jus Matrimoniale,* n. 502; Vlaming, *Praelectiones Juris Matrimonii,* n. 540; Cerato, *Matrimonium,* n. 83; Payen, *De Matrimonio,* II, n. 1689; Leitner, *Katholisches Eherecht,* p. 100; Linneborn, *Eherecht,* p. 291; Triebs, *Kanonisches Eherecht,* III, 513; Augustine, *Commentary,* V, 244.

tinct advantage and profit from his injustice. This conclusion, however, is altogether inconsistent with the dictates of right reason and the operation of the natural law. Therefore, the natural law in the interests of justice, i.e., to provide a remedy against the injustice inflicted, must nullify the marriage in its very inception by never permitting it to exist as a valid contract.[6]

(b) Marriage of its very nature is a voluntary association of bodies and souls united in a mutual bond of love and affection. Such a bond becomes impossible, however, when grave fear is present, because the two are incompatible. Since fear, therefore, is opposed to the marital bond and destructive of its nature, a marriage contracted under its influence must be invalid by the natural law.[7] The same conclusion is reached from a consideration of the threefold end of marriage. The union is ordained primarily for the procreation and education of children, and secondarily for the mutual help of the parties and as a remedy for concupiscence. Fear, which is directed toward the frustration of these ends, is repugnant to the natural law and therefore must invalidate marriage by reason of that law. Finally, natural law has a nullifying force in regard to acts which contain not only a transient but a perpetual moral baseness and depravity. But if marriage is contracted because of a grave fear, it has this depravity not only in the transient act of celebration, but retains it also afterwards as long as the fear continues. For the evils which originate from fear against the threefold good of marriage have their source in the act of consent given at the outset.[8]

(c) The law of the Decretals confirms this opinion. Alexander III expressly states that matrimonial consent cannot obtain where fear or force intervenes.[9] Since consent is required by the natural law for a valid marriage, the latter must be invalid by the same law where it is lacking because of fear. Moreover, when the Roman

[6] St. Thomas, *Summa Theologica,* Suppl., q. 47, a. 3; Ballerini-Palmieri, *Opus Theologicum Morale,* VI, tr. X, n. 1122; Lehmkuhl, *Theologia Moralis,* II, n. 965; Payen, *De Matrimonio,* II, n. 1689.

[7] St. Alphonsus, *Theologia Moralis,* lib. VI, n. 1054.

[8] Wernz-Vidal, *Jus Matrimoniale,* n. 502.

[9] C. 14, X, *de spons. et matr.,* IV, 1.

Pontiffs in this and other canonical texts [10] declare that marriage contracted on account of fear is invalid, they do not speak as making an innovation in ecclesiastical discipline, but rather as declaring and promulgating the natural law.[11] Neither can they be said to base their decisions on some older positive law, written or customary, but rather on reasons sought from the nature of defective consent and compulsory marriage.[12] The natural law, therefore, must be the source of the invalidity.

(d) The opinion that grave fear invalidates marriage by the natural law is further supported by the approval it receives in official ecclesiastical documents and judicial pronouncements. Among many instances which might be cited is an Instruction dealing with the impediment of ***raptus.*** In this it is clearly stated that the impediment of fear ***reapse consensum afficit, proinde in ipso jure naturali fundamentum habet.***[13] A typical recommendation is to be found in a decision of the Congregation of the Council. Treating of the freedom which matrimonial consent requires, it declares: ***quamvis metus non faciat simpliciter cessare consensum, tamen tollit qualitatem libertatis in matrimonium requisitam, quae libertas jure naturae necessaria omnino est.***[14]

§ 2. *The Ecclesiastical Law Opinion.*

Opposed to the opinion that the natural law is the source of the invalidity are many [15] who claim that the impediment of fear is

[10] Cc. 15, 28, X, *de spons. et matr.*, IV, 1.

[11] St. Alphonsus, *Theologia Moralis,* lib. VI, n. 1054.

[12] Wernz-Vidal, *Jus Matrimoniale,* n. 502.

[13] S. C. S. Inquis., *Instructio ad Episc. Albanen.,* 15 Feb. 1901—*ASS,* XXXIII (1901), 547. Cf. *Fontes,* n. 1250.

[14] S. C. C., *Nullit. Matrim.,* 10 Jun. 1865—*ASS,* II (1865), 19, note 3.

[15] Sanchez, *De Matrimonii Sacramento,* lib. IV, disp. XIV, n. 2; Pichler, *Jus Canonicum,* lib. IV, tit. I, n. 113; Pirhing, *Jus Canonicum,* lib. IV, tit. I, n. 106; Schmalzgrueber, *Jus Ecclesiasticum Universum,* lib. IV, tit. I, nn. 406-407; Lugo, *De Justitia et Jure,* disp. XXII, n. 120; De Angelis, *Praelectiones Juris Canonici,* lib. I, tit. XL, n. 4; Feije, *De Impedimentis et Dispensationibus Matrimonialibus,* nn. 136-142; Lega, *De Judiciis Ecclesiasticis,* I, p. 296, note 1; Santi, *Praelectiones Juris Canonici,* IV, n. 148; Gasparri, *De Matrimonio,* n. 935; Heiss, *De Matrimonio,* pp. 96-97; De Becker, *De Sponsalibus et Matrimonio,* p. 65; Chelodi, *Jus Matrimoniale,* n. 120; Genicot, *Institutiones Theologiae Moralis,* II, n. 463; Vermeersch-Creusen, *Epitome,* II, n. 376;

founded solely on ecclesiastical law. Among the reasons advanced to fortify this opinion are:

(a) If the impediment of fear were based on the natural law, the nullity would be due to absence of consent, or to lack of liberty in consent, or to the injury suffered by the innocent party. The nullifying force of grave fear, however, cannot be attributed to absence of consent. Even though the will is influenced by fear, consent is always present: *coacta voluntas est semper voluntas.* Voluntariness is diminished but not entirely destroyed. For the same reason, the invalidity is not due to a lack of liberty in consent. Furthermore, if marriage is null and void on either of these grounds, then the same should hold true in all cases of fear, whether from an intrinsic or extrinsic cause, whether justly or unjustly inflicted. But no one sustains such an absurd claim. Finally, the invalidity cannot be owing to the injury sustained by the innocent party. Other acts carrying with them grave injury are not necessarily invalid by natural law. Deceit or fraud which do not involve substantial error or error redounding to person do not *per se* invalidate marriage. The innocent party is irrevocably bound to the contract regardless of the evils entailed. Moreover, the natural law has no need to invalidate the marriage in order to protect the innocent party. Sufficient protection is afforded by the prohibition of force and compulsion and by the obligation placed on those guilty of injustice to make reparation. The natural law further provides for the interests of the injured party by granting to legitimate authority the power to annul marriage contracted under the influence of fear. Since the Catholic concept of the marital bond does not admit of annulment, ecclesiastical law determines that under certain conditions the marriage will be null and void *ab initio.*[16]

(*b*) For the matrimonial contract, as for any contract, the natural law requires nothing more than a just title and voluntary consent. Grave fear excludes neither of these elements. It does

Vromant, *De Matrimonio,* n. 192; Knecht, *Katholisches Eherecht,* p. 579; De Smet, *Betrothment and Marriage,* n. 535; Woywod, *Practical Commentary,* I, n. 1088.

[16] Feije, *De Impedimentis et Dispensationibus Matrimonialibus,* nn. 138, 141; Vromant, *De Matrimonio,* n. 192. Cf. Pruemmer, *Manuale Theologiae Moralis,* III, n. 795.

not exclude the title since it does not prevent the mutual transfer and acceptance of rights on the part of the contracting parties. As for voluntariness of consent, this is merely diminished and not entirely destroyed. But inasmuch as the natural law is so vague and general, it devolves upon the positive law to determine under what circumstances a diminished voluntary consent is insufficient to conclude the matrimonial contract. Ecclesiastical law does this when it declares the specific conditions under which fear invalidates matrimonial consent.[17]

(*c*) The presence of fear is an obstacle to the mutual love and affection which makes for a happy and successful marriage, but which is in no way necessary for a valid union.[18] Similarly as fear diminishes but does not destroy volition, so it in no way entirely destroys the union of bodies and souls or the ends for which that association is entered. The argument based on mutual love as advanced by the advocates of the other opinion simply shows how expedient it is for positive law to establish the impediment of fear if the institution of marriage was to be properly safeguarded.[19]

(*d*) As far as the canonical texts are concerned, they merely declare that fear interferes with the consent required by law in general. If they speak of the impediment as already existing, the reference can just as well be to some positive law regulating the matter. Many points of ecclesiastical discipline are referred to as existing in the law and, although their original enactment has been lost to view, they are undoubtedly of ecclesiastical origin. Moreover, those who subject the decision of Alexander III to so rigorous an interpretation as to exclude consent entirely should remember that, whenever an act is performed under the influence of fear, volition and consent are not necessarily lacking. Hence the texts of the Decretals are more correctly understood as speaking of the

[17] Schmalzgrueber, *Jus Ecclesiasticum Universum,* lib. IV, tit. I, n. 406.

[18] This point has been frequently emphasized by the Roman Rota in its judicial decisions. Cf. e.g., S. R. R., *Nullit. Matrim.*, 9 Mar. 1915—*Decisiones,* VII (1915), dec. VIII, n. 18; S. R. R., *Causa Ambianen.*, 3 Jan. 1917—*Decisiones,* IX (1917), dec. I, n. 7; S. R. R., *Causa Tarvisin.*, 9 Mar. 1917—*Decisiones,* IX (1917), dec. V, n. 13; S. R. R., *Nullit. Matrim.*, 12 Jul. 1922—*Decisiones,* XIV (1922), dec. XXIV, n. 5.

[19] Gasparri, *De Matrimonio,* n. 935.

consent which now *de facto* is required by ecclesiastical law, not however, of that which is demanded by natural law.[20]

(*e*) Evidence can likewise be drawn from the judicial pronouncements of ecclesiastical jurisprudence in favor of the assertion that in positive law alone is found the reason for the nullity of compulsory marriage. A few random citations will sustain this contention. After reviewing the general principles governing acts performed under the influence of fear and applying them to the particular case of marriage, one decision continues: *Coacta voluntas est semper voluntas. Et si, hoc minime obstante, matrimonium fit irritum, non ex consensus absoluto defectu est repetendum, sed a juris dispositione, qua laeso sucurritur et injuria reparatur. Hanc ob causam metum passo actio datur, quod metus causa . . . quae actio, cum locum non possit habere in matrimonio indissolubili, cautum est a jure ut laeso succuratur ope nullitatis contractus matrimonialis.*[21] The controversy is fully discussed in another judgment and the marriage in question declared invalid *ex jure ecclesiastico ob claram et explicitam dispositionem cap. 14, de spons. et matrim.*[22] Again, it is stated: *theoria canonica omnium doctorum consensu recepta, quod, saltem de jure ecclesiastico, metus dirimit matrimonium.*[23] It is apparent, therefore, that little can be gained from these sources to confirm the opinion that the invalidity of compulsory marriage has its origin in the natural law. As for the quotation from the Instruction to the Bishops of Albania, the words may just as correctly be understood as meaning that, while the natural law urges nullity, the norm for determining it depends on positive law.[24]

§ 3. *Conclusions*

These summary reviews of the two conflicting opinions reveal

[20] Feije, *De Impedimentis et Dispensationibus Matrimonialibus*, n. 139; De Becker, *De Sponsalibus et Matrimonio*, p. 65.

[21] S. R. R., *Nullit. Matrim.*, 2 Jul. 1918—*Decisiones*, X (1918), dec. VIII, n. 3.

[22] S. R. R., *Causa Vic. Apostol. Nyanzae Septentr.*, 10 Maii, 1918—*Decisiones*, X (1918), dec. V, n. 2.

[23] S. R. R., *Causa Parisien.*, 13 Mar. 1911—*AAS*, III (1911), 167. Cf. also S. R. R., *Causa Tunkinen.*, 7 Jul. 1911—*AAS*, III (1911), 663; S. R. R., *Causa Tarvisin.*, 11 Mar. 1912—*AAS*, IV, (1912), 504.

[24] De Smet, *Betrothment and Marriage*, n. 535.

clearly why the controversy is practically impossible of solution. Because of the almost even division of canonists and moralists who lend the weight of their authority to one or the other theory, both opinions enjoy great extrinsic probability. An appraisal of the objective worth of the arguments advanced to fortify either position leads to no more definite conclusion, mainly because none of the reasons are peremptory [25] and some, which it has been deemed fitting to omit, are tenuous and unconvincing.[26] It will be observed that the element of negation is present to a large extent in arguments offered in support of the ecclesiastical law opinion. This is accounted for by the fact that its adherents do not proceed so far in their claims as the natural law protagonists. Since these seem to prove too much, and consequently prove nothing,[27] the mere refutation of their arguments establishes the contention that the ecclesiastical law is the reason for the invalidity of marriage contracted under the influence of fear.

The present legislation of the Code cannot be said to settle the controversy. Nothing in favor of the opinion that the invalidation proceeds from the natural law can be gathered from canon 1087,[28] although Cerato [29] holds the contrary. His first reason is that fear is no longer listed among the impediments proper but among the natural obstacles besetting matrimonial consent. Therefore, it is not to be regarded as an impediment properly so-called of ecclesiastical law affecting the capacity of persons to contract marriage. It is rather a defect vitiating the act of consent itself, which should be fully free according to the natural law.[30] The nature of grave fear is not such that it renders the parties concerned incompetent to contract marriage, but simply makes the act null and void due to the privation of the constitutive element of marriage, free consent on the part of the parties to the contract. That fear invalidates marriage by the natural law might also be established from a correlation of canon 1087 with canon 1038, § 1 which states that the supreme

[25] Cappello, *De Matrimonio,* n. 609.
[26] Cf. Wernz-Vidal, *Jus Matrimoniale,* p. 590, note 33.
[27] Gougnard, *De Matrimonio,* p. 170.
[28] Cappello, *De Matrimonio,* n. 609.
[29] *Matrimonium,* n. 83.
[30] Cf. Farrugia, *De Matrimonio,* n. 31.

authority of the Church is competent to declare authentically when divine law forbids or invalidates marriage.

Cappello,[31] though adhering to the natural law theory, is of the opinion that this line of argumentation is without solid foundation. On the other hand, no certain argument can be derived from the Code in support of the opinion that ecclesiastical law is the sole source of the nullity. Since canon 103, §2 declares that acts which are the result of grave fear unjustly inflicted are valid, unless the law provides otherwise, De Smet [32] thinks that a valid argument can be drawn for the second opinion by understanding canon 1087 as a provision of ecclesiastical law. But the words *nisi aliud jure caveatur* should be understood of natural as well as positive law.[33]

Hence, while the natural law opinion may appear to some to enjoy a greater probability from the Code, it cannot be said that it actually favors either opinion or brings an end to the old controversy.[34]

It seems beyond dispute that one definite conclusion follows from a study of the conflicting opinions. The natural law at least persuades that the Church should provide for the full liberty of marriage by invalidating the contract entered through grave fear. This is deduced from the fact that the natural law of itself cannot always and with certainty invalidate a marriage contracted because of compulsion.[35] Who, for instance, would dare to establish from merely the natural law the line of demarcation between slight fear and grave fear? In order that the law may be certain and to do away with all ambiguity, or at least to reduce it to a minimum, some disposition of positive law is necessary.[36] Ecclesiastical law recognizes this necessity and provides accordingly. For these reasons a conciliation might be effected between the two opinions by holding that the nullity of matrimonial consent extorted by grave

[31] *De Matrimonio,* p. 658, note 23.

[32] *Betrothment and Marriage,* n. 535.

[33] Cappello, *De Matrimonio,* n. 609. Cf. Payen, *De Matrimonio,* II, p. 88, note 2.

[34] Farrugia, *De Matrimonio,* n. 31.

[35] Payen, *De Matrimonio,* II, n. 1688; De Smet, *Betrothment and Marriage,* n. 535.

[36] Heiss, *De Matrimonio,* pp. 96-97.

fear is *radicaliter* contained in the natural law, but *formaliter* in ecclesiastical law.[37]

ARTICLE II.—THE MARRIAGES OF INFIDELS

The practical importance of the above controversy in relation to the marriages of infidels, whether between themselves or with baptized persons, is apparent. Where marriage is contracted between two unbaptized persons under the influence of grave fear, if the civil law to which they are subject declares void or voidable marriages of that kind, then the parties are certainly obliged by that law and cannot give a valid consent.[38] In the absence of civil legislation, according to the first opinion the marriage is null and void, according to the second it is valid. On account of the strong probability of both opinions, such a marriage may not be declared certainly valid or invalid, so that in the external forum the principle *in dubio standum est pro valore matrimonii* must be applied.[39] It is evident that the same holds true where the doubt is one of fact, for instance, whether fear in a particular case is grave or slight.

In either case, should one of the unbaptized parties to a forced marriage be converted and wish to contract marriage with a baptized person, since a positive doubt exists as to the validity of the first marriage, the law favors the privilege or liberty of the convert.[40] The first marriage, accordingly, may certainly be dissolved and the second marriage contracted with the usual interrogations of the infidel party omitted, even if it is known that the latter is willing to live peacefully, i. e., without interfering with the religious obligations of the convert.[41]

Where a baptized Catholic and an unbaptized person contract marriage under the influence of grave fear but with a dispensation

[37] Cf. Gasparri, *De Matrimonio*, n. 935.

[38] Cf. Gasparri, *De Matrimonio*, nn. 290-292.

[39] Cappello, *De Matrimonio*, n. 610; Vromant, *De Matrimonio*, n. 193; Gougnard, *De Matrimonio*, p. 171; Knecht, *Katholisches Eherecht*, p. 579.

[40] *Codex Juris Canonici*, cc. 1014, 1127. Cf. Cappello, *De Matrimonio*, n. 788.

[41] Payen, *De Matrimonio*, II, n. 1690; Vromant, *De Matrimonio*, nn. 193, 288-289. Vlaming (*Praelectiones Juris Matrimonii*, n. 540) is of the opinion that the case should be referred to the Holy See.

from the impediment of disparity of cult, if the baptized party suffers the fear, the marriage is certainly invalid. The latter is directly subject to ecclesiastical law and therefore is prevented from giving a valid consent when he suffers a grave and unjustly inflicted fear.[42]

If the unbaptized party contracts under the influence of grave fear, some [43] assert that the marriage is valid because ecclesiastical authority does not extend itself or exercise its jurisdiction over the consent of one not subject to its laws. This opinion certainly cannot be admitted by those who claim that compulsory marriage is invalid by the natural law, to which both baptized and unbaptized are equally subject. But even admitting that ecclesiastical law is the sole reason for the invalidity, the opinion by far the more probable[44] maintains that, should fear compel the unbaptized party exclusively, the marriage is nevertheless null and void.[45]

The reasons are sound and convincing. The law of canon 1087 seems directly and immediately to regulate not the persons involved but the contract itself.[46] Furthermore, though the Church cannot oblige infidels directly by her laws, she can do this indirectly by a restriction placed on the faithful. Baptized persons are prevented by ecclesiastical law from contracting a valid marriage when grave fear influences consent. This inability affects the infidel party also, since competence is required in both parties for a valid matrimonial contract. Lastly, the purpose of the invalidating law is to safeguard the liberty of marriage. The law would fall short of its aim, however, if a marriage which is the result of fear unjustly inflicted on the infidel by the baptized party or by a third person should be valid. The baptized party would profit by his malice and injustice or, because of the unjust coercion of a third person, both the baptized and unbaptized parties would be exposed to the gravest evils and

[42] Gasparri, *De Matrimonio,* n. 936; Vromant, *De Matrimonio,* n. 194; Payen, *De Matrimonio,* II, n. 1690.

[43] Gasparri, *De Matrimonio,* n. 936; Gougnard, *De Matrimonio,* p. 171.

[44] Payen, *De Matrimonio,* II, n. 1690.

[45] Wernz, *Jus Matrimoniale,* p. 394, note 27; Cappello, *De Matrimonio,* n. 610; Chelodi, *Jus Matrimoniale,* n. 120; Vromant, *De Matrimonio,* n. 194; Wernz-Vidal, *Jus Matrimoniale,* p. 588, note 29; Knecht, *Katholisches Eherecht,* p. 579; Triebs, *Kanonisches Eherecht,* III, 514.

[46] Vromant, *De Matrimonio,* n. 194.

dangers which usually follow from a marriage unwillingly contracted.[47]

Nevertheless, because of this difference of opinion, the validity of a marriage between a baptized person and an infidel, in which the latter suffers a grave and unjustly inflicted fear, remains doubtful. In practice, if the fear ceases, convalidation should be effected *ad cautelam* in accordance with the principles of canon 1136. Should this be impossible, a declaration of nullity cannot be given without the intervention of the Holy See.[48] Vromant [49] suggests that the case be referred to the Holy See in order that the marriage, which is not accounted as *ratum et consummatum,* may be dissolved *ad cautelam.*

If a Catholic contracts marriage with a baptized non-Catholic, or if two baptized non-Catholics contract marriage under the influence of grave and unjustly inflicted fear, the eccleciastical law of invalidity applies by virtue of canon 87.[50] The records reveal that judicial decisions have been rendered by the Roman Rota in the cases of baptized non-Catholics.[51]

Article III.—Dispensation

The question of dispensation offers no difficulty. As long as the controversy concerning the origin of the impediment of fear continues, it is easily understood why the Church never dispenses, not even after marriage has been contracted. In the first place, it is doubtful whether a dispensation can be given. Until the controversy is definitely settled, a *dubium juris,* divine or positive, exists. For this reason the power of the Pope to dispense from the law remains

[47] Wernz-Vidal, *Jus Matrimoniale,* p. 588, note 29; Cappello, *De Matrimonio,* n. 610.

[48] Payen, *De Matrimonio,* II, n. 1690.

[49] *De Matrimonio,* n. 194. This author (*op. cit.,* p. 160, note 1) likewise points out that the *privilegium fidei* in its strict sense can never be applied to the doubtful marriage of a baptized person with an infidel. Cf. *Codex Juris Canonici,* cc. 1120, § 2, 1127.

[50] Payen, *De Matrimonio,* II, n. 1690; Vromant, *De Matrimonio,* n. 195.

[51] Cf. S. R. R., *Causa Osnabrucen.,* 11 Jan. 1912—*AAS,* IV (1912), 182-186; S. R. R., *Nullit. Matrim.,* 1 Jul. 1912—*Decisiones,* IV (1912), dec. XXVII, 314-328; S. R. R., *Causa Colonien.,* 1 Jul. 1912—*AAS,* IV (1912), 670-675; S. R. R., *Causa Southwarcen.,* 29 Jul. 1926—*AAS,* XVIII (1926), 501-507.

in question. If, despite this doubt, a dispensation were to be granted, he would expose himself to the danger of violating the divine law from which he cannot dispense.[52] Whenever such a doubt exists, the Church, in order to avoid the least possibility of violating the divine law, always acts in practice as though that law is in force.[53] For the same reason canons 15, 81, 1043, 1044, and 1045 can have no application in the case of marriage invalid because of fear. The power of dispensation is granted only for impediments of ecclesiastical law, or at least those from which the Holy See usually dispenses.[54]

Furthermore, even admitting that the certainty of the second opinion should be established, it may safely be said that the Church would never remove the nullity by dispensing from the law. To do so would not only place the party who suffered the compulsion under an unwilling obligation, but the person responsible for the injustice would gain a distinct advantage from his malicious action. *Metum comprobare contra bonos mores est.* This alone is sufficient reason for never permitting a dispensation where marriage will be, or already has been, contracted under the influence of grave fear.[55]

[52] Wernz, *Jus Matrimoniale,* n. 267.

[53] Cf. Triebs, *Kanonisches Eherecht,* I, 150.

[54] Maroto, *Institutiones,* I, n. 230; Michiels, *Normae Generales,* I, p. 338, note 2; Wernz-Vidal, *Jus Matrimoniale,* n. 413; Knecht, *Katholisches Eherecht,* p. 221, note 3.

[55] Gasparri, *De Matrimonio,* n. 937; Chelodi, *Jus Matrimoniale,* n. 120; Triebs, *Kanonisches Eherecht,* III, 514; Petrovits, *Church Law on Matrimony,* n. 427.

CHAPTER IX

CONVALIDATION

MARRIAGE which is null and void because of grave and unjustly inflicted fear is convalidated in the same manner as any marriage whose invalidity is due to defective consent. Four conditions may be distinguished: the removal of the cause of nullity, knowledge that the contract was null and void, legitimate renewal of consent, and the union of this consent to that of the party who has not suffered compulsion. The meaning and content of these requisites will receive consideration in the articles which follow.

ARTICLE I.— CESSATION OF FEAR

As long as fear continues to exert its influence, marriage cannot be convalidated either by an implicit or explicit renewal of consent. Unless fear is dispelled, the will can no more effectively give a valid consent than when the marriage was first contracted under its influence.[1] The act would merely be a repetition of the first consent vitiated by the defect of fear and be equally unqualified to have juridic effect. Moreover, the law which requires for convalidation the cessation of an impediment, should dispensation be impossible,[2] has an equivalent application in the case of fear and coercion. Consequently, in order to elicit a new and valid act of consent, it is necessary that fear must cease to exercise its influence over the will.[3]

The question arises whether it is required that the actual cause of fear be removed, or whether it is sufficient for the fear itself to cease. An illustration will clarify the distinction. A girl under the influence of a grave fear inspired by the threats of her parents marries a man concerning whose moral character she has grave doubts. After the marriage has been celebrated, the girl discovers her suspicions

[1] Ballerini-Palmieri, *Opus Theologicum Morale,* VI, tr. X, n. 1119.

[2] *Codex Juris Canonici,* c. 1133, § 1.

[3] Sanchez, *De Matrimonii Sacramento,* lib. IV, disp. XVIII, n. 7; D'Annibale, *Summula Theologiae Moralis,* III, n. 484; Gasparri, *De Matrimonio,* n. 1416; Cappello, *De Matrimonio,* n. 846; Vlaming, *Praelectiones Juris Matrimonii,* n. 772.

of the man's uprightness are unfounded and, although the cause of fear, as far as her parents are concerned, continues to exist, she gives a free and true consent to the union. The question is whether with the cause of fear still existing but the fear itself ceasing the marriage is convalidated.

As long as the total cause of fear endures, fear continues to exist even though the external act appears to be performed with complete freedom.[4] But when the cause of fear partially discontinues, it is possible for fear to cease entirely. In the above case, the reason for fearing was twofold: threats made by the parents and the erroneous judgment concerning the man's character. After the latter was rectified, only a partial cause of fear remained, the parents' threats. The fear itself, however, was entirely dispelled and consequently an efficacious renewal of consent became possible.[5] Hence, there seems to be no reason for denying an effective convalidation.

Neither an implicit nor an explicit renewal of consent can convalidate the marriage until fear ceases to exert its influence on the act of the will. Conjugal relations therefore with matrimonial intent and even cohabitation over a considerable length of time have no convalidating effect.[6] The same must be said of an explicit renewal of consent, privately by the use of words[7] or publicly by means of the prescribed ecclesiastical form.

Authors once discussed whether a marriage which had been contracted under the influence of a grave and unjustly inflicted fear was convalidated by an oath added to the act of consent.[8] Basing their arguments on the law of the Decretals,[9] they generally denied that convalidation could be effected in this manner. Any doubt in the matter seems definitely ended by current ecclesiastical legislation. Matrimonial consent extorted by grave fear is declared invalid not only for the protection of the individual but also in the interests of

[4] Sanchez, *De Matrimonii Sacramento,* lib. IV, disp. XVIII, n. 7.

[5] Payen, *De Matrimonio,* II, n. 1695.

[6] Sanchez, *De Matrimonii Sacramento,* lib. IV, disp. XVIII, nn. 1, 13-15; Schmalzgrueber, *Jus Ecclesiasticum Universum,* lib. IV, tit. I, nn. 416, 419.

[7] Cf. St. Alphonsus, *Theologia Moralis,* lib. VI, n. 1117.

[8] Sanchez, *De Matrimonii Sacramento,* lib. IV, disp. XX, nn. 11-12; Schmalzgrueber, *Jus Ecclesiasticum Universum,* lib. IV, tit. I, nn. 411-413; Ballerini-Palmieri, *Opus Theologicum Morale,* VI, tr. X, n. 1117.

[9] C. 2, X, *de eo, qui duxit,* IV, 7.

the public good. But any private oath or agreement loses its binding force when appended to an act tending to the harm of others and injurious to the common good.[10]

Furthermore, the character of an oath is that it is an accessory act and partakes of the nature of the principal act to which it is appended: *accessorium naturam sequi congruit principalis.*[11] If the chief obligation is null and void, so also the oath which is given to strengthen it.[12] One who is coerced to give matrimonial consent can equally be forced to take an oath. The law of invalidity would easily be frustrated and little protection would be afforded the party suffering the fear if a solemn attestation of this nature were to convalidate matrimonial consent.[13]

Marriage which is null and void on account of grave fear can never be convalidated by the forcible exacting of marital rights. *Quum quid una via prohibetur alicui, ad id alia non debet admitti.*[14] This practice would be a complete circumvention of ecclesiastical law and serve to deprive it of its intended effect. Moreover, on the principle that *praesumptio non potest plus operari quam veritas,* a presumed consent to forced conjugal relations cannot have the effect denied to an extorted and expressed consent. Finally, the possibility of convalidation in this manner is excluded for the same reasons which prevent an oath from having this effect.[15] Neither can matrimonial intent be presumed. Usually the coerced party is ignorant that the marital bond is non-existent, in which case he erroneously has this intention and cannot give voluntary consent: *nihil consensui magis obest quam error;* or, granting knowledge of the invalidity, he can have the intent only by giving voluntary consent to the union.[16] What has been said of forced consummation applies equally to forced cohabitation. As long as fear endures and

[10] *Codex Juris Canonici,* c. 1318, § 2.

[11] *Reg.* 42, R. J., in VI.°

[12] Payen, *De Matrimonio,* II, n. 1695; Knecht, *Katholisches Eherecht,* p. 576, note 4.

[13] Wernz-Vidal, *Jus Matrimoniale,* n. 504.

[14] *Reg.* 84, R. J., in VI°.

[15] Sanchez, *De Matrimonii Sacramento,* lib. IV, disp. XVIII, nn. 13-15; Schmalzgrueber, *Jus Ecclesiasticum Universum,* lib. IV, tit. I, n. 416; Reiffenstuel, *Jus Canonicum Universum,* lib. IV, tit. I, n. 334.

[16] Ballerini-Palmieri, *Opus Theologicum Morale,* VI, tr. X, n. 1118.

the will is opposed to the situation, the marriage cannot be convalidated by either of these methods.

Another disputed point in this connection is whether it is possible, in circumstances which are prejudicial to a person's rights or interests, e. g., proximate danger of death or mortal sin, for an invalid marriage to be convalidated without the cessation of fear. Such a case occurs when a man threatens death or grave bodily injury in order to extort marital relations after marriage has been contracted through fear, and the woman fears that she will commit grievous sin by consenting to the act.

Lehmkuhl,[17] favoring the opinion of many older authors whom he cites, maintains that the impediment, even though publicly known, ceases in the case where a woman, who has been compelled to marry and forced to the consummation of the union, sincerely consents. Seeing that the consummation of the marriage cannot be avoided, she prefers to contract marriage rather than offend God and thus completely although reflexly gives consent. This reflex consent is sufficient to convalidate the marriage, otherwise it would be necessary for her either to commit sin or abstain from the use of marriage and she could not choose what seems the lesser of two evils.[18] Sanchez [19] and Schmalzgrueber [20] admit the probability of this opinion, and among modern writers Payen [21] defends it for the same reasons.

According to Chelodi [22] the opinion may now be termed certainly improbable. Consent of this kind receives no recognition in the external forum. To admit it would mean that the marriage *objectively* considered would be at one and the same time valid and invalid according to the difference of forum. Not only is this hypothesis inconsistent, but the Church cannot be supposed either to wish or permit such an anomaly.[23] Besides, admitting that the law of invalidity is for the immediate protection of the individual party, the

[17] *Theologia Moralis,* II, n. 968.

[18] Gasparri, *De Matrimonio,* n. 929; D'Annibale, *Summula Theologiae Moralis,* III, n. 445.

[19] *De Matrimonii Sacramento,* lib. IV, disp. V, n. 3; disp. XVIII, nn. 13, 17.

[20] *Jus Ecclesiasticum Universum,* lib. IV, tit. I, n. 417.

[21] *De Matrimonio,* II, n. 1695.

[22] *Jus Matrimoniale,* p. 130, note 4.

[23] Cappello, *De Matrimonio,* n. 848.

principal reason for its enactment is to be found in the nature of marriage as a public and social institution. The favor of law which marriage enjoys as such cannot be renounced by any private agreements.[24]

Nor is the gravest necessity a reason for admitting the opposite view, because the woman can hold herself passive in the presence of violence. Since fear is no longer enumerated among the impediments, but among the obstacles to the validity of matrimonial consent, the fundamental reason for the opinion favoring convalidation fails. Canon 1136, §3 likewise seems to remove all doubt in the matter. But whatever opinion is adopted, once coercion has been employed, a valid matrimonial consent is not to be presumed.[25] It is apparent that a marriage is certainly not convalidated in the above hypothesis if, in addition to fear, some other impediment is a cause of invalidity.[26]

Article II.—Knowledge of Nullity

The second requisite for convalidation is knowledge on the part of the coerced party that the marriage was null and void from the beginning.[27] *Nil volitum nisi praecognitum.* Hence the coerced party cannot be said to consent voluntarily to the marriage with a new and valid act of the will unless he knows that the marriage is null and void. Any manifestation of matrimonial intentions, whether by conjugal relations or cohabitation, would be nothing else than a continuation and confirmation of the previous invalid and defective consent.[28]

This condition is clearly intimated by the terms of canon 1134: *quod constet ab initio nullum fuisse,* and canons 1133, § 1 and 1135, § 3: *pars impedimenti conscia.* That convalidation is not admitted as possible unless the person has knowledge of the invalidity is ap-

[24] Wernz-Vidal, *Jus Matrimoniale,* n. 504.

[25] Gasparri, *De Matrimonio,* n. 929.

[26] Wernz-Vidal, *Jus Matrimoniale,* p. 593, note 42.

[27] Cappello, *De Matrimonio,* n. 846; Vlaming, *Praelectiones Juris Matrimonii,* n. 772.

[28] Sanchez, *De Matrimonii Sacramento,* lib. II, disp. XXXIV, n. 2, lib. IV, disp. XVIII, n. 5; Reiffenstuel, lib. IV, Append., n. 590; St. Alphonsus, *Theologia Moralis,* lib. VI, n. 1114; Gasparri, *De Matrimonio,* n. 1397; D'Annibale, *Summula Theologiae Moralis,* III, n. 483.

parent from decisions in favor of nullity given by the Roman Rota in which this condition existed.[29] In a trial for invalidity of a marriage on grounds of violence and fear, possibility of subsequent convalidation of the marriage is excluded when evidence shows that the party was ignorant of an ecclesiastical law decreeing nullity. But if it is evident that the party knew or became aware of the invalidity and nevertheless continued cohabitation and omitted to make use of his right to accuse the marriage, a strong presumption exists in favor of convalidation.

Article III.—Renewal of Consent

Inasmuch as matrimonial consent cannot be supplied by the law [30] and since a dispensation from the defect is out of the question, the only means for making valid a compulsory marriage is for the party to give the consent which is lacking. This act of consent is absolutely required for revalidation. Since a grave doubt exists whether the consent first given suffices naturally to constitute the contract,[31] a *sanatio in radice* can never be granted.[32]

As in the case of all marriages null and void from the beginning, the act of consent to be effective must be a new act of the will.[33] According to natural law, any actual renewal of consent by the coerced party would suffice *ex natura rei* to convalidate the contract. Positive ecclesiastical law, however, has made various regulations designed to safeguard the parties and to establish the validity in the external forum.[34] These directions, which concern the method of manifesting the new act of consent, must be conformed to if a marriage, once null and void because of fear, is to be recognized as convalidated in the eyes of the Church.[35] After the cessation of fear

[29] Cf. S. R. R., *Causa Osnabrugen.*, 11 Jan. 1912—*AAS*, IV, (1912), 186; S. R. R., *Nullit. Matrim.*, 21 Dec. 1912—*Decisiones*, IV (1912), dec. XXXXI, n. 7; S. R. R., *Causa Vicariat. Apost. Novae Pomeran.*, 30 Apr. 1913—*AAS*, V (1913), 472; S. R. R., *Causa Southwarcen.*, 29 Jul. 1926—*AAS*, XVIII (1926), 505.

[30] *Codex Juris Canonici*, c. 1081, § 1.

[31] Payen, *De Matrimonio*, II, n. 1696.

[32] *Codex Juris Canonici*, c. 1140, § 1.

[33] *Codex Juris Canonici*, c. 1134.

[34] *Codex Juris Canonici*, c. 1136.

[35] Vlaming, *Praelectiones Juris Matrimonii*, n. 773; Cappello, *De Matrimonio*, n. 847.

and supposing the knowledge of nullity, renewal of consent according to this law suffices, because the marriage is not invalid from an incapacity of the person in the strict sense but from a defect of consent.[36]

It is possible in a rare case for the defect of consent to be merely internal, although the cause of fear is always external. The marriage is then convalidated when the party whose consent was wanting gives interior consent.[37] The want of merely internal consent is supplied by the person who has suffered the fear by a positive internal act of the will. No external manifestation of the renewal is necessary in this case.[38] From what will be stated in the following article, it will be clear that the other party must not necessarily be informed of the invalidity in this case. Performance of the ordinary duties of conjugal life with matrimonial intent will be a sufficient indication of a new and valid act of consent.

Considering the nature of coercion and fear, however, and the circumstances in which a compulsory marriage is for the most part contracted, the defect in question is not merely internal but also external in the sense that it manifests itself exteriorly in the act of giving consent. For this reason it is necessary to externalize the renewal of consent in some manner. The method of doing this depends upon whether the fact of compulsion and fear is public or occult, according as it can or can not be juridically proven by two trustworthy witnesses in the external forum.[39]

In the case where the defect of consent is occult, the renewal of consent must be expressed externally, but any manifestation, even though privately and secretly made, will suffice.[40] This means that the marriage may be convalidated without making use of the form

[36] Payen, *De Matrimonio,* II, n. 1696.

[37] *Codex Juris Canonici,* c. 1136, § 2.

[38] Sanchez, *De Matrimonii Sacramento,* lib. II, disp. XXXII, n. 11; D'Annibale, *Summula Theologiae Moralis,* III, n. 484, note 23; Gasparri, *De Matrimonio,* n. 1417. Sanchez *(loc. cit.)* seems to favor some external manifestation in addition to supplying the wanting internal consent. This opinion need no longer be held in view of the terms of the Code.

[39] *Codex Juris Canonici,* c. 1037.

[40] *Codex Juris Canonici,* c. 1136, § 3. Cf. S. C. S. Off., *Instr. ad Vic. Ap. Ocean.,* 6 Apr. 1843—*Fontes,* n. 894; Sanchez, *De Matrimonii Sacramento,* lib. II, disp. XXXVII, n. 4.

prescribed by law, ordinary or extraordinary,[41] and without others having knowledge of it. Hence, as long as the party truly consents with a new act of the will to the marriage, the new consent may be given expressly, by words or equivalent signs or tacitly, by conjugal acts voluntarily performed with matrimonial intent, by free and continued cohabitation as man and wife, or by the exhibition of the ordinary signs of marital association.[42]

When the fact is publicly known, however, that the marriage has been contracted because of grave coercion and fear, the new act of consent cannot be validly given and the marriage cannot be convalidated except by resorting to the prescribed ecclesiastical form.[43] Marriage of its very nature is a public and social transaction. If its nullity is a matter of public knowledge, a public process of convalidation is required. In order that the marriage, no less than its first celebration, may be possible of proof in the external forum, whether for the avoidance of scandal, the protection of the parties and offspring, or the sanctity of the sacrament, a public renewal of consent is absolutely necessary. This end can only be obtained by the use of the proper ecclesiastical form of marriage, ordinary or extraordinary as circumstances demand.[44] Until consent has been

[41] *Codex Juris Canonici,* cc. 1094, 1098.

[42] Sanchez, *De Matrimonii Sacramento,* lib. II, disp. XXXVII, n. 14; lib. IV, disp. XVIII, nn. 2-4, 12; Schmalzgrueber, *Jus Ecclesiasticum Universum,* lib. IV, tit. I, nn. 415, 419; Feije, *De Impedimentis et Dispensationibus Matrimonialibus,* n. 143; Gasparri, *De Matrimonio,* 1418; Wernz-Vidal, *Jus Matrimoniale,* n. 504; Cappello, *De Matrimonio,* n. 847; Payen, *De Matrimonio,* II, n. 1696; cf. S. R. R., *Causa Vicariat. Apost. Novae Pomeran.,* 30 Apr. 1913—*AAS,* V (1913), 467.

[43] *Codex Juris Canonici,* c. 1136, § 3.

[44] Benedict XIV, *Quaestiones Canonicae,* 317; *Institutiones Ecclesiasticae,* 87, n. 62; Sanchez, *De Matrimonii Sacramento,* lib. II, disp. XXXVII, n. 11; D'Annibale, *Summula Theologiae Moralis,* n. 483; Gasparri, *De Matrimonio,* n. 1418; Wernz-Vidal, *Jus Matrimoniale,* nn. 504, 654; Vlaming, *Praelectiones Juris Matrimonii,* n. 773; Farrugia, *De Matrimonio,* n. 344; cf. S. R. R., *Causa Parisien.,* 21 Maii, 1915—*Decisiones,* VII (1915), dec. XXII, n. 18; S. R. R., *Nullit. Matrim.,* 19 Jun. 1915—*Decisiones,* VII (1915), dec. XXIII, n. 5; S. R. R., *Nullit. Matrim.,* 9 Aug. 1915—*Decisiones,* VII (1915), dec. XXXV, n. 9; S. R. R., *Causa Calatanisiaden.,* 28 Jul. 1916—*Decisiones,* VIII (1916), dec. XXI, n. 14; S. R. R., *Causa Parisien.,* 11 Dec. 1916—*Decisiones,* VIII (1916), dec. XXXII, n. 13; S. R. R., *Causa Parisien.,* 12 Jun. 1919—*Decisiones,* XI (1919), dec. XI, n. 4; S. R. R., *Nullit. Matrim.,* 9 Jan. 1922—*Decisiones,* XIV (1922), dec. I, n. 12.

manifested in this public fashion, even though the fact of fear has been dispelled in some secret and private way and the union is naturally valid, the marriage remains juridically null and void and can be so declared at any moment by an ecclesiastical judge.[45]

For this reason, both the Congregation of the Council[46] in early days and the Roman Rota[47] in recent times have not hesitated to declare null and void marriages for failure to comply with this condition. Notwithstanding apparent private ratification in the form of voluntary cohabitation and conjugal life extending over a score of years, convalidation was not effected according to the legitimate form and the marriage remained juridically invalid.

When the only witnesses to a compulsory marriage have died and public knowledge of the circumstances in which consent was given may be said to have ceased, thus leaving the fact of defective consent occult, some authors[48] are of the opinion that the law of public renewal of consent may be dispensed with and the marriage convalidated in any private and secret fashion. Their reason is that, since it has become impossible juridically to prove defective consent, public convalidation would be of no practical advantage and therefore the Church does not urge it. Exception may be taken to this proposal because, even with eye-witnesses to the fact of coercion and fear removed by death, it is difficult to determine exactly when juridical proof of defective consent becomes impossible in the ex-

[45] Cappello, *De Matrimonio*, n. 847.

[46] S. C. C., *Causa Hispalen.*, 20 Jun. 1609—*Fontes*, n. 2378; S. C. C., *Causa Constantinopolitana*, 16 Dec. 1634—*Fontes*, n. 2567; S. C. C., *Causa Panormitana*, 30 Sept. 1719—*Thesaurus Resolut.* S. C. C., I, 229-230; *Fontes*, n. 3192. Reference may be made to a condition which was possible before the *Ne Temere* Decree went into force on April 19, 1908. In those dioceses and places where the Decree *Tametsi* of the Council of Trent had not been promulgated in the manner prescribed, a marriage null and void because of moral compulsion and fear could be convalidated without resorting to the ecclesiastical form. Even though coercion was a matter of public knowledge, the new act of consent could be manifested in private, expressly or tacitly, by cohabitation or association as husband and wife. Cf. Gasparri, *De Matrimonio*, n. 1418; Wernz, *Jus Matrimoniale*, n. 648; Smith, *Marriage Process*, n. 171.

[47] S. R. R., *Causa Parisien.*, 26 Feb. 1910—*AAS*, II (1910), 348-353; S. R. R., *Causa Veszprimien.*, 2 Jun. 1911—*AAS*, IV, (1912), 108-118; S. R. R., *Causa Tarvisin.*, 11 Mar. 1912—*AAS*, IV (1912), 503-519.

[48] Cappello, *De Matrimonio*, n. 848; Farrugia, *De Matrimonio*, n. 344.

ternal forum as long as the parties to the forced marriage survive.[49] It seems better, therefore, in practice at least, to adhere to the letter of the law and use the prescribed juridical form even in so rare a situation.

ARTICLE IV.—PERSEVERANCE OF OTHER'S CONSENT

The final condition required for effective convalidation of a forced marriage is the union of the new act of consent, elicited as described above, with the consent of the party who has not been influenced by fear. This means that the consent of the party who has freely contracted the marriage must still persevere.[50] Union of the two consents is necessary in order to have that mutual consent which is the essential element of the matrimonial contract. The ordinary case of compulsory marriage supposes that the consent of only one party has been defective on account of coercion. Consequently, the new act of consent must be elicited by that party alone. The other need not renew his consent for the purpose of mutuality, since that which he gave in the first celebration of the marriage is sufficient, provided it still perseveres.[51]

Previous to the Code it was commonly held that the party who had contracted the marriage with full liberty was not under any obligation to renew the consent once freely and validly given.[52]

[49] Cf., e.g., S. R. R., *Nullit. Matrim.*, 16 Aug. 1922—*Decisiones,* XIV (1922), dec. XXXII, nn. 6-7. Of three possible witnesses who alone were in a position to give trustworthy evidence to the circumstances of force and coercion, two were dead when the marriage was attacked and the one surviving was excused from testifying for grave reasons. One of the dead persons, however, the mother of the *actrix,* had written letters, *tempore non suspecto,* which described events as they had actually occurred previous to the marriage. The judges admitted the documents into the evidence as being her own testimony: "dici quodammodo potest, ipsam matrem in hac causa testari." Although the nullity of the marriage was not established, due in no small measure to the contradictory evidence resulting from the depositions of witnesses and the testimony offered by the letters, the case illustrates how practically impossible it is to determine when facts of compulsion and fear cease to be public knowledge.

[50] Payen, *De Matrimonio,* II, n. 1694.

[51] *Codex Juris Canonici,* c. 1136, § 1.

[52] Sanchez, *De Matrimonii Sacramento,* lib. II, disp. XXXII, n. 9; lib. IV, disp. XV, n. 2; Schmalzgrueber, *Jus Ecclesiasticum Universum,* lib. IV, tit. I, n. 272; St. Alphonsus, *Theologia Moralis,* lib. VI, n. 1114; D'Annibale, *Sum-*

This opinion now apparently receives the force of law by reason of its canonical sanction.[53] The law likewise ends the former controversy whether the other party, supposing him to be ignorant that coercive measures were employed to effect the marriage, had to be informed of the nullity of the contract.[54] Since the new act of consent is to be elicited only by the party who contracted the marriage under the influence of fear, it is not necessary to inform him of the nullity for the purpose of having him repeat his previous act of consent.[55] The marital consent once given is considered to exert its original efficacy, provided it still perseveres when the other party renews consent.

This continuance of the original matrimonial consent of the party who has not contracted through fear is absolutely necessary, otherwise the marriage is not convalidated and remains in its former status of nullity.[56] How is its perseverance to be ascertained? Even though marriage is invalidly contracted, matrimonial consent once given is presumed to continue until its revocation be proved.[57] If and as long as consent has not positively been revoked or retracted by a contrary act of the will, it is construed as persevering.[58]

A hypothetical, interpretative, or habitual attitude of mind receives no consideration. The mere presumption, or even moral certitude, that the other party *would* recall his consent or withdraw from the marital pact, if he knew of the nullity, cannot in the least be interpreted as retraction by a positive contrary act. It is not a

mula Theologiae Moralis, III, n. 483; Santi, *Praelectiones Juris Canonici,* IV, Appendix I, n. 69; Feije, *De Impedimentis et Dispensationibus Matrimonialibus,* n. 760; Gasparri, *De Matrimonio,* n. 1415; Wernz, *Jus Matrimoniale,* n. 648.

[53] Cappello, *De Matrimonio,* n. 846; Vlaming, *Praelectiones Juris Matrimonii,* n. 772; Blat, *Commentarium,* III, n. 549; Wernz-Vidal, *Jus Matrimoniale,* n. 654; Augustine, *Commentary,* V, 382.

[54] Sanchez, *De Matrimonii Sacramento,* lib. II, disp. XXXV, nn. 1-2; St. Alphonsus, *Theologia Moralis,* lib. VI, n. 1115; Benedict XIV, *Institutiones Ecclesiasticae,* 87, n. 69; Ballerini-Palmieri, *Opus Theologicum Morale,* VI, tr. X, nn. 1327-1331; Wernz, *Jus Matrimoniale,* n. 648.

[55] Farrugia, *De Matrimonio,* n. 343; Chelodi, *Jus Matrimoniale,* n. 165; Cappello, *De Matrimonio,* n. 846; Wernz-Vidal, *Jus Matrimoniale,* n. 654.

[56] St. Thomas, *Summa Theologica,* Suppl., q. 47, a. 4, ad 2.

[57] *Codex Juris Canonici,* c. 1093.

[58] Schmalzgrueber, *Jus Ecclesiasticum Universum,* lib. IV, tit. I, n. 271; Reiffenstuel, *Jus Canonicum Universum,* lib. IV, Appendix, n. 591.

new act of the will positively recalling the first act of consent and accordingly cannot destroy the consent already given.[59] It must also be noted that knowledge or belief on the part of the party who has not suffered fear that the marriage will be null and void does not necessarily exclude matrimonial consent.[60] The presumption of the law interprets the intention in favor of validity. Granting, therefore, the continuance of consent, as soon as the new act of consent is elicited by the coerced party, it is morally united to the original consent of the other. From that moment a valid matrimonial contract exists and the originally invalid union is effectively convalidated. Moral simultaneity suffices, because the nature of the contract does not require physical co-existence of matter and form. A moral union of wills, in which the new consent of one party accedes to the positively unrevoked and virtually persevering consent of the other, permits a valid act of consent, even though a considerable period of time should intervene.[61]

Where the other party to the marriage has been unjustly the cause of coercion and fear, his obligation in regard to convalidation has been variously placed.[62] If he has not as yet positively retracted his consent, he seems obliged to the contract, should the other party demand its convalidation, at least if he can in no other way repair the injury he has caused. If *de facto* he has retracted his consent, e. g., by actual desertion, before the injured party informally convalidates the marriage by a new and legitimate act of consent or, where fear is a public fact, if he refuses renewal according to the prescribed form, the marriage remains invalid. A second marriage contracted with a third person would be valid, provided no other canonical impediments exist.[63]

[59] Feije, *De Impedimentis et Dispensationibus Matrimonialibus,* n. 760; Cappello, *De Matrimonio,* n. 845; Wernz-Vidal, *Jus Matrimoniale,* n. 866; p. 807, note 34; Augustine, *Commentary,* V, 263-264.

[60] Codex Juris Canonici, c. 1085.

[61] St. Alphonsus, *Theologia Moralis,* lib. VI, n. 1114; Gasparri, *De Matrimonio,* n. 1415; Wernz-Vidal, *Jus Matrimoniale,* n. 654; Vlaming, *Praelectiones Juris Matrimonii,* n. 772.

[62] Sanchez, *De Matrimonii Sacramento,* lib. IV, disp. XV, n. 5; Schmalzgrueber, *Jus Ecclesiasticum Universum,* lib. IV, tit. I, nn. 422-425.

[63] St. Alphonsus, *Theologia Moralis,* lib. VI, n. 1057; Lehmkuhl, *Theologia Moralis,* II, n. 967; Wernz-Vidal, *Jus Matrimoniale,* n. 504.

CHAPTER X

PROCEDURE FOR DECLARATION OF NULLITY

BEFORE discussing the matter of procedure for a declaration of nullity on grounds of violence and fear, it is only proper to emphasize the insistence of the Code in desiring that a trial for nullity be avoided whenever possible. This practice is preferable as being more conducive to the avoidance of scandal, the salvation of the parties, and the interests of the offspring.[1] Accordingly, should the vitiated consent which renders the marriage null and void be not irremediable in a particular case, the judge should first *ex officio,* personally or through another, attempt to effect a reconciliation of the parties and induce them to convalidate their marriage in accordance with the principles outlined in the preceding chapter.[2] Very frequently, however, the nature of a forced marriage precludes any negotiations of this kind, owing to the injustice already involved and the fact that any *coercive* measures may further add to the injury. If the coerced party, after having obtained his freedom, has no inclination towards convalidation, or absolutely refuses it, he cannot be compelled,[3] not even on the pretext of protecting a community from scandal.[4] He remains free to seek a declaration of nullity by a lawful introduction of the case before an ecclesiastical tribunal.

[1] Genicot, *Institutiones Theologiae Moralis,* II, n. 534.

[2] *Codex Juris Canonici,* c. 1965.

[3] Knecht, *Katholisches Eherecht,* p. 580.

[4] Cf. e.g., S. R. R., *Causa Vicariat. Apost. Nyanzae Septentr.*, 10 Maii, 1918—*Decisiones,* X (1918), dec. V, 36-40; *Sec. Inst.*, 13 Maii, 1919—*Decisiones,* XI 1919, dec. XI, 87-93. In this case evidence revealed that the Vicar Apostolic, fearing scandal would be caused among the faithful if the parties were to be separated after a long cohabitation, ordered them to renew their matrimonial consent. When the woman refused to obey, she was deprived of Holy Communion which she was in the habit of receiving daily. After suffering this punishment for a time, the woman finally agreed to renew her consent. The Roman Rota vigorously disapproved of the Vicar's coercive action: "haec autem coactio injusta fuit . . . non poterat cogi ad matrimonium ineundum sub praetextu, quod scandalum ex ipsorum separatione exortum fuisset inter fideles." Sentences in favor of nullity were granted in both instances.

The trial of a cause in which the validity of a marriage is attacked on grounds of coercion and constraint will follow the ordinary rules of procedure as set forth in the Code for all cases of nullity.[5] Once it is determined that a case is acceptable, the questions of competence, constitution of the tribunal, and the method of procedure regarding proofs, publication of the process, conclusion in the cause, and appeals will be determined by these regulations. Certain features of such a trial, however, require close attention. These concern the right of accusing the marriage on grounds of violence and fear, elements singular to the trial itself, and the declaratory sentence.

Article I.—The Right of Accusation

Ecclesiastical law declares that a collegiate tribunal cannot try or decide any matrimonial case unless a regular accusation has preceded.[6] This takes place when one of the parties attacks the validity of the marriage against the other party, who either asserts it is valid or is unwilling to have it attacked.[7] Under the old discipline, the right of accusation was restricted to the party who had been the victim of duress and coercion.[8] Both parties had the right only where they had been equally forced into the marriage.[9]

The present legislation, however, makes an innovation and ordains that the parties are capable of attacking a marriage in all cases of nullity, provided they were not the cause of the impedi-

[5] *Codex Juris Canonici,* cc. 1960-1989. In this connection it will be found helpful to consult the *Regulae pro usu S. Romanae Rotae (AAS,* II, (1910), 783-850). The study of various types of *vis et metus* cases tried before that Tribunal since its restoration and published from year to year as the *S. Romanae Rotae Decisiones seu Sententiae* will likewise be found invaluable.

[6] *Codex Juris Canonici,* c. 1970.

[7] Wernz-Vidal, *Jus Matrimoniale,* n. 698; Lanier, *Procedure Matrimoniale,* p. 19.

[8] Cc. 21, 28, X, *de spons. et matr.,* IV, 1; c. 4, X, *qui matr. accus.,* IV, 18. S. C. S. Inquis., *Instructio ad Episc. Orient.,* 20 Jun. 1883, n. 35—*ASS,* XVIII (1885), 356; S. C. de Prop. Fid., *Instructio pro Foed. Stat. Amer. Ordin.,* a. 1883, § 36—*ASS,* XVIII (1885), 379; *Instructio Austriaca,* § 116—*Collection Lacensis,* V, 1301; S. C. C., *Causa Gnesen. et Posnanien.,* 23 Jul. 1892, 1 Sept. 1894—*ASS* (1895), 524; S. C. C., *Causa Vasten.,* 23 Jun. 1895—*ASS* (1896), 400. Cf. Gasparri, *De Matrimonio,* n. 1479; Wernz, *Jus Matrimoniale,* n. 269; Schmalzgrueber, *Jus Ecclesiasticum Universum,* lib. IV, tit. I, n. 429; Feije, *De Impedimentis et Dispensationibus Matrimonialibus,* n. 143.

[9] Kutschker, *Eherecht,* IV, 214; Smith, *Marriage Process,* n. 164.

ment.[10] Because fear was no longer enumerated among matrimonial impediments in the strict sense, but listed as a substantial defect of consent, the question was raised as to whether a party who had been the cause of compulsion was deprived of the right of accusation in view of the terms of the law: *nisi ipsi fuerint causa impedimenti.* When the doubt was proposed to the Pontifical Commission, a decision was handed down that the law applied to impediments in both the strict and wide sense of the term.[11]

Consequently, not only the party who has suffered the fear but also the one who has freely consented and was not responsible for the constraint enjoys the right of attacking the marriage. This new regulation is of great practical value. Should a girl, for instance, who has been compelled to marry by her parents, afterwards desert her husband, the cause can be introduced by the latter in the event that she fails to accuse the marriage out of malice or ignorance.[12] But if he has been the author of the coercion, he does not enjoy this right.

It appears from the nature of the law, however, that the privation is suffered only when the party is culpably guilty of using coercive measures and not when he has acted without malicious intent or in good faith.[13] The purpose of the law apparently is to restrict the cause to malicious or at least guilty action,[14] on the principle that no one should benefit from a fraudulent act committed by himself,[15] it seeks to prevent all possibility of fraud and collusion. At any rate, even though one who has been the cause of

[10] *Codex Juris Canonici,* c. 1971, § 1, n. 1.

[11] *Resp. Pont. Comm.,* 12 Mar. 1929 (*AAS,* XXI (1929), 171): "Utrum vox impedimenti canonis 1971, § 1, n. 1 intelligenda sit tantum de impedimentis proprie dictis (cann. 1067-1080), an etiam de impedimentis improprie dictis matrimonii (cann. 1081-1103). R. Negative ad primam parten; affirmative ad secundam."

[12] Cf. S. C. C., *Causa Burdigalen.,* 7 Apr. 1900—*AAS,* XXXII (1900), 727; S. C. C., *Causa Burdigalen.,* 20 Dec. 1902—*ASS,* XXXV (1903), 323; S. R. R., *Causa Lugdunen.,* 28 Jun. 1912—*Decisiones,* IV (1912), dec. XXVI, n. 1; S. R. R., *Causa Massilien.,* 10 Aug. 1912—*Decisiones,* IV (1912), dec. XXXV, n. 1; S. R. R., *Causa Ambianen.,* 3 Jan. 1917—*Decisiones,* IX (1917), dec. 1, n. 1; S. R. R., *Causa Lugdunen.,* 5 Jun. 1917—*Decisiones,* IX (1917), dec. XIV, n. 1; S. R. R., *Causa Camenecen.,* 17 Maii, 1922—*Decisiones,* XIV (1922), dec. XVI, n. 1.

[13] Triebs, *Kanonisches Eherecht,* III, 458.

[14] Augustine, *Commentary,* V, 418.

[15] C. 15, X, *de rescriptis,* 1, 3: "fraus sua nemini patrocinari debet."

fear without malicious intent is embraced by the law and impeded from introducing the cause, there appears no reason why a dispensation could not be granted where circumstances warrant it.[16]

In addition to the parties, the promotor of justice or prosecuting attorney of the ecclesiastical court may attack a marriage because of an impediment which by nature is public.[16a] Whether this right extends to cases of violence and fear is not certain. Most authors offer no direct opinion in the matter. Payen [17] and Triebs [18] expressly deny the cumulative capacity of the promoter for the reason that fear is not an impediment *natura sua* public.

Canon 1037 terms an impediment public when it can be proved in the external forum; otherwise it is occult. But an impediment can be public either of its very nature, in that it is based on a fact which of itself is public, as consanguinity, affinity, or *ligamen;* or on account of circumstances, as when the fact of itself is occult but has become of public knowledge, or at least is known in such a way that its complete revelation is probable and juridical proof in the external forum possible.[19] Since the law requires that the impediment be *natura sua* public, fear cannot be understood as comprehended within its scope,[20] even granting that impediments in the wide sense are included in canon 1971, §1, n. 2.[21] Furthermore, the very nature of the matter allows at least perfect and certain knowledge of the existence of fear to be had only by the parties themselves.[22]

The opinion, however, which favors giving the promoter of justice the right of accusation cumulatively with the parties to the forced marriage is not without reasonable foundation. It is the office and duty of the promoter, as a public person, to see that the interests of justice are served, that the common good is protected,

[16] Triebs, *Kanonisches Eherecht,* III, 459; cf. Roberti, "De Jure Accusandi Matrimonium"—*Apollinaris,* III (1930), 57-58.

[16a] *Codex Juris Canonici,* c. 1971, § 1, n. 2.

[17] *De Matrimonio,* II, n. 1691.

[18] *Kanonisches Eherecht,* III, 515.

[19] Cappello, *De Matrimonio,* n. 200; De Smet, *Betrothment and Marriage,* n. 465.

[20] Cf. De Smet, *Betrothment and Marriage,* II, p. 3, note 6.

[21] Noval, *Commentarium,* n. 850.

[22] Wernz-Vidal, *Jus Matrimoniale,* n. 147; Vlaming, *Praelectiones Juris Matrimonii,* n. 877.

and that the faithful in the diocese are safeguarded as far as possible from whatever is or will become a source of scandal.[23] Moreover, an impediment may be termed *natura sua* public when it is possible of proof in the external forum and public knowledge concerning it is either already certain, or the fact will regularly, in the ordinary course of events, be divulged with certainty and scandal. While fear of its nature may be occult, because of accidental circumstances it may and easily does become public. This happens when the fact of coercion can be proved juridically and is of prejudicial interest to the public ecclesiastical good due to being divulged with scandal actually given or necessarily resulting from knowledge of it.[24] Interpreting the law in accordance with these notions, the very nature of the situation requires that the promoter of justice enjoy the right of accusation.

An evaluation of these opinions shows the first as being in complete accord with the letter of the law and consequently it may seem preferable until some authoritative decision is made in the matter. Nevertheless, the second opinion appears to be more in harmony with the spirit and sense of the law and therefore may be accepted as admissible in practice. Unless the promoter of justice have the right of accusation, a marriage null and void because of an impediment or defect *natura sua* occult but *de facto* public might never be accused or even denounced. Since the validity or invalidity of marriage is always a matter of prime importance to the public good, particularly when the fact of nullity becomes commonly known, it can readily occur that welfare of the faithful and the ends of justice can be served in no other way than by the action of the person intended for that purpose, the promoter of justice.[25]

All others, even blood relations, enjoy only the right of informing the Ordinary or the promoter of justice concerning the invalidity of marriage due to force and fear.[26] It will then be his duty, if he judges it opportune and advisable, either to seek the convalidation of the

[23] Blat, *Commentarium,* IV, n. 526.

[24] Noval, *Commentarium,* n. 850.

[25] Cf. Roberti, "De Jure Accusandi Matrimonium"—*Apollinaris,* III (1930), 58, 250.

[26] *Codex Juris Canonici,* c. 1971, § 2.

union or obtain a declaration of nullity.[27] *The reliqui omnes* of the canon refers in the first place to relatives of the party. They are presumed to have better knowledge than others of the circumstances pointing to coercion.[28] Besides these every Catholic is permitted to denounce such a marriage. The former law deprived of the right of denunciation those who had acted from dishonest and fraudulent motives.[29] But it is now certain from an authentic interpretation of the Pontifical Commission that no one is excluded from this privilege, not even the party who has maliciously been the cause of fear and compulsion.[30]

How long the right of accusation endures is not precisely possible of determination. It has been observed that a marriage contracted under the influence of grave fear is not only invalid from the beginning, but remains so as long as the fear perdures to prevent convalidation in accordance with the terms of the law or the party, due to ignorance of his rights or of the nullity of the contract, has omitted to seek a declaration of invalidity.[31] On the other hand, a presumption exists in favor of convalidation and loss of right to accuse the marriage if a party, upon the cessation of fear, the acquisition of liberty, and knowledge of the nullity, voluntarily continues the conjugal life and omits the introduction of the cause.[32] This supposes,

[27] Noval, *Commentarium*, n. 850; Cappello, *De Matrimonio*, n. 878; Farrugia, *De Matrimonio*, n. 367.

[28] C. 2, C. XXXV, q. 6; c. 3, X, *qui matrim. accus.*, IV, 18.

[29] C. 6. X, *qui matrim. accus.*, IV, 18.

[30] *Resp. Pont. Comm.*, 17 Feb. 1930 (*AAS*, XXII (1930), 196): "An conjuges qui, juxta canonem 1971, § 1, n. 1 et interpretationem diei 12 Mar. 1929, habiles non sunt ad accusandum matrimonium, vi ejusdem canonis § 2 jus saltem habeant nullitatem matrimonii Ordinario vel promotori justitiae denuntiandi?—R. Affirmative." Cf. Roberti, "De Jure Denuntiandi Nullitatem Matrimonii"—*Apollinaris*, III (1930), 248-250.

[31] Sanchez, *De Matrimonii Sacramento*, lib. IV, disp. XVIII, nn. 7, 15; Wernz, *Jus Matrimoniale*, n. 269; cf. S. C. C., 14 Maii, 1746—Richter, *Canones et Decreta Concilii Tridentini*, p. 242, n. 79; S. C. C., *Nullit. Matrim.*, 10 Jun. 1865—*ASS*, II (1866), 6; S. C. C., *Causa Veneten.*, 4 Maii, 1889—*ASS*, XXII (1890), 97; S. R. R., *Causa Veszprimien.*, 2 Jun. 1911—*AAS*, IV (1912), 115.

[32] C. 21, X, *de spons. et matr.*, IV, 1; c. 4, X, *qui matrim. accus.*, IV, 18; S. C. C. Inquis., *Instructio ad Episc. Orient.*, 20 Jun. 1883, n. 35—*ASS*, XVIII (1885), 356-357; S. C. de Prop. Fid., *Instructio pro Foed. Stat. Amer. Ordin.*, a. 1883, § 36—*ASS*, XVIII (1885), 379.

of course, that the fact of coercion was not of public knowledge and consent had not to be formally renewed.

The period of a year and a half mentioned in the Decretals [33] formed the basis for many strict opinions among the older canonists.[34] This length of time, however, cannot be adopted as a definite norm, since it applies to the narration of a fact and the presumption established in a particular case, rather than an absolute and general disposition of law.[35] Moreover, inasmuch as prescription has no place where there is question of the validity of marriage,[36] the right of accusation cannot be lost by the mere passage of time.[37] Hence there seems no reason for any longer insisting upon the former severe opinions of canonists.[38]

Accordingly, since the Code maintains silence as to when conjugal cohabitation is presumed *per se* to indicate convalidation, the length of time will depend upon circumstances in each particular case. The determination as to whether the right of accusation has been lost is left to the prudent discretion of the judge.[39] Certainly, in the internal forum a determined length of time is not required. The marriage is convalidated the moment that consent is legitimately renewed. In the external forum a continuation of cohabitation, without conjugal relations, is not presumed done with matrimonial intent unless extending over a considerable period of time and even a long cohabitation is of no value in the internal forum if there is really wanting the intention of convalidation.[40] Hence, even after many years of apparent conjugal life the parties may be admitted to

[33] C. 21, X, *de spons. et matr.*, IV, 1.

[34] Cf. e.g., *Instructio Austriaca*, §§ 116, 120, 136—*Collectio Lacensis*, V, 1301-1303; Smith, *Marriage Process*, nn. 168-170.

[35] Schmalzgrueber, *Jus Ecclesiasticum Universum*, lib. IV, tit. I, n. 421; Wernz-Vidal, *Jus Matrimoniale*, p. 596, note 52.

[36] C. 7, X, *de sent. et re judic.*, II, 27; *Codex Juris Canonici*, cc. 1701, 1902.

[37] Vlaming, *Praelectiones Juris Matrimonii*, n. 798; Farrugia, *De Matrimonio*, n. 367; Wernz-Vidal, *Jus Matrimoniale*, n. 698.

[38] Wernz-Vidal, *Jus Matrimoniale*, p. 835, note 40.

[39] Schmalzgrueber, *Jus Ecclesiasticum Universum*, lib. IV, tit. I, n. 339; Smith, *Marriage Process*, n. 169; Knecht, *Katholisches Eherecht*, p. 582.

[40] Sanchez, *De Matrimonii Sacramento*, lib. IV, disp. XVIII, n. 6; Schmalzgrueber, *Jus Ecclesiasticum Universum*, lib. IV, tit. I, n. 421; Reiffenstuel, *Jus Canonicum Universum*, lib. IV, tit. I, n. 339.

accuse the marriage.[41] An extorted renewal of consent, or even that made voluntarily but not according to the prescriptions of canon 1136, even though cohabitation extends over a lengthy period, does not deprive one of the right to accuse the marriage. The same must be said if the party has been living an immoral life, e. g., in concubinage, or has contracted another marriage with a civil or non-Catholic ceremony.[42]

Article II.—Remarks on the Process

The burden of proving that a marriage was contracted under the influence of grave fear rests with the one making that assertion.[43] According to canon 1086, §1, the internal consent of the will is always presumed to correspond to the words or signs used in the celebration of marriage. Besides, fear proceeds from an injurious fact and therefore cannot be presumed. Finally, the one who alleges fear has against himself the presumption of the law that the marriage is valid. Consequently, there is incumbent upon him the burden of more conclusive and stronger proof to the contrary.[44] This proof must give clear evidence that neither before nor at the time of the ceremony the coerced party was willing to marry; moreover, that only under the influence of a grave and unjustly inflicted fear induced by an unavoidable evil he gave his consent; lastly, that after the celebration he did not manifest consent according to the prescriptions of the law but, on the contrary, as soon as he obtained his liberty, strove for a dissociation of the relationship and made use of his right of accusation.[45]

[41] Cf. S. R. R., *Nullit. Matrim.*, 9 Aug. 1915—*Decisiones,* VII (1915), dec. XXXV, n. 14; S. R. R., *Nullit. Matrim.*, 19 Feb. 1916—*Decisiones,* VIII (1916), dec. III, n. 18; S. R. R., *Causa Parisien.*, 11 Dec. 1916—*Decisiones,* VIII (1916), dec. XXXII, n. 14; S. R. R., *Nullit. Matrim.*, 2 Apr. 1917—*Decisiones,* IX (1917), dec. VII, n. 8; S. R. R., *Causa Parisien.*, 26 Feb. 1910—*Decisiones,* II (1910), dec. VIII, n. 10.

[42] Knecht, *Katholisches Eherecht,* p. 580. Cf. S. C. C., *Causa Massilien.*, 23 Jul. 1892—*ASS,* XXV (1893), 194; *Causa Gnesen. et Posnanien.*, 23 Jul. 1892, 1 Sept. 1894—*ASS,* XXVII (1895), 525.

[43] *Codex Juris Canonici,* c. 1748, § 1.

[44] Farrugia, *De Matrimonio,* n. 32; Cerato, *Matrimonium,* 83, f.

[45] Knecht, *Katholisches Eherecht,* p. 580, note. 3.

The proof of the existence of fear, qualified by the conditions of canon 1087, is exceedingly difficult. It is an internal fact for the one who suffers it; the one inflicting it for the most part acts secretly, especially in the case of reverential fear. Still, indirect though the proof must be, it is not entirely impossible. Because of the nature of the matter, the proof required is not physical or metaphysical, which excludes all possibility of the contrary, but moral, i. e., that which can produce persuasion.[46] Where coercion and constraint are in question, less rigid evidence than ordinarily demanded will suffice, provided it gives moral certitude.[47] The latter is produced by means of presumptions. These are gathered from facts, argumentations, and indications which frequently happen. When the presumptions are consistent, reasonable, relevant, serious and strongly probable, they are admitted by the law as proof sufficiently certain to overthrow the queen of presumptions: the favor which matrimony enjoys.[48] Until this moral certitude is established, however, sentence can never be pronounced against the marriage alleged to have been contracted under duress.[49]

Evidence admissible for this purpose includes all the facts and circumstances which preceded, accompanied, and followed the marriage celebration. In compliance with the directions of the Holy See [50] and in accordance with the practice of the Roman Rota and the

[46] Roberti, *De Processibus,* n. 324.

[47] Reiffenstuel, *Jus Canonicum Universum,* lib. I, tit. XL, n. 78. Cf. S. R. R., *Causa Tarvisina,* 11 Mar. 1912—*Decisiones,* IV (1912), dec. XI, n. 4; S. R. R., *Nullit. Matrim.,* 2 Jul. 1918—*Decisiones,* X (1918), dec. VIII, n. 6; S. R. R., *Causa Parisien.,* 12 Jun. 1919—*Decisiones,* XI (1919), dec. XI, n. 5; S. R. R., *Nullit. Matrim.,* 9 Jan. 1922—*Decisiones,* XIV (1922), dec. I, n. 13.

[48] Cf. Reiffenstuel, *Jus Canonicum Universum,* lib. II, tit. XXIII, n. 91: "praesumptio ilia quae valere facit actum, est regina aliarum praesumptionum; ac proinde praesumitur pro validitate actus donec probetur invalidus."

[49] Sanchez, *De Matrimonii Sacramento,* lib. IV, disp. XXVII, n. 1; Reiffenstuel, *Jus Canonicum Universum,* lib. I, tit. XL, nn. 78-80; Gasparri, *De Matrimonio,* n. 954; Payen, *De Matrimonio,* II, 1692; *Codex Juris Canonici,* c. 1869.

[50] S. C. S. Inquis., *Instructio ad Episc. Orient.,* 20 Jun. 1883, nn. 36-37—*ASS,* XVIII (1885), 357-359; S. C. de Prop. Fid., *Instructio pro Foed. Stat. Amer. Ordin.,* a. 1883, §§ 37-38—*ASS,* XVIII (1885), 379-381.

suggestions of authors,[51] the following points should furnish the basis of the investigation:

(a) the nature, age, sex, health, character, disposition, environment, training and education of the coerced party;
(b) the nature, character, and qualities of the parents or alleged authors of the fear and constraint;
(c) the reasons on account of which the coerced party was opposed to the marriage—in particular, whether there were plans of marriage with another, possible engagement, intentions of never marrying, etc.;
(d) the motives that inspired the authors of the compulsion and fear;
(e) the means employed to compel marriage: threats, ill treatment, physical violence, etc.;
(f) Circumstances preceding the celebration of marriage: constant use of coercive measures, continual resistance, aversion to the other party, attempts to avoid the marriage or obtain assistance, etc.;
(g) circumstances accompanying the celebration of marriage; actions and appearance of the coerced party;
(h) circumstances subsequent to the celebration of marriage—in particular, the facts of cohabitation, consummation, separation, and the precise reasons therefor;
(i) reasons for not sooner attacking the marriage, or at least bringing it to the attention of the proper authorities.

Since the proof of fear differs from other proofs in general, testimony on the above points is to be secured from all persons who have any knowledge of the matter of coercion and fear. Hence those are to be admitted as witnesses who otherwise *de jure* would not be admitted. Among these are the parents, brothers and sisters, the alleged authors of the coercion, blood relations, friends and associates of the party accusing the marriage, the pastor of the latter or the priest who assisted at the marriage, those who were present at the

[51] Wernz-Vidal, *Jus Matrimoniale*, p. 595, note 47; Lanier, *Procedure Matrimoniale*, p. 51; Triebs, *Kanonisches Eherecht*, III, 515-516; Knecht, *Katholisches Eherecht*, p. 580, note 3; Labouré-Byrne, *Procedure*, pp. 182-184.

ceremony, and all who have been in a position to know of the facts in the case.[52]

Household servants or employees are not prohibited from testifying: their work does not make them suspect, unless there is a well-grounded suspicion to that effect.[53] *Periti*, e. g., physicians, lawyers, or others serving in a professional capacity, can occasionally give helpful testimony.[54] Under certain circumstances, one who was *impubes* at the time the coercion was exercised may be admitted and the exception of age overruled or neglected.[55] Non-Catholics, if they are credible, without suspicion, and testify under oath, are not to be excluded.[56] One who has been leading a scandalous or immoral life is not prevented from offering testimony.[57]

Witnesses may be visual or auricular, but the former and those testifying *ex propria scientia* are preferable.[58] Witnesses *de auditu* are especially to be heard if the eye-witnesses are dead, or if they are trustworthy and have heard the facts from the latter, or if the facts are well-known.[59] Finally, even such witnesses are to be heard who *tempore non suspecto* received information from the coerced party on the matter of compulsion.[60]

The testimony given by those who act as witnesses in violence and

[52] Gasparri, *De Matrimonio*, n. 954; *Codex Juris Canonici*, c. 1974. S. C. S. Inquis., *Instructio*, n. 38; S. C. de Prop. Fid., *Instructio*, § 39.

[53] Cf. S. R. R., *Nullit. Matrim.*, 6 Jun. 1918—*Decisiones*, X (1918), dec. VI, n. 5; S. R. R., *Nullit. Matrim.*, 11 Apr. 1922—*Decisiones*, XIV (1922), dec. XI, n. 5.

[54] Cf. S. R. R., *Nullit. Matrim.*, 8 Mar. 1919—*Decisiones*, XI (1919), dec. VII, n. 6; S. R. R., *Nullit. Matrim.*, 8 Jul. 1919—*Decisiones*, XI (1919), dec. XIII, n. 4.

[55] Cf. S. R. R., *Causa Tarvisina*, 11 Mar. 1912—*Decisiones*, IV (1912), dec. XI, n. 16; S. R. R., *Nullit. Matrim.*, 9 Aug. 1915—*Decisiones*, VII (1915), dec. XXXV, n. 12; S. R. R., *Nullit. Matrim.*, 27 Jul. 1918—*Decisiones*, X (1918), dec. XII, n. 4. Cf. *Codex Juris Canonici*, c. 1757, § 1.

[56] Wernz, *Jus Matrimoniale*, n. 745; cf. S. R. R., *Causa Osnabrugen.*, 11 Jan. 1912—*Decisiones*, IV (1912), dec. III, n. 6.

[57] Cf. S. R. R., *Nullit. Matrim.*, 2 Jul. 1918—*Decisiones*, X (1918), dec. VIII, n. 8.

[58] Cf. S. R. R., *Causa Parisien.*, 31 Jan. 1922—*Decisiones*, XIV (1922), dec. III, n. 10.

[59] Cf. S. R. R., *Causa Parisien.*, 26 Feb. 1910—*Decisiones*, II (1910), dec. VIII, n. 9; S. R. R., *Causa Tarvisina*, 11 Mar. 1912—*Decisiones*, IV (1912), dec. XI, n. 11.

[60] Triebs, *Kanonisches Eherecht*, III, 515.

fear cases is to be variously evaluated. In the first place, it is the duty of the judge carefully to watch for any cause leading to a suspicion of fraud, prejury, or collusion. Besides putting the witnesses under oath, the tribunal should make efforts to obtain testimonials from their pastors or other responsible persons concerning their credibility and honesty.[61] At least two trustworthy witnesses are required and will suffice. One witness, especially if suspect, is of no value.[62]

Careful consideration must be given to their depositions. The testimony of two, trustworthy and beyond all exception, who offer evidence to the fact of coercion, is of no more value than many who testify to freedom of consent.[63] The reason lies in the fact that those who bear witness to fear speak of what can be perceived by the senses; the others give testimony to an internal fact, an invisible act of the will. This axiom, however, does not always prevail. As Sanchez[64] points out, it does not hold true where presumptions and conjectures make favorable the testimony of those witnessing to free consent, or where the testimony is not simply negative, but also restricted to a certain place and time. Consequently, the principle cannot be applied absolutely and its limitations must not be overlooked. The depositions of those who deny compulsion cannot be called merely negative if e. g., they were so intimate with the principals that they would have known or seen evidences of coercion. Their testimony is of greater weight than that of those not so closely associated.[65]

Furthermore, the testimony adduced should concern external facts which have been seen or heard. General affirmations without

[61] S. C. S. Inquis., *Instructio*, n. 38; S. C. de Prop. Fid., *Instructio*, § 39.

[62] Cf. S. R. R., *Nullit. Matrim.*, 6 Jun. 1918—*Decisiones,* X (1918), dec. VI, n. 7; S. R. R., *Nullit. Matrim.*, 24 Mar. 1922—*Decisiones,* XIV (1922), dec. VIII, n. 7.

[63] "Plus est credendum duobus testibus de metu in specie deponentibus, quam mille testibus in genere tantum spontaneam voluntatem affirmantibus." Cf. Sanchez, *De Matrimonii Sacramento,* lib. IV, disp. XXVII, n. 1; Wernz-Vidal, *Jus Matrimoniale,* p. 595, note 47; Payen, *De Matrimonio,* II, 1692.

[64] *De Matrimonii Sacramento,* lib. IV, disp. XXVII, nn. 2-3.

[65] S. R. R., *Nullit. Matrim.,* 11 Jun. 1918—*Decisiones,* X (1918), dec. VII, n. 4; S. R. R., *Causa Parisien.,* 31 Jan. 1922—*Decisiones,* XIV (1922), dec. III, n. 10.

particular facts or specific instances are of no value as evidence, especially if there are other depositions to the contrary. Hence, when no reasons are assigned, nor even external acts or signs related, the testimony amounts to mere opinion or judgment and not evidence.[66] Accidental discrepancies do not necessarily harm a cause. Discordant testimony can sometimes be conciliated by distinguishing various times and places, the real purpose of threats, whether made e. g., to prevent a certain marriage rather than compel the one contracted, etc.[67] Extra-judicial declarations not given under oath carry no weight, especially if made *tempore suspecto,* and cannot overthrow judicial testimony. Letters may be offered as evidence, particularly when written *tempore non suspecto.*[68] In all cases the testimony must be distinguished as to whether it is merely negative, indifferent, improbable, or false.

Of especial importance is the deposition of the parent or author of the coercion.[69] Their testimony is not necessarily under suspicion if a declaration of nullity is to their advantage, though occasionally it cannot be admitted as trustworthy.[70] Consanguinity does not diminish but increases credibility, because of a presumption in favor

[66] Cf. S. R. R., *Causa Lugdunen.,* 28 Jun. 1912—*Decisiones,* IV (1912), dec. XXVI, n. 10; S. R. R., *Causa Colonien.,* 1 Jul. 1912—*Decisiones,* IV (1912), dec. XXVIII, n. 6; S. R. R., *Nullit. Matrim.,* 29 Nov. 1913—*Decisiones,* V (1913), dec. L, n. 25; S. R. R., *Causa Avenionen.,* 14 Jul. 1914—*Decisiones,* VI (1914), dec. XXV, n. 3; S. R. R., *Causa Parisien.,* 4 Nov. 1915 —*Decisiones,* VII (1915), dec. XL, n. 3; S. R. R., *Causa Gallipolitana,* 16 Aug. 1917—*Decisiones,* IX (1917), dec. XXII, n. 4.

[67] Cf. S. R. R., *Causa Tarvisina,* 11 Mar. 1912—*Decisiones,* IV (1912), dec. XI, n. 13; S. R. R., *Nullit. Matrim.,* 1 Aug. 1913—*Decisiones,* V (1913), dec. XLII, n. 6.

[68] S. R. R., *Causa Massilien.,* 26 Maii, 1913—*Decisiones,* V (1913), dec. XXIX, n. 13; S. R. R., *Causa Avenionen,* 14 Jul. 1914—*Decisiones,* VI (1914), dec. XXV, n. 3; S. R. R., *Nullit. Matrim.,* 9 Mar. 1915—*Decisiones,* VII (1915), dec. VIII, nn. 7, 10; S. R. R., *Causa Mediolanen.,* 17 Aug. 1916—*Decisiones,* VIII (1916), dec. XXVII, n. 9; S. R. R., *Nullit. Matrim.,* 24 Nov. 1917—*Decisiones,* IX (1917), dec. XXVIII, n. 6.

[69] S. R. R., *Causa Lugdunen.,* 2 Apr. 1917—*AAS,* X (1918), 73: "cum in causis matrimonialibus confessio eorum, qui metum incusserunt, sit omnibus aliis testibus praeferenda, cum deponant de facto proprio."

[70] Cf. S. R. R., *Nullit. Matrim.,* 19 Feb. 1916—*Decisiones,* VIII (1916), dec. III, n. 21; S. R. R., *Causa Parisien.,* 31 Jan. 1922—*Decisiones,* XIV (1922), dec. III, n. 10; S. R. R., *Nullit. Matrim.,* 24 Mar. 1922—*Decisiones,* XIV (1922), dec. VIII, n. 7.

of knowledge and veracity.[71] The confession alone of the party who asserts the fact of fear is no proof of its existence because of the evident danger of collusion and fraud.[72]

Nemo testis in propria causa esse potest. Nevertheless, where other presumptions occur which favor his statements, his sworn deposition should be deferred to unless it is apprehended as false or is made after the accusation of the marriage.[73] Sometimes, however, the confession becomes a necessary element of proof, but it will have this value only if it is sufficiently established from another source that it contains the truth.[74]

The motive of the witnesses should be examined to determine whether they mean to tell the truth or wish to testify merely for some other reason, e. g., to be of assistance to a friend. Testimony that public report has it that the marriage was forced cannot prove the fact. Neither can proof be based on the possibility of some fact which would doubtlessly portend fear if it were true. An admission or statement made *tempore non suspecto* will be of great weight. Lastly, the testimony of a *de auditu* witness can only furnish weak presumptions. It merits as much credence as its author and if the latter's name is refused it is of little or no value.[75]

Article III.—The Sentence

A diligent and careful investigation of the evidence in each particular case will determine whether fear, in the event that its exist-

[71] S. R. R., *Causa Varsavien. sive Lublinen.*, 21 Jul. 1910—*AAS*, II (1910), 889: "Testimonia haec attendenda maxime sunt, quia consanguinitas non minuit, imo auget fidem ratione praesumptae scientiae et veritatis."

[72] C. 5, X, *de eo, qui duxit,* IV, 13; *Instructio Austriaca,* §§ 148, 169—*Collectio Lacensis,* V, 1305, 1307; Wernz, *Jus Matrimoniale,* n. 769; *Codex Juris Canonici,* c. 1751.

[73] Gasparri, *De Matrimonio,* n. 954; Reiffenstuel, *Jus Canonicum Universum,* lib. II, tit. XVIII, n. 20. Cf. S. R. R., *Nullit. Matrim.*, 2 Jul. 1918—*Decisiones,* X (1918), dec. VIII, n. 10; S. R. R., *Nullit Matrim.*, 7 Mar. 1922—*Decisiones,* XIV (1922), dec. VI, n. 5; S. R. R., *Nullit. Matrim.*, 7 Aug. 1922—*Decisiones,* XIV (1922), dec. XXVIII, nn. 7-8.

[74] Sanchez, *De Matrimonii Sacramento,* lib. II, disp. XLV, n. 15; S. R. R., *Causa Colonien.*, 1 Jul. 1912—Decisiones, IV (1912), dec. XXVIII, n. 3.

[75] Cf. S. R. R., *Nullit. Matrim.*, 24 Mar. 1922—*Decisiones,* XIV (1922), dec. VIII, n. 5; S. R. R., Nullit. Matrim., 6 Jun. 1918—*Decisiones,* X (1918), dec. VI, n. 12; S. R. R., *Nullit. Matrim.*, 14 Aug. 1922—*Decisiones,* XIV (1922), dec. XXXII, nn. 9, 13.

ence has been proven, is qualified with the conditions required by canon 1087 to vitiate matrimonial consent and thereby invalidate marriage. Unless the evidence submitted, however, excludes every prudent doubt to the contrary, judgment is never to be pronounced against the marriage.[76]

The matrimonial contract is a solemn and public transaction which, in view of its nature of a permanent and indissoluble union, should be surrounded with the greatest freedom and entered with complete liberty of will. Once it has been concluded, however, it must be judged valid rather than invalid until the contrary is demonstrated. Not only the favor which it enjoys before the law, but the reverence due to the sacrament, the interests of the common good, and the welfare of the offspring, require that this stand be taken.[77] Every presumption, accordingly, should militate in favor of the matrimonial bond. No consideration is to be given to opposing presumptions unless they are so strong and convincing as to prove beyond doubt the alleged nullity on grounds of coercion and constraint.

Nevertheless, while the verification of canon 1087 must be certain, moral certitude suffices. As has been indicated above, this will be established from the presumptions produced by the evidence furnished to show the existence of a juridically qualified fear. Strong as is the presumption in favor of marriage, it must yield to a stronger, and the strongest presumption must yield to the truth. It must be noted, furthermore, that the conclusion against the validity of marriage is not to be drawn from this or that deposition made by one or the other of the witnesses, but from their joint testimony taken as a whole.[78] The strongest presumption that a particular marriage was most undesirable to a certain party and that he submitted through fear to the imperious will of another does not in the least

[76] S. C. S., Inquis., *Instructio*, n. 39; S. C. de Prop. Fid., *Instructio*, § 40; cf. *Codex Juris Canonici*, c. 1869.

[77] Schmalzgrueber, *Jus Ecclesiasticum Universum*, lib. IV, tit. I, n. 432; Laymann, *Theologia Moralis*, lib. V, tr. X, c. 5, n. 4; Ballerini-Palmieri, *Opus Theologicum Morale*, VI, tr. X, n. 1125; Cappello, *De Matrimonio*, n. 606; Triebs, *Kanonisches Eherecht*, III, 505.

[78] S. R. R., *Causa Calatanisiaden.*, 28 Jul. 1916—*Decisiones*, VIII (1916), dec. XXI, n. 13.

suffice to declare the nullity of the marriage. Moral certitude must arise from the entire *acta* that the person was really opposed to the marriage and merely contracted it through a grave and unavoidable fear unjustly inflicted by another.[79]

Consequently, where the invalidity of the marriage has been certainly established, and a declaration of nullity requested, then the marriage is to be declared null and void. Where the proofs are such as to leave a reasonable doubt, or make it reasonably uncertain whether the requirements of the law are fulfilled, the marriage cannot be declared invalid on grounds of force and fear. Finally, if the evidence certainly fails to demonstrate the nullity, sentence must be pronounced in favor of the bond. Should the parties have separated, further efforts might be made to effect a reconciliation and secure renewal of consent as a final precaution. If this is impossible, a separation *a thoro et mensa* may be advisable.[80]

While the testimony may not suffice to establish invalidity on the score of coercion, still it sometimes demonstrates the fact of non-consummation. In this hypothesis the case may be referred to the Holy See for a dispensation *super rato non consummato.* It will not be necessary to secure special permission for the process.[81] A like procedure may be followed where a marriage is certainly valid in regard to the consent given but has never been consummated.

The principle having application in cases where the defect of fear is not juridically proved is that of the Decretals:[82] *Tolerabilius est enim aliquos contra statuta hominum dimittere copulatos, quam conjunctos legitime contra statuta Domini separare.* This rule of action holds for a doubt of fact, i.e., whether fear in a particular case fulfills all the conditions of the law, as well as for a doubt of law, e.g., whether fear unjustly inflicted *quoad modum* for the purpose of extorting matrimonial consent invalidates marriage. Until the legislator makes further definite dispositions, sentence must always be

[79] S. R. R., *Nullit. Matrim.*, 19 Dec. 1922—*Decisiones,* XIV (1922), dec. XXXVIII, n. 7.

[80] Smith, *Marriage Process,* n. 175; Payen, *De Matrimonio,* II, n. 1693.

[81] Cf. *S. C. de discipl. Sacram.*, "De Processibus in Causis Dispensationis super Matrimonio Sato et non Consummato," 7 Maii, 1923, n. 4—*AAS,* XV (1923), 392; Viscont, *De Matrimonio Rato et non Consummato,* p. 15.

[82] C. 47, X, *de testibus,* XI, 20.

pronounced in favor of validity where the latter doubt is encountered.[83]

In conclusion it may be said that the judge in cases of violence and fear can do no more than act according to the axiom: *jus dicere secundum leges et probata.* He has to apply the existing law and pronounce sentence on the basis of the evidence submitted. If this fails to establish nullity, the decision must be in favor of validity. If it clearly demonstrates that matrimonial consent was extorted under the influence of a grave and unjustly inflicted fear, he must declare the marriage null and void.

[83] Cf. Wernz-Vidal, *Jus Matrimoniale,* n. 505; p. 595, note 47.

BIBLIOGRAPHY

SOURCES

Acta Apostolicae Sedis (AAS), Romae, 1909-

Acta et Decreta Conciliorum Recentiorum (Collectio Lacensis), 7 vols., Friburgi Brisgoviae, 1870-1890.

Acta Sanctae Sedis (ASS), 41 vols., Romae, 1865-1908.

Bullarium Diplomatum et Privilegiorum Sanctorum Pontificum Taurinensis Editio, 24 vols., Augustae Taurinorum, 1857-1872.

Canones et Decreta Concilii Tridentini, 19. ed., Taurini, 1913.

Codex Juris Canonici Pii X Pontificis Maximi jussu digestus Benedicti Papae XV auctoritate promulgatus, Romae, 1918.

Codex Theodosianus, ed. P. Kruger, Th. Mommsen, P. M. Meyer, 3 vols., Berolini, 1905.

Codicis Juris Canonici Fontes, cura Emi. Petri Card. Gasparri editi, 5 vols., Romae, 1925-1930.

Collectanea S. Congregationis de Propaganda Fide, 2 vols., Romae, 1907.

Concilii Plenarii Baltimorensis III (1884), Acta et Decreta, Baltimorae, 1886.

Corpus Juris Canonici, Editio Lipsiensis II (Richter-Friedberg), 2 vols., Lipsiae, 1922.

Corpus Juris Civilis, ed. P. Krueger, Berolini, 1922.

Harduin, J., *Conciliorum Collectio Regia Maxima*, 12 vols., Parisiis, 1715.

Jaffé, Philippus, *Regesta Pontificum Romanorum*, 2. ed., 2 vols., Lipsiae, 1881.

Mansi, Joannes, *Sacrorum Conciliorum Nova et Amplissima Collectio*, 53 vols., Parisiis, 1901-1927.

Migne, Jacques, *Patrologiae Cursus Completus,—Series Latina*, 221 vols., *(MPL)*, Parisiis, 1844-1855; *Series Graeca*, 161 vols., *(MPG)*, Parisiis, 1858-1864.

Pallottini, Salvator, *Collectio Omnium Conclusionum et Resolutionum quae in causis propositis apud S. Cong. Cardinalium S. Concilii Tridentini Interpretum prodierunt ab anno 1564 ad annum 1860*, 17 vols., Romae, 1868-1893.

Richter, Aemilius, *Canones et Decreta Concilii Tridentini*, Lipsiae, 1853.

S. Romanae Rotae Decisiones seu Sententia, Romae, 1909-

Thesaurus Resolutionum Sacrae Congregationis Concilii, 167 vols., Romae, 1718-1908.

Thiel, Andreas, *Epistolae Romanorum Pontificum Genuinae*, Brunsbergae, 1868.

AUTHORS

Alphonsus, De Liguori, *Theologia Moralis*, 5 vols., Taurini, 1872.

Ayrinhac, *Marriage Legislation in the New Code of Canon Law*, New York, 1918.

[Bachofen], Charles Augustine, *A Commentary on the New Code of Canon Law*, 4. ed., 8 vols., St. Louis, 1918-1929.

Bain, Alexander, *The Emotions and the Will*, New York, 1888.
Ballerini, Antonius—Palmieri, Dominicus, *Opus Theologicum Morale*, 7 vols., Prati, 1889.
Bangen, Joannes, *De Sponsalibus et Matrimonio*, 4 vols., Aschendorffia, 1858-1860.
Baronius, Caesar, *Annales Ecclesiastici* (*ed.* Aug. Theiner), 37 vols., Barri-Ducis, 1864-1883.
Benedictus XIV, *Opera Omnia*, 17 vols., Prati, 1839-1847.
Berardi, Carolus, *Gratiani Canones Genuini ab Apocryphis Discreti, Corrupti ad emendationem Codicum Fidem Exacti, Difficiliores Commoda interpretatione illustrati*, 4 vols., Venetiis, 1777.
Bernard, Fernand, *The First Year of Roman Law*, trans. by Chas. P. Sherman, New York, 1906.
Billot, Ludovicus, *De Ecclesiae Sacramentis*, 2. ed., 2 vols., Romae, 1897.
Blat, Albertus, *Commentarium Textus Codicis Juris Canonici*, 6 vols., Romae, 1921-1927.
Bouquillon, Thomas, *Institutiones Theologiae Moralis Fundamentalis*, Brugis, 1873.
Brunnemann, Joannes, *Commentarius in Codicem Justinianeum*, Lipsiae, 1699.
Callan, Charles—McHugh, John, *Moral Theology*, 2 vols., New York, 1929.
Cappello, Felix M., *Tractatus Canonico-Moralis De Sacramentis*, vol. III, *De Matrimonio*, 2. ed., 1927.
Catholic Encyclopedia, 15 vols., New York, 1907-1912.
Cerato, Prosdocimus, *Matrimonium a Codice I. C. Integre Desumptum*, 4. ed., Patavii, 1929.
Chelodi, Joannes, *Jus Matrimoniale, juxta Codicem Juris Canonici*, 3. ed., Tridenti, 1921.
Chenon, E., *La Rôle Sociale de l'Eglise*, Paris, 1922.
Clark, William, *Handbook of the Law of Contracts*, 2 ed., St. Paul, 1904.
Corbett, Percy E., *The Roman Law of Marriage*, Oxford, 1930.
Corpus Scriptorum Ecclesiasticorum Latinorum, Vienna, 1866-
Cosci, Christopher, *De Separatione Tori Conjugalis tam nullo existente seu Soluto quam salvo Vinculo Matrimonii ejusque Effectibus*, 4. ed., Florentiae, 1856.
D'Annibale, Josephus, *Summula Theologiae Moralis*, 3. ed., 3 vols., Romae, 1892.
De Becker, Julius, *De Sponsalibus et Matrimonio Praelectiones Canonicae*, 2. ed. Lovanii, 1903.
Desforges, L., *Etude Historique sur la Formation du Mariage en Droit Romaine et en Droit Français*, Paris, 1887.
De Smet, Aloysius, *Betrothment and Marriage*, trans. by A. Owens, 2. ed., 2 vols., St. Louis, 1925.
Dictionnaire de Théologie Catholique, 18 vols., Paris, 1903-1927.
Duchesne, L., *Early History of the Church*, New York, 1912.
Engel, Ludovicus, *Collegium Universi Juris Canonici*, Venetiis, 1760.
Ernouf, *Histoire de Waldrade et de Lothaire II*, Paris, 1858.
Esmein, A., *Le Mariage en Droit Canonique*, 2 vols., Paris, 1891.
Farrugia, Nicolaus, *De Matrimonio et Causis Matrimonialibus, tractatus canonico-moralis juxta Codicem Juris Canonici*, Romae, 1924.

Feije, Henricus, *De Impedimentis et Dispensationibus Matrimonialibus,* 3. ed., Lovanii, 1885.

Ferreres, Joannes, *Compendium Theologiae Moralis,* 7. ed., 2 vols., Barcinone, 1928.

Freisen, *Geschichte des Canonischen Eherechts,* 2. ed., Paderborn, 1893.

Fulton, John, *The Laws of Marriage,* London, n.d.

Funk, F. X., *Manual of Church History,* trans. by Luigi Cappadelta, 2 vols., London, 1910.

Fustel de Coulanges, N. D., *The Ancient City,* trans. by W. Small, Boston, 1874.

Gasparri, Petrus, *Tractatus Canonicus de Matrimonio,* 3. ed., 2 vols., Parisiis, 1904.

Genicot, E.—Salsmans, I., *Institutiones Theologiae Moralis,* 11. ed., 2 vols., Bruxellis, 1927.

Girard, *Manuel Elementaire de Droit Romain,* 7. ed., Paris, 1924.

Gothofredus, Jacobus, *Codex Theodosianus cum Perpetuis Commentariis,* 6 vols., Lipsiae, 1736.

Gougnard, Armando, *Tractatus De Matrimonio ad Normam Codicis Recognita,* 7. ed., Mechliniae, 1931.

Hefele, C., *Conciliengeschichte,* 2. ed., 9 vols., Freiburg, 1873-1890.

Hefele-Leclercq, *Histoire des Conciles,* 9 vols., Paris, 1907-1930.

Heiss, M., *De Matrimonio,* Monachii, 1861.

Hinschius, P., *Decretales Pseudo-Isidorianae,* Berlin, 1863.

——*System des Katholischen Kirchenrechts,* 6 vols., Berlin, 1869.

Knecht, August, *Handbuch des Katholischen Eherechts,* Freiburg, 1928.

Kutschker, Johann, *Das Eherecht der Katholischen Kirche,* 4 vols., Wien, 1857.

Laboulaye, Ed., *Recherches sur la Condition Civile et Politique des Femmes,* Paris, 1843.

Lanier, Henri, *Guide Pratique de la Procedure Matrimoniale en Droit Canonique,* Paris, 1927.

Laymann, Paulus, *Theologia Moralis,* Venetiis, 1719.

Leage, R. W., *Roman Private Law,* London, 1924.

Lega, Michael, *Coram Lega Habitae S. R. Rotae Decisiones seu Sententiae,* Romae, 1926.

——*Praelectiones in Textum Juris Canonici de Judiciis Ecclesiasticis,* 2 vols., Romae, 1896.

Lehmkuhl, Augustinus, *Theologia Moralis,* 12. ed., 2 vols., Friburgi Brisgoviae, 1914.

Leitner, Martin, *Lehrbuch des Katholischen Eherechts,* 3. ed., Paderborn, 1920.

Lessius, Leonardus, *De Justitia et Jure Caeterisque Virtutibus Cardinalibus,* 3. ed., Antwerpiae, 1612.

Linneborn, Johannes, *Grundriss des Ehrechts,* 3. ed., Paderborn, 1922.

Lugo, Johannes de, *Disputationes de Justitia et Jure,* 2 vols., Lugduni, 1670.

Mackensie, Thomas, *Studies in Roman Law,* Edinburgh, 1886.

Maher, Michael, *Psychology,* New York, n.d.

Maine, H. J. S., *Ancient Law,* London, 1885.

Mann, Horace K., *Lives of the Popes,* 15 vols., St. Louis, 1902-1929.

Maroto, Philippo, *Institutiones Juris Canonici,* 3. ed., 2 vols., Romae, 1921.

May, Geoffrey, *Marriage Laws and Decisions in the United States,* New York, 1929.

Meyer, *Institutiones Juris Naturalis,* Freiburg, 1900.
Michiels, Gommarus, *Normae Generales Juris Canonici,* 2 vols., Dublin, 1929.
Mommsen, Theodore, *History of Rome,* trans. by W. P. Dickson, 6 vols., London, 1868-1886.
Morey, William C., *Outlines of Roman Law,* 2. ed., New York, 1914.
Moy, C. E., *Das Eherecht der Christen in der Morgenlaendischen und Abendlaendischen Kirche bis zur Zeit Karls des Grossen,* Regensburg, 1833.
Noldin, H., *Summa Theologiae Moralis,* 18. ed., 4 vols., Oeniponte, 1926.
Noval, Josephus, *Commentarium Codicis Juris Canonici, De Judiciis,* Romae, 1920.
Ojetti, B., *Commentarium in Codicem Juris Canonici,* Romae, 1929.
Panormitanus, Abbas, *Commentaria in quinque Libros Decretalium,* 8 vols., Venetiis, 1578.
Payen, G., *De Matrimonio in Missionibus ac Potissimum in Sinis Tractatus Practicus et Casus,* 3 vols., Zi-ka-wei, 1929.
Pennacchi, J., *Commentaria in Constitutionem "Apostolicae Sedis,"* 2 vols., Romae, 1883.
Perrin-Klein, *Psychology,* New York, 1926.
Petrovits, Joseph, *The New Church Law on Matrimony,* Philadelphia, 1921.
Pichler, Vitus, *Jus Canonicum,* 2 vols., Ravennae, 1741.
Pirhing, Enricus, *Jus Canonicum Nova Methodo Explicatum,* 2 vols., Delingae, 1678.
Pollock-Maitland, *History of English Law before the Time of Edward I,* Cambridge, 1895.
Pontius, Basilius, *De Sacramento Matrimonii Tractatus cum Appendice de Matrimonio Catholici cum Haeretico,* 2. ed., Bruxellis, 1627.
Probst, Ferdinand, *Sakramente und Sakramentalien,* Tübingen, 1872.
Pruemmer, M., *Manuale Theologiae Moralis,* 3. ed., 3 vols., Freiburg, 1928.
Reiffenstuel, Anacletus, *Jus Canonicum Universum,* 4 vols., Romae, 1838.
Roberti, Franciscus, *De Processibus,* 2 vols., Romae, 1926.
Roby, Henry J., *Roman Private Law,* 2 vols., Cambridge, 1902.
Salmanticenses, *Cursus Theologiae Moralis,* 3 vols., Venetiis, 1728.
Sanchez, Thomas, *De Sancto Matrimonii Sacramento Disputationum, Tomi Tres,* Lugduni, 1669.
Santi, Franciscus, *Praelectiones Juris Canonici,* 4. ed., 5 vols., Ratisbonae, 1885.
Schaff, Philip, *History of the Christian Church,* 7 vols., New York, 1904.
Schmalzgrueber, Franciscus, *Jus Ecclesiasticum Universum,* 12 vols., Romae, 1844.
Schmitz, H., *Die Bussbuecher und die Bussdisciplin der Kirche,* Mainz, 1883.
Schoensteiner, Ferdinand, *Grundriss des Kirchlichen Eherechts,* Wien, 1925.
Schoepf, Joseph, *Handbuch des Katholischen Kirchenrechts,* 2. ed., 4 vols., Schaffhausen, 1866.
Schulte, Friederich, *Handbuch des Katholischen Eherecht,* Giessen, 1885.
Sherman, Charles P., *Roman Law in the Modern World,* 2. ed., 3 vols., New York, 1924.
Slater, Thomas, *A Manual of Moral Theology,* 2 vols., London, 1928.
Smisniewicz, Leon, *Die Lehre von den Ehehindernissen bei Petrus Lombardus und bei seinen Kommentatoren,* Posen, 1927.
Smith, S. B., *The Marriage Process in the United States,* New York, 1893.

Smith, William—Cheetham, Samuel, *Dictionary of Christian Antiquities*, 2 vols., Hartford, 1880.

Sohm, Rudolph, *The Institutes*, trans. by James C. Ledlie, 3. ed., Oxford, 1926.

Tanquery, Ad., *Synopsis Theologiae Moralis et Pastoralis*, 8. ed., 3 vols., Rome, 1921.

Thomas, Acquinas, *Opera Omnia*, (*ed.* Frette), Parisiis, 1873-1879.

Triebs, Franz, *Praktisches Handbuch des Geltenden Kanonischen Eherechts*, 2. ed., 3 vols., 1927-1929.

Troplong, M., *De L'Influence du Christianisme sur le Droit Civil des Romains*, Louvain, 1844.

Van Espen, Z. B., *Jus Ecclesiasticum Universum*, 5 vols., Lugduni, 1778.

Vermeersch, A.—Creusen, J., *Epitome Juris Canonici*, 3. ed., 3 vols., Mechliniae, 1927.

Vermeersch, Arthur, *Theologiae Moralis, Principia, Responsa, Consilia*, 2. ed., 3 vols., Romae, 1927.

Vidal, Petrus, *Institutiones Juris Civilis Romani*, Prati, 1915.

Viscont, Antonius, *Tractatus Canonicus de Matrimonio Rato et non Consummato*, Romae, 1928.

Vlaming, Th. M., *Praelectiones Juris Matrimonii*, 3. ed., 2 vols., Bussum in Hollandia, 1921.

Vromant, G., *Jus Missionariorum*, vol. V: *De Matrimonio*, Louvain, 1931.

Walsh, William J., *Tractatus de Actibus Humanis*, Dublin, 1880.

Wernz, F. X., *Jus Decretalium*, 2. ed., 6 vols., Prati, 1912.

Wernz, F. X.,—Vidal, Petrus, *Jus Canonicum ad Codicis Normam Exactum*, 3 vols., vol. V, *Jus Matrimoniale*, Romae, 1923-1928.

Westermarck, Edward, *History of Human Marriage*, London, 1891.

Woywod, Stanislaus, *A Practical Commentary on the Code of Canon Law*, 2 vols., New York, 1925.

Zhishman, *Das Eherecht der Orientalischen Kirche*, Wien, 1864.

PERIODICALS

American Ecclesiastical Review, The, (AER), Philadelphia, 1889—

American Journal of Psychology, Albany, 1889—

Analecta Ecclesiastica, Romae, 1893-1911.

Apollinaris, Commentarium Juridico-Canonicum, Romae, 1928—

Archiv für katholisches Kirchenrecht, Mainz, 1857—

Collationes Brugenses, Brugis Flandorum, 1896—

Jus Pontificium, Romae, 1921—

Nouvelle Revue Théologique, Tournai, 1869—

Periodica de re canonica et morali utili praesertim Religiosis et Missionariis, Brugis, 1905—

Theologisch-praktische Quartalschrift, (LQR), Linz, 1832—

UNIVERSITAS CATHOLICA AMERICAE

WASHINGTON, D. C.

FACULTAS JURIS CANONICI

No. 80

1932

DEUS LUX MEA

TITULI

QUOS

AD DOCTORATUS GRADUM

IN

JURE CANONICO

APUD UNIVERSITATEM CATHOLICAM AMERICAE

CONSEQUENDUM

PUBLICE PROPUGNABIT

JOSEPH V. SANGMEISTER

SACERDOS ARCHIDIOECESIS PHILADELPHIENSIS

JURIS CANONICI LICENTIATUS

HORA XI, A. M. DIE XXIII MAII MCMXXXII

TITULI

IN JURE CANONICO

I.	De Dissertatione.	
II.	De Juris Canonici Historia.	
III.	Canones 1-7	De Ambitu Codicis.
IV.	Canones 8-24	De Legibus Ecclesiasticis.
V.	Canones 25-30	De Consuetudine.
VI.	Canones 31-35	De Temporis Supputatione.
VII.	Canones 36-62	De Rescriptis.
VIII.	Canones 118-123	De Juribus et Privilegiis Clericorum.
IX.	Canones 492-498	De Erectione et Suppressione Religionis, Provinciae, Domus.
X.	Canones 499-517	De Superioribus et de Capitulis.
XI.	Canones 518-530	De Confessariis et de Cappellanis.
XII.	Canones 531-537	De Bonis Temporalibus Eorumque Administratione.
XIII.	Canones 539-541	De Postulatu.
XIV.	Canones 542-552	De Requisitis ut Quis in Novitiatum Admittatur.
XV.	Canones 553-571	De Novitiorum Institutione.
XVI.	Canones 572-586	De Professione Religiosa.
XVII.	Canones 587-591	De Ratione Studiorum in Religionibus Clericalibus.
XVIII.	Canones 592-612	De Obligationibus Religiosorum.
XIX.	Canones 613-625	De Privilegiis Religiosorum.
XX.	Canones 737-779	De Baptismo.
XXI.	Canones 1012-1018	De Matrimonio in Genere.
XXII.	Canones 1058-1066	De Impedimentis Impedientibus.
XXIII.	Canones 1067-1080	De Impedimentis Dirimentibus.
XXIV.	Canones 1094-1103	De Forma Celebrationis Matrimonii.
XXV.	Canones 1104-1107	De Matrimonio Conscientiae.
XXVI.	Canones 1406-1408	De Fidei Professione.
XXVII.	Canones 1552-1568	De Notione Judicii et De Foro Competenti.
XXVIII.	Canones 1572-1593	De Tribunali Ordinario Primae Instantiae.
XXIX.	Canones 1608-1645	De Disciplina in Tribunalibus Servanda.
XXX.	Canones 1646-1666	De Partibus in Causa.
XXXI.	Canones 1706-1725	De Causae Introductione.
XXXII.	Canones 1726-1731	De Litis Instantia.
XXXIII.	Canones 1750-1753	De Confessione Partium.
XXXIV.	Canones 1770-1781	De Examine Testium.
XXXV.	Canones 1812-1824	De Probatione per Instrumenta.
XXXVI.	Canones 2162-2167	De Translatione Parochorum.
XXXVII.	Canones 2195-2198	De Natura Delicti.

XXXVIII. Canones 2214-2220 De Poenis in Genere.
XXXIX. Canones 2241-2285 De Censuris.
XL. Canones 2306-2311 De Poenalibus Remediis.

IN JURE ROMANO

XLI. The Periods of Roman Law.
XLII. The Sources of Roman Law.
XLIII. Personality.
XLIV. Slavery.
XLV. Citizenship.
XLVI. Patria Potestas.
XLVII. Personae in Manu.
XLVIII. Tutela et Cura.
XLIX. Personae in Mancipio.
L. Ownership.
LI. De Obligationibus in Genere.
LII. De Obligationibus Extra-Contractualibus.
LIII. Furtum.
LIV. Damnum Iniuria Datum.
LV. De Actionibus.

AMERICAN CHURCH—CIVIL LAW

LVI. Juridical Status of the Church in the United States.
LVII. Methods of Holding Church Property.
LVIII. Tax Exemption.
LIX. Marriage.
LX. Cemeteries.

Vidit Facultas:

VALENTINUS T. SCHAAF, O.F.M., J.C.D., Vice-Decanus.
LUDOVICUS H. MOTRY, S.T.D., J.C.D, a Secretis.
FRANCISCUS J. LARDONE, S.T.D., J.U.D.
JOHN McDILL FOX, A.B., LL.B.

Vidit Rector Magnificus Universitatis:

JACOBUS HUGO RYAN, S.T.D., PH.D., LL.D., LITT.D.

BIOGRAPHICAL NOTE

JOSEPH V. SANGMEISTER was born at Philadelphia, Pennsylvania, March 23, 1905. He attended the Parochial Schools and Roman Catholic High School, Philadelphia. His philosophical and theological studies were made at St. Charles' Seminary, Overbrook, Pennsylvania, where he received the degree of Bachelor of Arts. In September, 1930, he entered the Catholic University of America, Washington, D. C., to pursue a graduate course of studies in the School of Canon Law. He was ordained to the Priesthood on May 30, 1931.

CANON LAW STUDIES

1. Freriks, Rev. Celestine A., C.PP.S., J.C.D., Religious Congregations in Their External Relations, 121 pp., 1916.
2. Galliher, Rev. Daniel M., O.P., J.C.D., Canonical Elections, 117 pp., 1917.
3. Borkowski, Rev. Aurelius L., O.F.M., De Confraternitatibus Ecclesiasticis, 136 pp., 1918.
4. Castillo, Rev. Cayo, J.C.D., Disertacion Historico-canonica sobre la Potestad del Cabildo en Sede Vacante o Impedida del Vicario Capitular, 99 pp., 1919 (1918).
5. Kubelbeck, Rev. William J., S.T.B., J.C.D., The Sacred Penitentiaria and Its Relations to Faculties of Ordinaries and Priests, 129 pp., 1918.
6. Petrovits, Rev. Joseph J. C., S.T.D., J.C.D., The New Church Law on Matrimony, X-461 pp., 1919.
7. Hickey, Rev. John J., S.T.B., J.C.D., Irregularities and Simple Impediments in the New Code of Canon Law, 100 pp., 1920.
8. Klekotka, Rev. Peter J., S.T.B., J.C.D., Diocesan Consultors, 179 pp., 1920.
9. Wannenmacher, Rev. Francis, J.C.D., The Evidence in Ecclesiastical Procedure Affecting the Marriage Bond, 1920. (Not Printed.)
10. Golden, Rev. Henry Francis, J.C.D., Parochial Benefices in the New Code, IV-119 pp., 1921. (Printed 1925.)
11. Koudelka, Rev. Charles J., J.C.D., Pastors, Their Rights and Duties According to the New Code of Canon Law, 211 pp., 1921.
12. Melo, Rev. Antonius, O.F.M., J.C.D., De Exemptione Regularium, X-188 pp., 1921.
13. Schaaf, Rev. Valentine Theodore, O.F.M., S.T.B., J.C.D., The Cloister, X-180 pp., 1921.
14. Burke, Rev. Thomas Joseph, S.T.B., J.C.D., Competence in Ecclesiastical Tribunals, IV-117 pp., 1922.
15. Leech, Rev. George Leo, J.C.D., A Comparative Study of the Constitution "Apostolicae Sedis" and the "Codex Juris Canonici," 179 pp., 1922.
16. Motry, Rev. Hubert Louis, S.T.D., J.C.D., Diocesan Faculties according to the Code of Canon Law, II-167 pp., 1922.
17. Murphy, Rev. George Lawrence, J.C.D., Delinquencies and Penalties in the Administration and the Reception of the Sacraments, IV-121 pp., 1923.
18. O'Reilly, Rev. John Anthony, S.T.B., J.C.D., Ecclesiastical Sepulture in the New Code of Canon Law, II-129 pp., 1923.
19. Michalicka, Rev. Wenceslas Cyrill, O.S.B., J.C.D., Judicial Procedure in Dismissal of Clerical Exempt Religious, 107 pp., 1923.
20. Dargin, Rev. Edward Vincent, S.T.B., J.C.D., Reserved Cases According to the Code of Canon Law, IV-103 pp., 1924.
21. Godfrey, Rev. John A., S.T.B., J.C.D., The Right of Patronage According to the Code of Canon Law, 153 pp., 1924.
22. Hagedorn, Rev. Francis Edward, J.C.D., General Legislation on Indulgences, II-154 pp., 1924.

23. KING, REV. JAMES IGNATIUS, J.C.D., The Administration of the Sacraments to Dying Non-Catholics, V-141 pp., 1924.
24. WINSLOW, REV. FRANCIS JOSEPH, A.F.M., J.C.D., Vicars and Prefects Apostolic, IV-149 pp., 1924.
25. CORREA, REV. JOSE SERVELION, S.T.L., J.C.D., La Potestad Legislativa de la Iglesia Católica, IV-127 pp., 1925.
26. DUGAN, REV. HENRY FRANCIS, M.A., J.C.D., The Judiciary Department of the Diocesan Curia, 87 pp., 1925.
27. KELLER, REV. CHARLES FREDERICK, S.T.B., J.C.D., Mass Stipends, 167 pp., 1925.
28. PASCHANG, REV. JOHN LINUS, J.C.D., The Sacramentals According to the Code of Canon Law, 129 pp., 1925.
29. PIONTEK, REV. CYRILLUS, O.F.M., S.T.B., J.C.D., De Indulto Exclaustrationis necnon Saecularizationis, XIII-289 pp., 1925.
30. KEARNEY, REV. RICHARD JOSEPH, S.T.B., J.C.D., Sponsors at Baptism According to the Code of Canon Law, IV-127 pp., 1925.
31. BARTLETT, REV. CHESTER JOSEPH, A.M., LL.B., J.C.D., The Tenure of Parochial Property in the United States of America, V-108 pp., 1926.
32. KILKER, REV. ADRIAN JEROME, J.C.D., Extreme Unction, V-425 pp., 1926.
33. MCCORMICK, REV. ROBERT EMMETT, J.C.D., Confessors of Religious, VIII-266 pp., 1926.
34. MILLER, REV. NEWTON THOMAS, J.C.D., Founded Masses According to the Code of Canon Law, VII-93 pp., 1926.
35. ROELKER, REV. EDWARD G., S.T.D., J.C.D., Principles of Privilege According to the Code of Canon Law, XI-166 pp., 1926.
36. BAKALARCZYK, REV. RICHARDUS, M.I.C., J.U.D., De Novitiatu, VIII-208 pp., 1927.
37. PIZZUTI, REV. LAWRENCE, O.F.M., J.U.L., De Parochis Religiosis, 1927. (Not Printed.)
38. BLILEY, REV. NICHOLAS MARTIN, O.S.B., J.C.D., Altars According to the Code of Canon Law, XIX-132 pp., 1927.
39. BROWN, BRENDAN FRANCIS, A.B., LL.M., J.U.D., The Canonical Juristic Personality with Special Reference to its Status in the United States of America, V-212 pp., 1927.
40. CAVANAUGH, REV. WILLIAM THOMAS. C.P., J.U.D., The Reservation of the Blessed Sacrament, VIII-101 pp., 1927.
41. DOHENY, REV. WILLIAM J., C.S.C., A.B., J.U.D., Church Property: Modes of Acquisition, X-118 pp., 1927.
42. FELDHAUS, REV. ALOYSIUS H., C.PP.S., J.C.D., Oratories, IX-141 pp., 1927.
43. KELLY, REV. JAMES PATRICK, A.B., J.C.D., The Jurisdiction of the Simple Confessor, X-208 pp., 1927.
44. NEUBERGER, REV. NICHOLAS J., J.C.D., Canon 6 or the Relation of the Codex Juris Canonici to the Preceding Legislation, V-95 pp., 1927.
45. O'KEEFFE, REV. GERALD MICHAEL, J.C.D., Matrimonial Dispensations, Powers of Bishops, Priests, and Confessors, VIII-232 pp., 1927.
46. QUIGLEY, REV. JOSEPH, A.M., A.B., J.C.D., Condemned Societies, 139 pp., 1927.
47. ZAPLOTNIK, REV. IOANNES LEO, J.C.D., De Vicariis Foraneis, X-142 pp., 1927.

48. Duskie, Rev. John Aloysius, A.B., J.C.D., The Canonical Status of the Orientals in the United States, VIII-196 pp., 1928.
49. Hyland, Rev. Francis Edward, J.C.D., Excommunication, Its Nature, Historical Development and Effects, VIII-181 pp., 1928.
50. Reinmann, Rev. Gerald Joseph, O.M.C., J.C.D., The Third Order Secular of Saint Francis, 201 pp., 1928.
51. Schenk, Rev. Francis J., J.C.D., The Matrimonial Impediments of Mixed Religion and Disparity of Cult, XVI-318 pp., 1929.
52. Coady, Rev. John Joseph, S.T.D., J.U.D., A.M., The Appointment of Pastors, VIII-150 pp., 1929.
53. Kay, Rev. Thomas Henry, J.C.D., Competence in Matrimonial Procedure, VIII-164 pp., 1929.
54. Turner, Rev. Sidney Joseph, C.P., J.U.D., The Vow of Poverty, XLIX-217 pp., 1929.
55. Kearney, Rev. Raymond A., A.B., S.T.D., J.C.D., The Principles of Delegation, VII-149 pp., 1929.
56. Conran, Rev. Edward James, A.B., J.C.D., The Interdict, V-163 pp., 1930.
57. O'Neil, Rev. William H., J.C.D., Papal Rescripts of Favor, VII-218 pp.,
58. Bastnagel, Rev. Clement Vincent, J.U.D., The Appointment of Parochial Adjutants and Assistants, XV-257 pp., 1930.
59. Ferry, Rev. William A., A.B., J.C.D., Stole Fees, X-107 pp., 1930.
60. Costello, Rev. John Michael, A.B., J.C.D., Domicile and Quasi-Domicile, VII-201 pp., 1930.
61. Kremer, Rev. Michael Nicholas, A.B., S.T.B., J.C.D., Church Support in the United States, VI-136 pp., 1930.
62. Angulo, Rev. Luis, C.M., J.C.D., Legislación de la Iglesia sobre la intención en la aplicación de la Santa Misa, VII-104 pp., 1931.
63. Frey, Rev. Wolfgang Norbert, O.S.B., A.B., J.C.D., The Act of Religious Profession, VIII-174 pp., 1931.
64. Roberts, Rev. James Brendan, A.B., J.C.D., The Banns of Marriage, XIV-140 pp., 1931.
65. Ryder, Rev. Raymond Aloysius, A.B., J.C.D., Simony, IX-151 pp., 1931.
66. Campagna, Rev. Angelo, Ph.D., J.U.D., Il Vicario Generale del Vescovo, VII-205 pp., 1931.
67. Cox, Rev. Joseph Godfrey, A.B., J.C.D., The Administration of Seminaries, VI-124 pp., 1931.
68. Gregory, Rev. Donald J., J.U.D., The Pauline Privilege, XV-165 pp., 1931.
60. Donohue, Rev. John F., J.C.D., The Impediment of Crime, VIII-110 pp., 1931.
70. Dooley, Rev. Eugene A., O.M.I., J.C.D., Church Law on Sacred Relics, IX-143 pp., 1931.
71. Orth, Rev. Clement Raymond, O.M.C., J.C.D., The Approbation of Religious Institutes, 171 pp., 1931.
72. Pernicone, Rev. Joseph M., A.B., J.C.D., The Ecclesiastical Prohibition of Books, XII-267 pp., 1932.
73. Clinton, Rev. Connell, A.B., J.C.L., The Paschal Precept, 1932.
74. Donnelly, Rev. Francis B., A.M., S.T.L., J.C.L., The Diocesan Synod, 1932

75. Torrente, Rev. Camilo, C.M.F., J.C.L., Las Processiones Sagradas, 1932.
76. Murphy, Rev. Edwin J., C.PP.S., J.C.L., Suspension Ex Informata Conscientia, 1932.
77. MacKenzie, Rev. Eric F., A.M., S.T.L., J.C.L., The Delict of Heresy in its Commission, Penalization, Absolution, 1932.
78. Lyons, Rev. Avitus E., S.T.B., J.C.L., The Collegiate Tribunal of First Instance, 1932.
79. Connolly, Rev. Thomas A., J.C.L., Appeals, 1932.
80. Sangmeister, Rev. Joseph V., A.B., J.C.L., Force and Fear as Precluding Matrimonial Consent, 1932.
81. Jaeger, Rev. Leo A., A.B., J.C.L., The Administration of Vacant and Quasi-Vacant Episcopal Sees in the United States, 1932.
82. Rimlinger, Rev. Herbert T., J.C.L., Error Invalidating Matrimonial Consent, 1932.
83. Barrett, Rev. John D. M., S.S., J.C.L., Comparative Study of the Third Plenary Council and the Code, 1932.

www.ingramcontent.com/pod-product-compliance
Lightning Source LLC
LaVergne TN
LVHW050244080826
844660LV00012B/592

* 9 7 8 0 8 1 3 2 2 2 6 9 1 *